NATURAL AUDIENCES

COMMUNICATION AND INFORMATION SCIENCE

A series of monographs, treatises, and texts
Edited by
BRENDA DERVIN
Ohio State University

Recent Titles:

Susanna Barber • News Cameras in the Courtrooms
Alan Baughcum and Gerald Faulhaber • Telecommunications Access and Public Policy
Lee Becker, Jeffrey Fruit, & Susan Caudill • The Training and Hiring of Journalists
Herbert Dordick, Helen Bradley, & Burt Nanus • The Emerging Network Marketplace
Sara Douglas • Labor's New Voice: Unions and the Mass Media
William Dutton & Kenneth Kraemer • Modeling as Negotiating
Fred Fejes • Imperialism, Media, and the Good Neighbor
Glen Fisher • American Communication in a Global Society
Howard Frederick • Cuban-American Radio Wars
Edmund Glenn • Man and Mankind: Conflict and Communication Between Cultures
Gerald Goldhaber, Harry Dennis III, Gary Richetto, & Osmo Wiio • Information Strategies
Bradley Greenberg, Michael Burgoon, Judee Burgoon, & Felipe Korzenny • Mexican Americans and
  the Mass Media
W. J. Howell, Jr. • World Broadcasting in the Age of the Satellite
Heather Hudson • When Telephones Reach the Village
Robert Landau, James Bair, & Jean Siegman • Emerging Office Systems
James Larson • Television's Window on the World
John Lawrence • The Electronic Scholar
Thomas Lindlof • Natural Audiences
Kenneth Mackenzie • Organizational Design
Armand Mattelart and Hector Schmucler • Communication and Information Technologies
Robert Meadow • Politics as Communication
Vincent Mosco • Policy Research in Telecommunications: Proceedings from the Eleventh Annual
  Telecommunications Policy Research Conference
Vincent Mosco • Pushbutton Fantasies
Kaarle Nordenstreng • The Mass Media Declaration of UNESCO
Kaarle Nordenstreng & Herbert Schiller • National Sovereignty and International Communication
David Paletz • Political Communication Research
Everett Rogers & Francis Balle • The Media Revolution in America and in Western Europe
Dan Schiller • Telematics and Government
Herbert Schiller • Information and the Crisis Economy
Herbert Schiller • Who Knows: Information in the Age of the Fortune 500
Jorge Schnitman • Film Industries in Latin America
Jennifer Daryl Slack • Communication Technologies and Society
Jennifer Daryl Slack & Fred Fejes • The Ideology of the Information Age
Keith Stamm • Newspaper Use and Community Ties
Robert Taylor • Value-Added Processes in Information Systems
Sari Thomas • Studies in Mass Media and Technology, Volumes 1–3
Lea Stewart & Stella Ting-Toomey • Communication, Gender, and Sex Roles in Diverse Interaction
  Contexts
Tran Van Dinh • Independence, Liberation, Revolution
Barry Truax • Acoustic Communication
Georgette Wang and Wimal Dissanayake • Continuity and Change in Communication Systems
Frank Webster & Kevin Robins • Information Technology: A Luddite Analysis

NATURAL AUDIENCES:

Qualitative Research
of
Media Uses and Effects

edited by

Thomas R. Lindlof
University of Kentucky

ABLEX PUBLISHING COMPANY
NORWOOD, NEW JERSEY

Library of Congress Cataloging-in-Publication Data

Natural audiences.
  (Communication and information science)
  Bibliography: p.
  Includes index
  1. Mass media—Audiences. 2. Mass media and children. 3. Mass media—Research. I. Lindlof, Thomas R. II. Series.
P96.A83N38   1978   302.2'34   86-17425
ISBN 0-89391-341-3

Ablex Publishing Corporation
355 Chestnut Street
Norwood, New Jersey 07648

Contents

PART III SUBCULTURES AND INSTITUTIONS

Contributors

James A. Anderson (Ph.D., University of Iowa, 1965) is Professor of Communication at the University of Iowa. His current work concerns the family as an information processing environment focusing primarily on the accommodations of media by family members. He describes himself as a methodologist — one who studies the relationship between methods of research and the claims advanced. He has just completed *Communication Research: Issues and Methods,* a text examining quantitative and qualitative methods.

Jennifer Bryce received her Ed.D. in Family and Community Education from Teachers College, Columbia University, in 1980. After serving as National Institute of Mental Health Fellow, she taught 2 years at the University of New Hampshire before leaving for Beirut, where she is currently an Assistant Professor in the Faculty of Health Sciences. Her current research focuses on family functioning and its role in protecting children from the stresses of war.

Muriel G. Cantor earned her doctorate in sociology from the University of California, Los Angeles, in 1969, and now holds the rank of Professor in the Sociology Department at American University in Washington, D.C. She has published several books and reports as well as many articles and book reviews in the areas of mass communications, work and occupations, and the sociology of women. Several of these publications were generated from the research she conducted for the National Institute of Mental Health, Corporation for Public Broadcasting, and the Office of Education. Her latest book (with Suzanne Pingree), *The Soap Opera,* was published in 1983. Along with Joel M. Cantor, she is now studying the influence of American entertainment television in Western Europe.

Michael Griffin received the M.A. and Ph.D. in Communications from the Annenburg School of Communications, University of Pennsylvania, and is currently teaching courses in visual media studies as a Lecturer at the University of Minnesota. He has published articles on children's acquisition of visual media skills, the influence of commercial entertainment forms upon television content, and the history of pictorial description and picture use. He is currently completing a book on the role of amateur photography organizations in the historical shaping of photographic aesthetics.

Dafna Lemish received her Ph.D. degree from the Ohio State University in 1982. She is currently teaching at the University of Haifa in Israel and consulting for the research department of the Israeli Instructional Television Center. Her current research interests are in media use, children and television, and application of naturalistic forms of inquiry in mass media research.

Thomas R. Lindlof received the Ph.D. from the University of Texas at Austin in 1980, and is now Associate Professor of Telecommunications at the University of Kentucky. His research interests include the uses of media in family and subcultural settings, and interpretive processes of television viewing. He is completing a study of the incorporation of microcomputer technology into family life.

Cynthia M. Lont is an Associate Professor in the Communication Department at George Mason University. Her research interests include music as a cultural commodity and women and the media, as well as theory building in cultural studies and political economy. Dr. Lont received her M.A. from Southern Illinois University and a Ph.D. from the University of Iowa.

James Lull received the Ph.D. degree from the University of Wisconsin in 1976. He is now Associate Professor in the Radio-Television-Film program of the Department of Theatre Arts at San Jose State University. His research interests focus on social and cultural variations in the uses and effects of media, particularly music and television, as they are revealed through ethnographic documentation.

Paul Messaris received his Ph.D. from the University of Pennsylvania in 1975. He is Associate Professor of Communications at the Annenberg School of Communications, University of Pennsylvania. His teaching and research are concerned with visual communication, and the current focus of his research is on visual "literacy."

Timothy P. Meyer is Professor of Communication and the Arts at the University of Wisconsin, Green Bay. He has published nearly 100 book chapters and journal articles. Recent qualitative research has been published in *Journal of Broadcasting* and *Critical Studies in Mass Communication*. Current research interests also include the media/marketing channels for Hispanics.

Dona Schwartz received her Ph.D. in Communications from the Annenberg School of Communications, University of Pennsylvania. She is an Assistant Professor in the School of Journalism and Mass Communication, University of Minnesota. Dr. Schwartz is currently engaged in a study examining the role of photographic materials in the presentation of ethnographic research. Generally, her research interests center in the area of sociology of visual media production and use.

Paul J. Traudt is an Assistant Professor in the Department of Speech Communication at the University of New Mexico. Dr. Traudt's research interests center on the relationship between the mass media and social-reality construction as well as video criticism utilizing sociocultural approaches. He earned his M.A. from the University of Utah and a Ph.D. from the University of Texas at Austin.

Ellen Wartella is a Research Associate Professor at the Institute of Communications Research, University of Illinois. During 1985–1986, she is a Fellow at the Gannett Center for Media Studies, Columbia University. She does research on children and media.

Michelle A. Wolf is an Assistant Professor in the Department of Broadcast Communication Arts at San Francisco State University. Her research is primarily focused on the various ways in which individuals and families integrate media into their lives. She has conducted several long-term qualitative studies of how children process and use televised content, and has observed and analyzed family uses of media. Dr. Wolf is currently developing and using nontraditional research procedures to explore how members of different "sub-cultures" within the United States use music.

Preface

When presented with proposals for unconventional methodologies or concepts, it is not unusual for members of a scholarly community to respond with some trepidation, if not skepticism. Even in a "variable" field like communications, where an eclecticism of approaches is normal, the prospect of foundational shifts in the ways that phenomena are studied and described can be unsettling. The coming of qualitative methods to the study of mediated communication has in fact been met with trepidation and skepticism in some quarters, but also with a healthy curiosity. The term that is used here, *qualitative research*, subsumes many enterprises (e.g., ethnography, ethnomethodology, naturalistic inquiry) that have long experienced acceptance and usage in such disciplines as cultural anthropology and sociology. As such, there is nothing very new about them—except in their applications to the phenomenal character of mediated communication.

The turn to qualitative research among those who are curious about its utility comes partly from a recognition that much quantitatively-based research takes for granted the very empirical "facts" that require fundamental examination. In critical studies, this has meant more emphasis on both the ideological apparatus of media industries and the latent functions of media content. In empirical studies of audiences, this has meant that the *acts* of mediated communication—how they are organized, practiced, and cognitively represented—move to the center stage of research attention. Qualitative inquiry is directed towards the processes by which individuals incorporate information technologies into their ongoing motives and goals. There is an interest in accounting for the actual unfolding of everyday interactions with media. There is, accordingly, a commitment to systematically investigating the situational contexts in which media are encountered and exploited. To stand some conventional terms on their heads, those who do naturalistic inquiry consider "audience members" to be social actors in many respects, and the "content" of communication events are the actors' interpretations of those occasions of use.

Fortunately, it is no longer controversial to claim that much can be learned from using observational data, actors' accounts, and informants' reports as evidence of media uses and effects. Conference papers arguing for consideration of qualitative research methods in mass communication began to be presented at the International Communication Association, the Speech Communication Association, and other meetings in the late 1970s. Book chapters and journal articles detailing such arguments soon followed. The skepticism that greeted the idea that the study of communication through the perspectives and observed natural behaviors of social actors is potentially valuable has largely subsided. Although doubts are still entertained regarding its appropriateness for certain subjects, this first phase of introduction to the "innovation" is mostly over. The burden of proof for *demonstrating* the value of qualitative research, however, rests specifically and quite naturally with those making such claims. The primary purpose of this volume, therefore, is to present examples of the relevance and usefulness of qualitative research. Field projects form the heart of this book and reflect many of the concerns expressed about this type of research: how it gets done in the field, what questions it can profitably address, how data are analyzed and reported, and what it means in advancing knowledge of media uses and effects.

The structure of the volume's contents manifest in broad form the progression of qualitative work in mediated communication. The tripartite division of children, families, and subcultures and institutions recognizes the arenas in which mediated communication typically occurs. In seeking contributions for those three sections, I was interested in empirical projects that either focused on previously unexplored aspects of mediated communication or developed new understandings of more established topical domains. In the Children section, Dafna Lemish, Michelle A. Wolf, and Paul Messaris undertake in their various ways to explicate the meanings that children impart to television—as a physical appliance, as a play object, as a source of representations of stories and people, as a measure against which real world events and relationships are evaluated. Their studies elucidate many of the developmental origins of natural attitudes about the place of media in Western culture. The Family section exemplifies the complexity of interpersonal negotiation that occurs in the most familiar of media use settings. As Jennifer W. Bryce, and Paul J. Traudt and Cynthia M. Lont, reveal in their analyses, media become actively engaged in the ongoing definition of family members' roles and even the maintenance of family systems. Compared to the other two sections, the chapters constituting Subcultures and Institutions are the most disparate in their objectives, populations, and levels of analysis. Underlying the studies by Thomas R. Lindlof, Michael Griffin and Dona B. Schwartz, and James Lull, however, is the intention to document the uses of different media by individuals and groups for creating personal expressions in the context of larger systems of cultural definition. Taken as a whole, the studies reveal the methodological diversity and appropriateness of application that characterize naturalistic inquiry.

Although I held out the promise to the chapter contributors for more space than is generally given a journal article, it was perhaps inevitable that nearly all of them faced hard decisions in reducing their work to acceptable lengths. The issue of presentational format is especially vexing for qualitative research. Since most case studies follow a different form from quantitative reports—demonstrating claims by the use of verbal and/or behavioral specimens embedded in narratives—the preferred presentational formats have been the monograph and the book. While several social science journals provide regular outlets for the traditional article (e.g., *Qualitative Sociology, Urban Life, Human Science, Symbolic Interaction*), longer formats remain more viable for reporting the field study. As Lindlof and Meyer write in the introductory chapter, it may be time to consider some alternative means of dissemination of interpretive research.

In planning this volume, it became evident that attention needed to be given to providing cohesion within each section. The commentaries that follow the data-based chapters fulfill the need for conceptual perspective. The commentaries also create a colloquy of sorts by providing critiques of the substantive and procedural aspects of the projects. These critiques review the strengths, difficulties, and possibilities of doing qualitative research within each domain, and thereby provoke speculation into the future conduct of such research. The authors of these commentaries were chosen for their long familiarity with each of those research areas and their sympathy (if not first hand experience) with qualitative research. James A. Anderson, Ellen Wartella, and Muriel G. Cantor performed their multiple tasks admirably. Their thoughtful pieces suggest that naturalistic inquiry can lead to new ways of understanding media uses and effects without sacrificing continuity with some enduring concerns in communication research.

The introductory chapter by Thomas R. Lindlof and Timothy P. Meyer presents a synoptic view of the distinctive features of qualitative methods that recommend their use for certain research problems. The authors also pay ample attention to several issues that have not been considered very often in connection with mediated communication: the utilization of audio/visual and computing tools, institutional resistances to qualitative research, presentational format, and the kind of understanding that such inquiry should be expected to yield.

Many people contributed to the conception and realization of this volume. Among those who offered useful advice in the early stage were James A. Anderson, James Lull, Paul Messaris, Horace Newcomb, Stuart J. Sigman, and Paul J. Traudt. Mary S. Mander patiently schooled me in some of the strategies and arcane arts of book editing (although more had to be improvised than I would have suspected). Timothy P. Meyer provided help in focusing the overall purposes and structure of the volume. I would like to thank Robert S. Brubaker, former Head of the Department of Speech Communication at the Pennsylvania State University, and Thomas R. Donohue, former Chairman of the Department of Telecommunications at the University of Kentucky, for their support for the project. I want to commend Charlotte Hetzel for her fine work in typing and preparing the book manuscript and other materials. My wife, Valerie, merits the heartiest accolade for her steady encouragement.

Chapter 1

Mediated Communication as Ways of Seeing, Acting, and Constructing Culture: The Tools and Foundations of Qualitative Research

Thomas R. Lindlof

Department of Telecommunications
University of Kentucky

Timothy P. Meyer

College of Communication
University of Wisconsin at Green Bay

We begin this chapter with the proposition that many questions regarding the forms and consequences of mediated communication require research procedures that are unusually sensitive to the manner in which information is made available and diffused in advanced technology cultures. Following the ideas of the late Derek J. deSolla Price (55), advances in scientific understanding are as much due to the stimulative effects of new research technologies as to insight or ideation alone. Ethnography and related qualitative approaches comprise a set of procedures that may be very well suited to the highly situated and rule-bound features of mediated communication, and make it feasible to gain access to the meaningful constructs of media users. To be sure, there is no assurance that such procedures will lead to conceptual breakthroughs. The great investments of time and effort needed to achieve rigor in this type of research may also deter many would-be studies. It is hoped, however, that the promise of elucidating the rich complexities of mediated communication will spur the imaginative application of alternative approaches. This chapter examines the distinctive advantages of qualitative research and their specific relevance to the study of human communication and media.

Despite an extensive literature on media audience behavior, our knowledge of the social constitution and pragmatics of mediated communication remains at a primitive level. There is little understanding of such problems as how mediated communication is organized as a practical activity in local cultures, how content-decoding competence is defined and achieved, and how personhood develops from both selective and fortuitous uses of media resources. The lack of such knowledge is partly due to the received and usually unquestioned notion of the audience. Since mass communication is made possible by the sanction, investment, and guidance of large institutions, which require systematic evidence about the outcomes of their operations, it should not be surprising that the conditions of message reception have been typically viewed in terms of an audience constituted as an aggregate. The notion of the audience has long reflected its etymological derivation as an assembly of spectators or listeners, as at a concert. At a theater, of course, whatever behaviors are displayed by audience members are governed (or informed) by the overt and/or formal conventions specific to the entertainment (44). With the coming of mass media, modifiers were added—large, dispersed, heterogeneous, anonymous, etc. (42)—that both defined the generic aspects of the mass communication audience and made it possible to create audience profiles for particular media. Normative evaluation of audience size and segmentation for marketing purposes has proceeded with the audience-as-aggregate notion left fairly intact.

Mediated communication, however, is a quintessentially domestic activity. The fact that corporate media messages are usually received by people in private and familiar settings means that the selection and use of those messages will be shaped by the exigencies of those local environments. The various "theaters" in which these audiences congregate observe their own justificatory logics. Moreover, with the increasing adoption of technological add-ons for the basic media delivery systems, the messages can be edited, deleted, rescheduled, or skipped past with complete disregard for their original form. The received notion of the mass communication audience has simply little relevance for the reality of mediated communication.

Another difficulty in understanding the natural forms of mediated communication concerns the methods used in American mass communication scholarship. The dominant modes of audience inquiry have entailed hypothetico-deductive procedures to explain the uses and effects of manifest media content. This empirical tradition apparently relied on long term collaborations with government agencies, the communications industry, and older human science disciplines for developing its models of communication as well as its topical agenda (60). For the sake of simplicity, we can refer to two paradigms that emerged out of that tradition:

the deterministic and the functionalist.[1] The deterministic paradigm responds to the perceived need for universal probability statements regarding audience behavior that can be applied to transient social problems. Emphasis is placed on the types of attitudinal or behavioral effects that *can* be produced under certain optimal conditions. Extrapolation of such studies to what *actually* occurs in media reception situations, however, is heavily limited by such factors as the unusual environments for testing, the narrow range of permissible responses, and a verificationist orientation to theory construction.

The functionalist paradigm, on the other hand, casts the audience member as a "free-agent" media user whose goal is to assess the utility of more or less equivalent sources of social and psychological gratification. Here the idea of an active audience, forwarded by uses and gratifications proponents, seems more amenable to capturing the essential teleological character of what audience members actually do vis à vis many opportunities for media use. In the sense that mass communication is an activity in which audience members are not forced to comply with message producers, the enormous potential range of audience behaviors and interpretations thus implied is a subject that uses and gratifications claims to recognize. Moreover, uses and gratifications has been attempting to come to terms with some of the more fundamental criticisms of the functionalist approach, namely: that its assumptions are tautological (53), and that its findings are only valid in a stable, nondynamic system (53, 59).

Yet the reliance on verbal reports in the sample survey format by uses and gratifications and similar research approaches remains problematic on several counts. First, the ambivalent, happenstance, routinized, and class-determined character of much information seeking and exposure suggests that the active audience presumption overreaches in its conceptions of the everyday reality of media use. This raises the troubling idea that not only may the *individual* be an inappropriate unit of analysis, but that the discourse of uses and gratifications designs encourages respondents to think of themselves as sole initiators of action. Locus of control issues are put out of play. Second, as Messaris (45) has already pointed out, uses and gratifications measures may actually elicit sentiments or folk knowledge instead of the hoped-for media user's analysis of his or her motives and gratifications. Sentiments may be useful data for mapping

---

[1]We are not using the term "paradigm" in the strong Kuhnian sense. There is not a normal science in mass communication to the extent that consensus exists regarding a body of knowledge, nor has there ever been one. Rather, "paradigm" is used here as a framework of beliefs for operating in the world.

media-related cognitive frames or world views, as in the analysis of cultivation effects. But in light of considerable recent evidence that most people's reasoning heuristics and introspective analyses fall short of "lay scientist" criteria, although retrospective reports may be quite good in some situations (17), verbal reports are of dubious veridicality without further contextual or observational data. Finally, and particularly in their usual reductionist form for use in multivariate procedures, verbal reports give off a false sense of commensurability of media use motives and gratifications. The functional-systemic terms of the argument drain the behaviors constituting media use of their socio-historical origins. For example, a finding that two different age groups seek "cognitive orientation" in television news probably fails to discriminate what kind of cognition, for what particular purposes or news items (if any), and in what social nexus the orientation would be operative. It is vital to procure information about the symbolic constructions (i.e., the culture) and the range of social actions in which a communication medium and its content functions for an individual.

The paradigm that expresses the stance of this chapter, which we call the *interpretive* paradigm, takes it subject to be the fields of meaning that pervade the projects of human life. Precisely because people cognize their graspable and imagined environments in symbolic schemes, continually developing future courses of action and revising past acts, the phenomena of social life are fundamentally self-referential and require different paths of inquiry than the exact sciences. In his essay "Concept and Theory Formation in the Social Sciences," Alfred Schutz (63, p. 59) elaborates on the special subject of the social scientist:

> The world of nature, as explored by the natural scientist, does not "mean" anything to molecules, atoms, and electrons. But the observational field of the social scientist—social reality—has a specific meaning and relevance structure for the human beings living, acting, and thinking within it. By a series of common-sense constructs they have pre-selected and pre-interpreted this world which they experience as the reality of their daily lives. It is these thought objects of theirs which determine their behavior by motivating it. The thought objects constructed by the social scientist, in order to grasp this social reality, have to be founded upon the thought objects constructed by the common-sense thinking of men, living their daily life within the social world. Thus, the constructs of the social sciences are, so to speak, constructs of the second degree, that is, constructs of the constructs made by the actors on the social scene, whose behavior the social scientist has to observe and to explain in accordance with the procedural rules of his science.
>
> Thus, the exploration of the general principles according to which man in daily life organizes his experiences, and especially those of the social world, is the first task of the methodology of the social sciences.

The interpretive paradigm, as it is used for empirically studying meaning systems, is not monolithic, and indeed there are many varieties (30, 51, 64). The following review briefly illustrates the different emphases of some of those varieties. *Ethnomethodology* appropriated the aims of phenomenology in its studies of the logics-in-use of situated everyday behavior. The phenomenological method of "epoche" is a process of analyzing the presuppositions of the natural attitude (i.e., the cultural glosses on objects and relations that are unquestioningly used in everyday perception) by radically doubting the empirical premises of its existence (36). Ethnomethodologists attempt to show that communication (as an accomplishment) is "known only in the doing" (24). In other words, communication practices themselves sustain the participants' sense of their unproblematic reality. Since talk is typically considered the major resource for social actors' accounting practices, discourse analysis methods have contributed to the present diversity of studies in ethnomethodology. *Ecological psychology* also seeks to examine the situational influences on behavior through naturalistic inquiry (5, 10), although, unlike ethnomethodology, this approach conceptualizes those influences in terms of developmental effects of person–environment systems.

Among the symbols-and-meaning approaches to social inquiry, *symbolic interactionism* (8, 26, 27, 43) focuses on the production and negotiation of meaning in society, and specifically the ways in which "actors" manage their roles in social interaction. Emphasis is placed on examining how the self is defined by controlling access to, and possible interpretations of, social information. Using the ethnographic case study approach, the material, structural, and communicational features of such units as the family (33, 39), the ethnic subculture (23), and child communities (12) can be described in micro-systemic terms. On a larger scale, the belief systems of entire cultures may come under intensive *semiotic* analysis. Observations of ritual displays, public symbols, personal stories, and other records are analyzed to reveal the cognitive frames or dynamic collective personality of a people (25).

For all the varieties of the interpretive paradigm, human behavior becomes a topic of investigation when it signifies a person's intentional orientation to the world, or when observing others attribute significance to it. The behaviors constituting social relations are in turn derived from intersubjective constructs of the social actors (68), and can only be understood (or critiqued) through some "insider" knowledge of those constructs. This does not imply that the task of interpretive research should be re-creations of the actors' subjective constructions, or that the products of that research are somehow exempt from the rules of inference traditionally employed by the social sciences (46). Rather, the work of the interpretive researcher is directed towards ontological concerns about the organization of human experience (31), viz. under what conditions communicative acts occur, how it is that people account for their acts, what versions of the world are proposed and negotiated through communication. Although the scope of the resulting claims is normally idiographic, the evidence used to advance them is subject to evaluations of their completeness and adequacy that are not solipsistic.

The umbrella of "qualitative research" covers a number of methods that are designed to gain access to the natural domains where social actors carry out their characteristic activities. While some believe that quantitative methods are antithetical to the analysis of naturalistic phenomena, many observational techniques are in fact available for numerically coding linguistic and nonverbal behaviors (73) without necessarily stage-managing the conditions of their appearance. Anthropologists have regularly employed projective tests, sorting or ranking tasks, and other psychological instruments (54). Such techniques can usefully augment the more episodic behavioral and verbal specimens obtained in the field. Interpretive researchers have also recognized that microcomputers are adept at manipulating symbols of all types. Computer programs have proven feasible for the tasks of searching lengthy field notes and accounts for designated concepts, updating field records, and facilitating communication among researchers at different sites; applications of artificial intelligence may even someday aid in the systematic derivation of inferences from raw data (see 11).

For most empirical questions of concern to the researcher, however, the primary methods of choice will be those that are intended to apprehend the processual detail of social reality. Because mediated communication does not consist of discrete events that can be easily operationalized at a molar level, such methods should be sensitive to the temporal and interactive nuances of its enactments. Such methods should be maximally open to diverse indicators of concepts taken to the field, and should allow for the later refinement of variables for observation and testing. Such methods should make explicit the roles of the researcher in interacting with social actors. The methods that meet these requirements in varying degrees include participant observation, the life history interview, the depth interview, the informant interview, and unobtrusive measures—among which must be counted institutional and personal documents and artifacts, representational maps, diaries, and audio/visual records. There is continuing controversy regarding the extent to which these methods may be used individually or collectively. Denzin (13, p. 183), for example, defines participant observation quite inclusively as "a *field strategy* that simultaneously combines document analysis, interviewing of respondents and informants, direct participation and observation, and introspection" (emphasis added). For Anderson (2), participation in the social actors' world (and the actors' concomitant acceptance of that stance) is the sine qua non of naturalistic inquiry, in which light the uses of multiple observers or covert observing devices become highly problematic. For Douglas (15), "fronting" is a normal tactic employed by social actors to deflect the information-gathering advances of the social scientist; thus, the social scientist must also engage in fronting or other covert practices in order to penetrate certain social worlds. For Zelditch (78, p. 572), informant interviewing can not only save time and resources but also outperform direct observation in some cases, since "there exist parts of the social structure into which [the participant-observer] has not penetrated and probably will not, by virtue of the way he has defined himself to its members, because of limitations on the movement of those who sponsor him, etc." The upshot of all these perspectives is simply that, in the pursuit of an (always partial) understanding of unique social worlds, unique configurations of methods must be identified and applied. Qualitative research is therefore characterized by a catholicity of data-gathering tools that can be differentially applied to the specific demands of the social occasions, scenes, and settings.

Rather than focus attention on the individual methods, which are covered in many texts (e.g., 9, 54, 61), we will examine some distinctive features that recommend the use of qualitative methods. These four features—reflexivity, contextuality, meaning system explication, and theory development—will be discussed in terms of their importance for the study of mediated communication.

According to Hammersley and Atkinson (30), the logic of ethnography hinges on acknowledging that the social investigator, as inevitably a part of the social phenomena that are being studied, is "the research instrument *par excellence*" (p. 18). This *reflexivity*—the significant involvement of the research act as both a product of and a process in everyday life—provides the means of taking account of and usefully exploiting the effects of the procedures themselves. Inherent in the reflexivity principle is the exquisite notion that, while the researcher must be careful not to unduly impinge on the characteristic social patterns (once they are known), selective intrusions—via interviews, changes in the sampling of situations, etc.—can be highly revealing.

In the area of field relations, for example, it has been frequently noted that the researcher must continually negotiate a "marginal" status within the group. On the surface, this issue reduces to the question: Are my activities obtrusive to the integrity of the scenes I am observing? Obtrusiveness, of course, exists as a factor in all types of social research, although only the interpretive paradigm is interested in exploring all the ramifications of reactive effects. As we will discuss later, this concern begs more important questions regarding the researcher's schedule of contacts, the type of information sought, and the level of trust that is established.

More profoundly, the marginality issue—i.e., the researcher's ambiguously dual role as outsider and as novice insider to the social group—suggests that knowledge of the first order constructs of social actors may always be elusive. The researcher's own socialization and professional schemes of classification may prevent him or her from extrapolating "true" second-order constructs from the behaviors and accounts gathered in the field. To the extent that the researcher does not share a group's history, the accents of meaning that are exclusive to the group remain inaccessible. He or she is therefore doomed to selecting among explanatory glosses on what is observed. Yet it is also apparent that practical measures afford the capability to achieve some understanding of social actors' perspectives. For example, the use of audio-visual media by the people themselves can result in a sort of interface between meaning systems, particularly in difficult cross-cultural studies (7, 48, 76). The use of confirmatory contacts with social actors (47)—e.g., determining whether the researcher's incipient grasp of the social process in question is confirmed by the actors' own experience with all or part of that process—can also help in assessing the validity of conclusions (4, 47). The researcher's own talents of observation and judgment are continually called into play in the process of witnessing the mundane aspects of the social actors' routines (74). Reflexivity operates at the heart of the research activity as an extended discourse of stories told to sponsors, colleagues, research assistants, subjects, and the researcher him or herself in moments of introspection and deliberate inference (32).

Qualitative research departs from nomothetic social science in its attention to the historical and situational contexts in which the objects of interest are embedded. *Contextuality* refers to the multiple connections between the phenomena being studied and the inscribed data that contribute to an assessment of the latter's ecological validity. During data collection, contextuality will be indexed by means of in-situ observation, the employment of multiple data sources, and continuous reference to emergent explanations of observed events. The result is a "thick description" (25) of the layers of meaning that lend the events their significance for social actors. During data analysis, the interpretive researcher "revives" the natural forms of those events in order to reconstruct their underlying processes.

In practical terms, contextuality reveals its methodological utility in a number of ways, one of which is the problem of divergence. Divergence refers to the different results sometimes obtained from different methods in investigating a particular phenomenon. It has been frequently observed in media audience research, for example, that questionnaires yield data that diverge from evidence of the same phenomenon obtained from other sources (6, 69). The lack of congruence between actions and attitudes may well be symptomatic of people's situational stances toward the expectations of different research approaches (14). The same interview technique used with different parties to the *same* event may also yield very different reports; in the case of parent–child interactions, observational methods may be the most viable way of reconciling perspectives (77). Triangulation is a general technique for reconciling "facts" obtained during data collection; it involves "the comparison of data relating to the same phenomenon but deriving from different phases of the fieldwork, different points in the temporal cycles occurring in the setting, or, as in respondent validation, the accounts of different participants (including the ethnographer) in the setting" (30, p. 198). Triangulation does not carry the presumptive burden of coming up with a high-fidelity reconstruction of an event. Divergent results from multiple methods can shed valuable light on such phenomena as sex-role stereotyping (38) that would remain obscured if only one method was relied on. In fact, it has been argued that conventional concepts of reliability must be violated in qualitative research in order that the use of multiple instruments, observers, and sampling points enhance validity (49, pp. 595–597).

In qualitative research, then, higher-order contextual descriptions find their indexicality in both the convergence and divergence of data. The reflexivity of the research act—the continual interpretation of the researcher's position in the setting, his or her procedures, and analytic constructs—provides the means of deciding the admissability of divergent evidence.

In developing their topics and resources for investigation, interpretive researchers attempt to *explicate the meaning systems* operating in a particular group or culture. From the accounts, terminologies, and situated actions of social actors derived from the research process, the researcher builds an argument for the symbolic alignments that motivate or inform overt behavior. Meaning explication is especially problematic in the study of media. Mass communication is usually distinguished by the separation in time and space between message producers and receivers. Changes in audience-imputed meanings of programs, characters, and other content bits can occur quite independently of producers' intentions. A program that is produced this year may be interpreted as "nostalgic" 10 years from now. A program considered "realistic" today (by the realism standards operative for a particular individual or group) may be judged quite differently by revisionist standards a generation later. Similarly, a program at a single point in time can be "enjoyed" and "used" quite differently by individuals in varying cognitive-developmental, socio-economic, and subcultural positions. The accents of reality that are imputed to television therefore suggest a larger system of coordinated meanings of reality used for social practices. It is up to the interpretive researcher not only to document instances of reference to television's "reality" or any other first-order construct, but also to explain how it is talked about and applied in everyday life.

In terms of research procedure, meaning systems are often explicated by looking for evidence of competence among culture members. That is, if we assume that social action is coordinated by intersubjective constructs held in common by members of a particular community, then there should exist specific behaviors that publicly demonstrate to those members certain levels of competence in handling meanings. The view that there are rule-governed competencies carries with it the assumption that particular acts may be classified as attempts, successes, or failures—as judged by members of the community (70). For example, Fine (19, p. 461) identified three uses of popular culture for "establishing, confirming, and reifying group beliefs and attitudes":

> First, group members may use the *form* of popular culture products as a mechanism for expressing opinions and arriving at consensus. Second, members may use the *topics* of popular culture products to express viewpoints. Third, members may employ the specific *content* of popular culture as a topic or to express an opinion in the course of group interaction—i.e., employ popular culture as an analogy for ongoing interaction.

In all of these uses, situational rules may be operative in defining acceptable topics in the group context and the interactional methods for expressing them. Within the family, strategic and tactical rules define the sorts of media-related behaviors that exemplify and/or validate certain family roles (41). Between children of different ages, competence in the narrative decoding of motion pictures is demonstrated by knowledge of special effects, stereotypical character roles, and the use of suspense devices (21). Qualitative methods are especially useful in determining the existence of competence values as indicated in behavioral regularities (and the exceptions that prove the rules), as well as the distribution of those meanings in society.

Ethnography and related qualitative approaches are frequently depicted as delivering "only" case studies, with questionable generality beyond the time and place they were conducted, seldom contributing to a comprehensive theory. Yet *theory development* constitutes one of the outstanding strengths of qualitative research. That strength lies partly in its ability to interleave concept formation, data collection, and hypothesis testing throughout many phases of the project. Data collection and analysis are not strictly confined to hypothesis-testing, as is the case with the hypothetico-deductive approach. Because data analysis in qualitative research involves a more dynamic involvement of inductive reasoning, the theoretical product tends to be models of processes rather than confirmations of deductively-argued effects.

A qualitative project is typically conceived in terms of sensitizing concepts (13) – i.e., concepts that attune the researcher "to discover what is unique about each empirical instance of the concept while uncovering what it displays in common across many different settings" (13, p. 17). Thus, the interpretive researcher rarely enters the field with fully-operationalized or standardized measuring instruments, unless they are to be used in a diagnostic fashion to determine the physical, cognitive, or personality states of the social actors (see 47). By forestalling formal operationalization until after preliminary data collection is over, the researcher has the opportunity to become acclimated to the setting in a number of ways: learning the prominent symbols and the codified and informal rules of the group, developing rapport, etc. Hammersley and Atkinson (30, p. 175) describe the general structure of this process:

> Ethnographic research has a characteristic "funnel" structure, being progressively focused over its course. Progressive focusing has two analytically distinct components. First, over time the research problem is developed or transformed, and eventually its scope is clarified and delimited and its internal structure explored. In this sense, it is frequently only over the course of the research that one discovers what the research is really "about," and it is not uncommon for it to turn out to be about something quite remote from the initial foreshadowed problems.

Towards the conclusion of a project, the descriptive thrust will sometimes turn to explanation and testing. The steadily-crystallizing hypotheses may at that time be subjected to tests of disconfirmation through triangulation procedures, further observation of critical cases, or even experimentation. The analytic induction procedure (see 13, p. 191–196) represents a way to arrive at causal explanation through the progressive analysis of negative cases and modification of theoretical propositions until a universal relationship can be posited. This procedure approximates the most powerful advantage of the experimental method: researcher control of variables. Even without the rigor of analytic induction, some variant of the comparative method can be employed for pitting one explanation against another in accounting for field phenomena.

The theoretical product of many qualitative projects is the development or refinement of descriptive typologies. Following Pike's distinction of the emic and etic modes of anthropological analysis (see 54, pp. 54–66), typological (or taxonomic) emic analysis often intends to represent natural categories of "the native's point of view," mainly relying on interviews to categorize the ideational dimensions of a single culture. The emic insists on the incommensurability of cultural perspectives, in that its objects of study comprise the nonrational and arbitrary in human life. This "romantic" current in anthropology is well expressed by Shweder (65, p. 48). as:

> the specific presuppositions, values, and schemes of classification communicated by specific people to other specific people on specific occasions. Members of a common culture know each other not by the deep structures or hypothesized processes underlying their thoughts but rather by the surface content of what they say and do to each other in the here and now. The more we attend to surface content, the less common is the culture of man.

Etic analysis, on the other hand, mainly relies on observations by an outside investigator in striving to build structural, cross-cultural explanations of systems of "objective" behavior. The categories that emerge are entirely those of the researcher's and may be linked in ways that bear little or no connection to native definitions of reality. The etic is represented in sociology by Goffman's treatises on face to face interaction rituals, and in cognitive psychology by the work of Piaget and Kohlberg on universal stages of moral development.

The etic and emic modes are ideal types, and both are found in varying degrees in the procedures, if not the purposes, of most qualitative research. This is true of the field of mediated communication. Lull's (40) structural typology of social uses of television viewing, and Jaglom and Gardner's (35) developmental typology of children's television realism perceptions, lean heavily on etic assumptions of universally-applicable categories, although they are founded to some extent on informant-based cultural knowledge. Pacanowsky and Anderson's (52) study of the use of media-related information in the discourse of a police unit remains rather faithful to the emic perspective: the categories they propose are closely tied to the idioms and specific circumstances of the originating culture. Depending on what position on the emic–etic continuum the researcher decides to adopt, the case type used as evidence for theory construction will vary.

What areas of mediated communication can be usefully studied through the interpretive paradigm? This brief section addresses that question by expanding on the theme of this chapter and this book—that mediated communication can be approached as ways of acting, seeing, and constructing culture. In other words, the topical domains to which qualitative methods are most suited are those in which people draw on communications media for creatively engaging the world. The following areas are meant as neither a prescriptive agenda for research nor an exhaustive ordering of topics. They do indicate some aspects of media use that we believe are amenable to qualitative inquiry.

Media use that defines subcultures. Subculture life often centers on specialized, even ritualistic methods of media attendance and use. Subcultures are marked by a reflexive and highly-refined sense of their members as distinctive vis a vis mainstream modes of socialization. The subculture represents a very robust interactional arena for research, since the members' communication activity often relies on a restricted code or language and makes continuing reference to shared information sets, modes of group initiation, and lines of action (see 20, 71). Gans' (23) participant observation description of urban Italian-Americans' self-conscious appropriation of mainstream media, and Roe and Salomonsson's (58) recent interview study of Swedish adolescents' use of video cassettes, illustrate some avenues in media research of subculture. Radway's (56) related concept of the "interpretive community" in her study of romance novel readers suggests that textual genres can operate as cultural propositions on which a shared group life is based.

Media use as "frames" for understanding life concerns and experiences. How individuals make use of the forms and content of media for making decisions or inferences about the nature of their world is a domain that can be usefully explored through an interpretive framework. Among the specific areas subsumed here are the reality status of media characters, events, and stories; the types of involvement engaged in by the media user; and the relationship of cognitive-affective attributions of media characters to the media user's everyday behavior (16, 18). Typically, qualitative research in this vein also considers the social contexts of media attendance as key conditions on the development of interpretive frames (62). In Great Britain, several researchers have attempted to discern television decoding strategies systematically as they relate to viewers' ideological positions and life experiences (34, 50). These efforts owe much of their impetus to the theoretical work of Stuart Hall and others of the "Birmingham Centre" (29, 67), and indicate a growing interest on both sides of the Atlantic in applying semiotics to the study of mediated communication (22).

Media use as constitutive of ongoing social interactions and relationships. This area concerns the myriad ways in which individuals relate to each other, practice impression management, and organize their time through situational engagements with media. In this sense, media are often employed for non-content-related ends, for example, as a temporal device for linking social scenes. Additionally, ongoing content flow from media may be abstracted by individuals for managing conversations or for referring to subtextual themes in close relationships (40, 75). This research area generally relies on observations of so-called micro social situations. The formulation of communication rules is a normal consequence of much research in this area. The diversity of this research is indicated by recent studies of sibling interactions (1), public televiewing (37), institutional media use (66), and children's play behavior (57).

Media use as influencing the development of expressive competence. The interest here is with the impact of both long-term and sudden experiences with particular media on different kinds of personal expression. In contrast with the other three domains, this one has antecedents in anthropological studies of technology transfer, as well as studies of the effects of media exposure regimens on children's perceptual discrimination, role-taking, and other indices of communicative competence. Some recent attention has focused on the ways in which culturally-accepted forms of media (mainly in the commercial sector) affect individuals' organization of their perpetual worlds (28, 76).

In this section, we turn our attention to those key issues which are inherent in the assumptions, hypotheses, procedures, and inferences made by researchers who do qualitative inquiry. While the problems we have identified are also frequently applicable to traditional hypothetico-deductive research, the emphasis here is on unique aspects of naturalistic approaches. Limitations that encumber research generally will, however, be noted.

Researcher obtrusiveness. Most research procedures represent obtrusions into the arenas of social interactions that form the focus of inquiry. Only those nefarious methods which observe and/or record others via electronic surveillance technologies would be considered unobtrusive. The mere presentation of a questionnaire and its instructions presents a violation of ordinary routines. The entry of a researcher (whether known as such by the group or not) is an obtrusion of a different kind. It is assumed, of course, that the researcher's presence will indeed alter the subsequent interactions in the setting, but that, eventually, the researcher will become just another member or an accepted part of the scenery (for those whose primary role is observational but not active participation).

Media use settings are ideal for ethnographers in the sense that they nearly overflow with ritualized behavioral patterns (perhaps cognitive as well); but such settings are also usually quite private and even intimate. The obtrusion of a participant-observer into such private spheres of activity certainly causes or demands a change in the rituals. Some aspects which may be part of the ritual may never be displayed at all or even verbally alluded to, escaping the researcher's awareness. Obvious examples would include activities such as drug use, intimate sexual behavior, more romantic moments that members may be used to sharing (e.g., a couple watching a favorite movie together), or more emotional or emotion-arousing uses. And, if such uses are only referred to by participants in verbal accounts, the ability of the researcher to observe the ritual and interpret it is quite obviously jeopardized (in any valid sense, at least). For example, a couple may watch David Letterman or even *Hawaii 5-0* reruns together, enjoying the opportunity to be with one another and away from the children and demands of the day that has nearly ended. The act of sharing and the opportunity to share may thus be the most significant aspect of the couple's pattern. But a researcher would be unable to observe and/or directly participate in what may be a truly significant mediated event for that couple.

Getting access to such social settings may present a nearly insurmountable barrier. There are some alternatives worth exploring, however. Researchers might get participants to prepare their own narrative accounts which describe their activities in some detail and provide participants' own interpretations of what the accounts mean to them. If each of the two persons follows such a procedure, the researcher has some grasp of activities that would otherwise remain hidden. Less practical but perhaps somewhat effective would be an audio-only or video recording of the event, which could become a source of data for the researcher/observer. The use and obtrusiveness of research instruments will, however, be commented upon in more detail in an upcoming section. Suffice to say, ethnographers need to be resourceful when trying to overcome ever-present barriers of privacy and intimacy.

Because mediated communication occurs in private and often intimate settings, the need for ethnographers to be willing to commit large blocks of time seems crucial. Unless the researcher's interests are limited to just a few, rather superficial aspects (e.g., repeated TV viewing patterns in prime time), the researcher must be willing to wait until he or she is readily accepted into the household and is treated as another "member of the family." To date, only Wolf, Meyer, and White (75) have reported a study where participant observers actually spent enough time to clearly be considered family members. The prospect of spending 6 months to a year or more with one or two families is not a pleasant prospect, especially for relatively inexperienced (usually untenured) researchers who face institutional pressure to produce in a perhaps unrealistically short amount of time. Nonetheless, time spent is critical for mediated communication contexts if the barriers of privacy and intimacy are to be circumvented or reduced to a substantial degree.

Status differences between researcher and subjects. The mere mention of the researcher as a "researcher" or as a "college professor" may be enough to make subjects in an ethnographic inquiry shudder, refuse to participate at all, try to act much differently than usual, or feel as if their every move is being scrutinized and analyzed. Most people have an enormous dislike for being monitored, as if in a fishbowl. Couple that with the status of the researcher as allegedly blessed with superior intellect and mental capabilities, and a problem of major proportions may have arisen.

Status differences also present an inescapable problem when child subjects are part of the inquiry. The researcher is both stranger and adult to the child or adolescent. As such, a certain amount of reticence and skepticism is present as "givens" for the researcher. And, given young children's limited ability to use language and adolescents' unwillingness to verbalize, especially to "strange" adults, use of subjects' verbal accounts would be limited and somewhat unreliable.

To ameliorate status problems, ethnographers need to spend a large block of time with subjects to become accepted and, more importantly, to be trusted. Researchers must be willing to share their observations and some preliminary inferences to assure subjects that researcher motivations are not sinister or likely to portray subjects as inept or in any way inadequate. Being straightforward and completely honest from the initial contact seem mandatory parts of the research protocol. A researcher needs to make subjects fully aware that they are the "experts" at doing what they do—not the researcher, despite all of his or her credentials and training. Young children are far less skeptical of improper motives, but they may be reticent to talk to or with the researcher. Regular presence breeds familiarity and acceptance by subjects of all ages, but especially children when they also see the researcher accepted by other family members.

Ethnographic teams: Pitfalls and advantages of collaboration. Research in the social sciences pursuing hypothetico-deductive models has a long history of using multiple observers or a team of investigators to attack a certain problem. These collaborative efforts have obvious practical advantages in that they expand the amount of ground covered and reduce the amount of time spent (at least potentially) by any individual in collecting data. Indeed, one of the hallmarks of "good" or sound research designs is the establishment of high levels of inter-observer reliability. Consensus among multiple observers of the same phenomenon is the desired goal: i.e., all observers saw the same things happen in the same day. Procedures are carefully designed; observers are briefed and trained in terms of what to look for and what constitutes an occurrence of interest (to the investigator). Researchers try to avoid the common experience of five accident witnesses with five different, conflicting accounts of what happened. The underlying assumption, of course, is that there are common interpretations of phenomena if observers are carefully trained in what to look for and how to recognize various displays of behavior.

For the most part, naturalistic observation rejects the idea of multiple observers producing a single interpretation. "What is going on here?" is a question to be answered differently by different respondents and by different observers, all reflecting their own frames of reference and their own individual frameworks of interpretation. In analogy to the accident observers, there is no one "correct" account of what happened, but multiple accounts of the event interpreted by the different observers from different vantage points and with different interpretive frameworks. Of course, when there is overlap and agreement on what was perceived to have happened, a legal version of the "truth" may emerge, but no standard of veridicality in fact exists which in essence says, "This is what really happened."

In qualitative inquiry, multiple observers can be used with some degree of reliability. When a researcher seeks to document the occurrence of more concrete, overt behaviors, a research team can be deployed to amass such data. Lull (40), for example, used a team to study family uses and rules for using television. Observations by researchers in households occurred over the same time period and with the same set of predetermined categories to classify the observations. The interpretation of data, once collected, however, remains the province of the researcher, who will develop a case for what such findings mean and what is implied by them. The "team" does not make any overall inferences and interpretations. Even under such conditions of efficiency, though, the researcher loses a great deal by not observing and interacting with each of the families on a first-hand basis. What results is a different kind of narrative which more closely resembles a hypothetico-deductive study with the appearance of a naturalistic framework (a sheep in wolves' clothing?) or a compromise between two largely competitive and antithetical perspectives.

The major drawback of collaborative efforts to study naturalistic phenomena is that the researcher is the instrument "par excellence" (30). The benefit for readers or users of such research is the researcher's explication of his or her own interpretive framework brought to bear upon a given phenomenon. "What is going on here?" is a question with many, many answers. One should always be skeptical of two or more researchers, approaching a situation filled with a horde of uncertainties and unknowns, who come up with, independently, the same basic narrative. Interests, approaches, perspectives, and insights should likely vary, and, in some instances, vary a great deal. What one sees is a function of what one is looking for, and when one is uncertain of what is "there," what is reported should bring in the background, experiences, and interests of each researcher, and each one ought to have an effect, as a participant, on the nature of the interactions among those observed. Thus, what one sees would differ, perhaps substantially, from what is observed and interpreted by others.

Research technologies and naturalistic inquiry: New opportunities. In its rich history, qualitative researchers doing participant observation have relied mainly upon the venerable but simple tools of paper and pencil to take notes on the spot or to jot them at a later point while events were still fresh in the mind. Other researchers made use of audio recordings to increase the ability to keep accurate records of at least some aspects of the inquiry (aurally recorded). In anthropology, the ethnographic film has been used with some frequency as part of a written narrative or as a means of representing the essence of the inquiry. Film or video stock becomes the equivalent of field notes. Photographs have been the only tool, or one of several tools, used by other naturalistic researchers (64). The written record remains the most frequently used tool for naturalistic inquiry—a curious occurrence, especially in the area of mediated communication, where knowledge of how various new technologies can be used should be at a high level of sophistication. Yet, with a few exceptions, naturalistic inquiry into mediated communication contexts has avoided the tools of video recording to collect data and/or as a format for narrative presentation. There are some reasons why this has happened.

Recalling our earlier comments on researcher obtrusiveness, it is easy to make an argument for tools becoming yet another major obstacle which interferes with observation and fundamentally alters the "natural" flow of events to the point where such events become artifacts of the research process (like any laboratory equipment). One can observe and participate somewhat unobtrusively while merely making notes with a pad and pencil, or by turning on an audio recorder and placing it out of sight while events transpire. But the presence of the researcher and his or her impact on what is being observed alters the event; writing in notepads while events transpire, or the presence of a recorder, also remind those being observed of what is going on and that what they are doing is the subject of examination and inference. Obtrusion and its reminders are inescapable parts of the research process.

Audio-visual equipment, it is argued, gives new meaning to the word "obtrusiveness." Indeed, it does. The presence of a camera, recorder, lights, the noise of the equipment running, the size of the equipment, and so on have been considered major drawbacks negating the usefulness of such tools (64). But changes in the capability levels, configuration, and size of the gear have occurred to the point where the obtrusion is not nearly as great as it once was. New developments render many of these limitations obsolete or at least reduced greatly in their significance and potential for distorting the phenomena under study.

Recent video technology enables naturalistic inquiry to proceed with substantially less obtrusion. Camcorders (camera and recorder all in one) weigh less than five pounds, accept full-size 2-hour videocassettes, and produce high quality color video under varying light conditions. The microphones are sensitive and almost miniscule. And, while a broadcast-quality signal is not produced, such video is not intended for broadcast and, therefore, requires a signal that is simply able to be viewed clearly. Audio recorders have also changed to the point where locations can be outfitted with hidden microphones, with machine stop-and-start via voice activation. Infrared cameras can operate in near total darkness. The point is that video gear is no longer the large obtrusion it once was. Researchers who continue to argue that it is obtrusive are only revealing their unwillingness to learn a new form of observation and data collections.

Others have argued that recording devices differ from the eyes and ears of humans:

> Eyes are not cameras; they cannot zoom, nor can they pan. Ears are not microphones. . . . But even if an individual had microphones for ears and cameras for eyes, he is always "situated" within a social environment at some space-time point. Depending on physical barriers, spacing patterns among those present, and his own patterns of locomotion, the same room can look and sound amazingly different to him than it does to others (64, p. 82).

These arguments miss several crucial points. First, video and audio gear are not meant to take the place of the researcher who would be present and interacting in the research setting; they provide an extremely rich source of additional data. Second, cameras and microphones are not eyes and ears; they do not have the same flexibility or sensitivity. But the camera can be used to unobtrusively gain access to positions and angles not possible with the human eye. The researcher, like the camera, can only be in one position at a time. If the camera has an operator, the fixed position point also diminishes in impact. The camera can zoom, selectively focus, and provide extreme closeups in ways neither possible nor practical for the human eye.

Video accounts provide researchers with the ability not only to visually collect data, but to assemble it through editing and production effects in unique ways. Showing a setting at different points in time can be effectively demonstrated by editing segments together; small but important nuances of behavior (72) are revealed by frame-by-frame analysis at different running speeds; split screen techniques offer the chance to see behaviors from different points in time or different locations presented simultaneously; breaking the screen up in four or more parts with separate video inputs also provides an experience of multiple perspectives in an unprecedented way. Linking up computer simulations and projections of actions via animation and image modification also hold a great deal of promise for new constructions of data heretofore unattainable via human observation. Innovations in procedures are always slow to be accepted, but qualitative researchers in other fields are beginning to experiment with video tools as new means to collect and interpret data. Mediated communication researchers should be leading the way in such endeavors, not merely following the lead of others far less knowledgable about the production capabilities of the medium. Video technology can capture and represent events in ways that would be missed by human observation in real time. While video technology's sensitivity is limited, the advantages it offers over the human eye are so overwhelming as to suggest a mandate for its use.

In addition to video and audio technology, it is imperative that we discuss the use of the computer in qualitative research. Computers, of course, have the enormous capacity for storage, retrieval, and editing of data files. In the field, a computer's advantage would be to prepare and file field notes and other pieces of information. Once data are collected, the computer comes in handy as an organizing tool—coding, cross-referencing, merging, and modifying data bases to arrange elements in different combinations. In the long run, computer files can serve an archival function, giving easy access to other users from remote locations, adding the information from other researchers, storing the narrative and updating versions as new findings emerge. In short, the computer offers qualitative researchers staggering control over volumes of data and can be used in a variety of productive ways.

Computers are also most beneficial to researchers who use video as part or all of their data collection. The computer can be used to store coded frames of video, which in turn allows for the analysis of time-coded video. Such time series analyses are especially appropriate for studying the many ongoing, interrelated processes of mediated communication. Linking up video records with computer capability represents another challenge for media naturalists, most notably those who are willing to be weaned from paper and pencil note-taking.

The Presentation of Naturalistic Inquiry. When qualitative researchers complete their analysis and set about the task of preparing a narrative, there are many critical decisions to be made regarding form, medium, length, cost, etc. Traditionally, the narrative has taken the form of books or monographs; on occasion, an article length manuscript is prepared. Again, however, new technological forms enable other forms of presentation. A working narrative could be stored for access by other researchers or interested readers in the same manner as one locates a printed resource on microforms or from the appropriate shelf in the library. Publication might be in the form of videocassette or disc, containing words and pictures (even video records). Raw video stock could also be transferred to a disc as part of the total "record" available to others who are concerned about the representativeness of what was included in a video version.

Traditional print publication does not bode well for media ethnographers. Book publishers are reluctant to commit to lengthy projects with little expectation of finding a fairly sizable market; production costs have been steadily rising, a fact which only worsens an already bad situation. Monographs remain an unlikely outlet, in that there are few opportunities from journals or publishers. (Market size is again the problem.) Journals present the severe handicap of space limitations; many narratives cannot be boiled down to 20-25 pages of manuscript without losing much of the "thick" description which is the primary outcome of the project.

One print alternative outlet is the novel. Some qualitative researchers have fictionalized their accounts and published them as paperback books. Indeed, many of the topics researched by media scholars would lend themselves to such a format. The problem with "fictions" is that they can provide a means to falsely highlight or unfairly emphasize events that did not actually occur that way in the context of data collection. Fictions can cover up weak evidence because they are cosmetically altered to maximize impact on readers. And, despite the qualification of the work as a fictional account based on actual field work, the reader may easily forget the qualifiers and be swept away through the creative uses of dramatic license. Novels may make for better (i.e., more entertaining) reading than nonfictional narratives, but the entertainment value may also make actual narratives pale by comparison and thus make them seem less believable or significant. This issue parallels television's cultivation of docudramas, based on fact but fictionalized to fill in a lot of gaps and to make the story more interesting. A fictional narrative is a "novel" idea that deserves consideration, but it seems to be a venture that carries with it considerable risks. Spelling out the restrictions on dramatic license is the major problem which needs to be solved if novels are to become an acceptable outlet for qualitative inquiry.

Professional and Institutional Constraints on Qualitative Researchers. We have already referred to the rigors of naturalistic inquiry, most notably the commitment and time spent in the field. And, given the limited opportunities for collaboration on a single project, there seems little recourse to expedite qualitative research. Like researchers who bemoan the paucity of longitudinal studies, communication scholars are confronted with institutional obstacles when planning for and implementing a naturalistic research agenda. The results, unfortunately, are similar to the sparse activities of long-term research: much talk and recognition of need, but little productivity.

Researchers doing hypothetico-deductive studies have the advantages of short-term projects and publication outlets well suited to reports of their findings. In a 6-year (or briefer) probationary period prior to tenure, these scholars are able to compile an impressive list of publications and scholarly papers. Funding institutions are problem-oriented and have changing agendas and funding levels, all of which encourage support for short-term projects with periodic reports of progress. Such frequent reports of success are correlated with the accountability of the agency in spending its budget wisely and productively. In essence, the system of support for, and recognition of, research is geared toward hypothetico-deductive inquiry.

In contrast, naturalistic inquiry, prior to the investigation, can offer little more than some general outcomes that might ensue and a long-term agenda with no completed experiments or studies along the way to completion. This basis for inquiry does not lend itself to either funding agencies' agendas or the expectations of faculty imposed by most colleges and universities.

Qualitative researchers face the additional burden of having few publication outlets readily available for their work (as previously described). Thus, even when a project has been completed, it may take an even longer time to finally achieve distribution and recognition. Institutions need to take all of these factors into account when making personnel decisions. The same expectations of vigorous scholarly pursuit and quality research can still be enforced, but the reliance on quantity of output needs to be carefully re-thought and reconsidered. Due recognition to the demands of qualitative methods must be given by administrators and colleagues alike. The present system in most universities seems to discourage such research. Notions of institutional and individual accountability will have to be redefined before any substantial increases in qualitative research in communication are to be forthcoming.

Changes must also take place in the profession: its publications and forums for the presentation of research. Journal and book editors need to be far more broadminded in their range of acceptable projects. The appearance of journals like *Critical Studies in Mass Communication* and special journal issues like *Journal of Broadcasting* in Fall 1982 are important steps in the direction of promoting and sanctioning the usefulness of qualitative research. Professional associations have also shown strong signs of acceptance of naturalistic inquiry. The formation of a Philosophy of Communication Division and a Popular Culture Interest Group in the International Communication Association are most encouraging. It would appear as if the field has begun to take strides in accepting naturalistic perspectives as an important and enlightening form of inquiry of value and interest to scholars and students alike.

Given a general lack of understanding of the complex nexus of interrelated processes of mediated communication, the field can be best served by the methods and theories of naturalistic inquiry in identifying the ontological and praxeological components and interactions. Naturalistic inquiry is well suited to answering key questions of what is going on and how the "what" gets done in everyday life. As such, the goal of this inquiry is to provide thick, rich descriptions (25) of social reality and how such realities are constructed and interpreted. At a later stage, epistemological ("why") questions could be answered at least in part, once a basic understanding of the underlying dimensions of mediated communication behaviors was achieved. Perhaps, at this point, hypothetico-deductive and interpretive paradigms could be used in tandem or in a complementary sense. It may be, however, that the two basic approaches are so different in their assumptions about the nature of social reality and how the world is organized that a blend is impossible. Whether or not each approach needs to choose and/or redefine its goals is debatable. Our comments on the agendas suggested by others in this regard follow.

Contributions of Qualitative Research. Qualitative sociologists have made several suggestions. One is to abandon the heretofore tradition of arbitrarily distinguishing between objectivity and subjectivity. In science concerning human behavior, this notion suggests that all "knowledge" is the product of subjective perceptions. Schwartz and Jacobs (64) encourage us to "not separate the 'real' order that exists in social dealings among humans from the interpretations and accounts of that order produced by society's members" (p. 374)—including, we might add, those of researchers themselves. This position posits an arguable premise which has, for qualitative researchers at least, an appealing face validity. But the two notions of subjective and objective realities are nearly inextricably linked. And, as Schwartz and Jacobs observe:

> We currently have neither an adequate vocabulary with which to describe on-going conscious life nor a scientific methodology for tapping it. Further, we have already seen the complexities involved in retrieving on-going subjective experiences and meanings by observation and/or interviewing. But this task is child's play compared to the job of retrieving members' knowledge, using the same resources. In summary, it is currently unclear what knowledge or competence is . . . and therefore how to retrieve it, whether scientifically or at all (pp. 374–375).

Schwartz and Jacobs also argue that inquiry into human behavior abandon the call of "traditional science," via the hypothetico-deductive models of the physical sciences, and pursue instead the "more modest goal of 'understanding' or 'interpretation' " (p. 376). Several assumptions are present here. First, it is assumed that traditional social science approaches have little chance to lead us to firm, law-like relationships comparable to the physical sciences. In a sense, the goal of traditional science is unattainable, because of the unique properties of the phenomena as complex occurrences. To date, social science has yet to offer a single "law" of human behavior (á la the physical sciences) and appears incapable, perhaps inherently, of accomplishing this end. Second, the pursuit of science as a goal may not be fostered at all by qualitative research methods. Schwartz and Jacobs (64) "see no optimistic signs" that qualitative inquiry "has unearthed the tools that will eventually make a science of society possible" (p. 377). In this regard, they argue that qualitative tools are neither appropriate for nor capable of leading to scientific constructs that can be scientifically validated. The goals, therefore, must be different.

Naturalistic inquiry might be best suited to meeting the goal of contributing to our understanding of exceedingly complex and interrelated processes and events. Whether by Geertz's (25) "thick description" or the explanation of rules (e.g., 75) or by ethnomethods, symbolic interaction, or frame analysis, the inquiry seeks to describe and interpret underlying dimensions and processes, all of which aid our sense of how communication phenomena produce or alter patterns of ongoing human behavior.

Anderson (3) has maintained that synthesizing interpretive and hypothetico-deductive perspectives would require the abandonment of both general modes as a prerequisite to action. One would then start anew, building a framework for understanding that draws only the desirable elements of both paradigms but is free of the restrictions and assumptions that are demanded by them separately. Anderson also suggests that such a synthesis would require a consensus on the key terms in communication inquiry. Included are terms like "locus of meaning," "reality," the concept of the "individual," and the purpose of "scientific explanation."

Regarding the purpose of scientific explanation, Anderson sees it as the choice between rules or laws as goals and that one is not compatible with the other. As he indicates:

> Rules theory itself is an inadequate formulation for dealing with explanation of the situated individual. Explanation from rules like that from laws is inherently reductionistic. Explanation from the situated individual is inherently expansionistic. Reductionistic explanation is not useful in preserving the individual and expansionistic explanation is not adequate for aggregate analysis.

It would seem that Anderson's position is closely aligned with Schwartz and Jacobs' in that both general modes of inquiry are seen as limited in their capacity to produce scientific laws or to contribute to a science of prediction, control, and explanation. Anderson, however, sees the need to construct a new synthetic perspective rather than opting merely for an agenda with understanding as its only primary goal.

In the search for a synthesis or in the adoption of understanding as a primary goal, the accommodation of hypothetico-deductive versus interpretive perspectives becomes a viable question. But the problems inherent with such an approach are many. Ethnomethodologists, for example, urge us to focus on discovering some of what we already know about the ordinary, taken-for-granted experiences of daily life. But, because these experiences are daily rituals, we are not accustomed to "thinking" about what we do and why. We just seem "to do it." Such experiences are thus hidden from us and are only rarely illuminated, and then only when examined in some considerable detail. Much of our ordinary communication behavior also demands a certain amount of "vagueness" which further impairs our ability to assess what is occurring and why. Ironically, vagueness is the arch villain of positivist science, where clarity and objectivity of interpretation are the embraced ideals. But vagueness is essential to daily patterns of social interaction. Without it, or worse with the pursuit of scientific clarity, social interactions as we have come to know and experience them would be nearly impossible. Consider the following conversational exchange:

FRED: You know, all these weather forecasters are full of baloney. They've got millions of dollars of equipment and they still never get it right.

ETHYL: Do you mean all weather forecasters in the world, here in town, on television or where? Do you mean that they give the wrong forecast every single time, most of the time, some of the time, or what?

FRED: You know what I mean. Stop being so picky. Who do you think you are, anyway, Perry Mason? These guys are jerks.

ETHYL: By "jerk," do you mean someone with below average intelligence, an IQ in the single digits, or what?

FRED: The way you're acting, I mean you. Now knock it off!

This exchange vividly illustrates the overwhelming degree to which we rely on vagueness to facilitate our patterns of social interaction. Ethyl's attempts to get Fred to be more precise and clear in his language results in a predictable response from Fred: annoyance over someone breaking the implicit conversational rules that participants in a culture come to quickly understand and apply. But, as mentioned earlier, vagueness, a staple of social interaction, presents a formidable barrier which must be penetrated in order to understand the meanings of communication behaviors for participants.

Another problem for qualitative research of behavioral routines or rituals occurs when much of the business of these rituals turns out to be rather trivial in the search for understanding; the myriad of details carefully considered and dutifully analyzed by researchers may well add up to what seems to be of little or no significance. Separating trivia from significant occurrences is a difficult task for the researcher.

One way of making the separation between trivia and important details requires investigators to move away from the comfortable and convenient mentality that states (á la Durkheim) that "big causes have big effects" or, conversely, that, if we observe big effects, there must be "big causes" preceding them. Big effects can be more usefully thought of as a culmination over time of a variety of causal factors, many of which by themselves may indeed be very small, almost inconsequential. But when conditions are right, chain reactions occur and produce "big" effects. Schwartz and Jacobs refer to the example of what can cause an individual to have a negative self-image, a so-called big effect, brought on by the initial awareness of skin blemishes, the feeling of embarrassment and withdrawal from social interactions, which in turn leads to awkward social encounters due to infrequent practice, which in turn leads to more entrenched feelings of social unacceptability, etc. Combinations of "small" causes interact under the right conditions over time to produce an apparent "big" effect.

Effects of media can be thought of in a parallel mode: 30 million people watching television tonight is a measurable big effect, but its causes are undoubtably quite varied from one person to the next. A hostile man beats his wife nearly senseless because she complains that he watches professional wrestling too much, or because she refuses to get him another six pack for the next bout. What caused the beating, however, may be a combination of factors and conditions which allowed the behavior to be triggered by what seems to be a trivial cause.

It is, of course, more convenient to think of big effects as having big causes; it is certainly more efficient to boil down causal factors to as few in number as possible. This "parsimony" is in fact the goal of the traditional physical sciences, where causes and specified conditions will invariably produce a given effect which can be verified through nearly countless replications. But, if we are to judge social sciences by the standards of achievement in the physical sciences, social science is, as Mazur refers to it, "the littlest science." No single law of human behavior has emerged from the totality of social science research. With such a poor track record, it seems clear that positivist science may never achieve "laws" in the same sense of the physical sciences.

Summary. Our goals for mediated communication research, thus, seem to reside down one of two divergent paths: to pursue science or to pursue understanding (i.e., a grasp of what is occurring and why, but devoid of the unattainable demands of positivist science). If understanding is the goal, then qualitative research methods hold considerable promise. But methods developed to date have presented a veritable horde of procedural and theoretical problems that need to be satisfactorily resolved or at least alleviated to enable them to create those tools which hold the keys to understanding communication behavior in all of its richness and complexity. And, as Harold Garfinkel has long maintained, using others' methods for studying unique phenomena is short-sighted and usually doomed to failure. *Unique phenomena demand the development of methods and theory unique to those phenomena.* The phenomena of mediated communication present an excellent case in point: unique, unprecedented, complex, ambiguous, ethereal, potent, dynamic, emergent, and interdependent with the fabric of social reality. We don't need to stop borrowing from the methods and perspectives of others; we do need to stop wholesale adoptions of others' methods and perspectives which have been developed for inquiry into other unique phenomena. Borrow what is insightful, but use it to develop new methods and theories that do justice to the unique phenomena at hand. Through such inquiry, the goal of increased understanding can be achieved. Its results, while perhaps less impressive than the laws of physical science, will be substantial.

REFERENCES

1. Alexander, A., M.S. Ryan, and P. Munoz. "Creating a Learning Context: Investigations on the Interaction of Siblings During Television Viewing." *Critical Studies in Mass Communication* 1, 1984, pp. 345–364.
2. Anderson, J.A. "Evaluative Principles for Naturalistic Inquiry, Or: How Do I Know That You Know What You're Talking About." Paper presented to the International Communication Association, Minneapolis, 1981.
3. Anderson, J.A. *Communication Research Methods.* New York: McGraw-Hill, in press.
4. Anderson, J.A., P.J. Traudt, S.R. Acker, T.P. Meyer, and T.R. Donohue. "An Ethnological Approach to the Study of Televiewing in Family Settings." Paper presented to the Western Speech Communication Association, Los Angeles, 1979.
5. Barker, R.G., and H.F. Wright. *Midwest and its Children.* Evanston, IL: Row, Peterson, 1954.
6. Bechtel, R.B., C. Achelpohl, and R. Akers. "Correlates Between Observed Behavior and Questionnaire Response on Television Viewing." In E.A. Rubenstein, G.A. Comstock, and J.P. Murray (Eds.), *Television and Social Behavior*, Vol. 4. Washington, DC: U.S. Government Printing Office, 1972, pp. 274–344.
7. Bellman, B.L., and Jules-Rossette, B. *A Paradigm for Looking: Cross-Cultural Research with Visual Media.* Norwood, NJ: Ablex, 1977.
8. Blumer, H. *Symbolic Interactionism.* Englewood Cliffs, NJ: Prentice-Hall, 1969.
9. Bogdan, R., and S. Taylor. *Introduction to Qualitative Methods: A Phenomenological Approach to the Social Sciences.* New York: Wiley, 1975.
10. Bronfrenbrenner, U. "Toward an Experimental Ecology of Human Development." *American Psychologist* 32, 1977, pp. 513–531.
11. "Computers and Qualitative Data" (Special issue). *Qualitative Sociology 7* (1 and 2), 1984.
12. Denzin, N. *Childhood Socialization.* San Francisco: Jossey-Bass, 1978.
13. Denzin, N. *The Research Act* (Second Edition). New York: McGraw-Hill, 1978.
14. Deutscher, I. "Words and Deeds: Social Science and Social Policy." *Social Problems* 13, 1966, pp. 235–254.
15. Douglas, J.D. *Investigative Social Research.* Beverly Hills, CA: Sage, 1976.

16. Durkin, K. "Children's Accounts of Sex-Role Stereotypes in Television." *Communication Research* 11, 1984, pp. 341–362.
17. Ericsson, K.A., and H.A. Simon. "Sources of Evidence on Cognition: A Historical Overview." In T.V. Merluzzi, C.R. Glass, and M. Genest (Eds.), *Cognitive Assessment.* New York: The Guildford Press, 1981, pp. 16–51.
18. Fernie, D.E. "Ordinary and Extraordinary People: Children's Understanding of Television and Real Life Models." In H. Kelly and H. Gardner (Eds.), *Viewing Children Through Television.* San Francisco: Jossey-Bass, 1981, pp. 47–58.
19. Fine, G.A. "Popular Culture and Social Interaction: Production, Consumption and Usage."*Journal of Popular Culture* 11, 1977, pp. 453–466.
20. Fine, G.A. *Shared Fantasy.* Chicago: University of Chicago Press, 1983.
21. Freidson, E. "Adult Discount: An Aspect of Children's Changing Taste." *Child Development* 24, 1953, pp. 39–49.
22. Fry, D.L., and V.H. Fry. "Elements of a Semiotic Model for the Study of Mass Communication." In M. McLaughlin (Ed.), *Communication Yearbook 9.* Beverly Hills, CA: Sage, in press.
23. Gans, H. *The Urban Villagers.* New York: Free Press, 1962.
24. Garfinkel, H. *Studies in Ethnomethodology.* Englewood Cliffs, NJ: Prentice-Hall, 1967.
25. Geertz, C. *The Interpretation of Cultures.* New York: Basic Books, 1973.
26. Goffman, E. *Interaction Ritual.* New York: Doubleday, 1967.
27. Goffman, E. *The Presentation of Self in Everyday Life.* Garden City, NY: Doubleday, 1969.
28. Griffin, M. "What Young Filmmakers Learn From Television: A Study of Structure in Films Made by Children." *Journal of Broadcasting & Electronic Media* 29, 1985, pp. 79–82.
29. Hall, S. "Encoding/Decoding." In S. Hall, D. Hobson, A. Lowe, and P. Willis (Eds.), *Culture, Media, Language.* London: Hutchinson and Co., 1980, pp. 128–138.
30. Hammersley, M., and P. Atkinson. *Ethnography: Principles in Practice.* London: Tavistock, 1983.
31. Hawes, L. "Toward a Hermeneutic Phenomenology of Communication." *Communication Quarterly* 25 (3), 1977, pp. 30–41.
32. Hawes, L. "The Reflexivity of Communication Research." *Western Journal of Speech Communication* 42, 1978, pp. 12–20.
33. Henry, J. *Pathways to Madness.* New York: Vintage, 1965.
34. Hobson, D. *Crossroads: The Drama of a Soap Opera.* London: Methuen, 1982.
35. Jaglom, L.M., and H. Gardner. "The Preschool Television Viewer as Anthropologist." In H. Kelly and H. Gardner (Eds.), *Viewing Children Through Television.* San Francisco: Jossey-Bass, 1981, pp. 9–30.
36. Kockelmans, J.J. "Some Fundamental Themes of Husserl's Phenomenology." In J.J. Kockelmans (Ed.), *Phenomenology: The Philosophy of Edmund Husserl.* Garden City, NY: Anchor, 1967, pp. 24–36.
37. Lemish, D. "Television Viewing in Public Places." *Journal of Broadcasting* 26, 1982, pp. 757–782.
38. Lever, J. "Multiple Methods of Data Collection: A Note on Divergence." *Urban Life* 10, 1981, pp. 199–213.
39. Lewis, O. *Five Families.* New York: Mentor, 1959.
40. Lull, J. "The Social Uses of Television." *Human Communication Research* 6, 1980, pp. 197–209.
41. Lull, J. "A Rules Approach to the Study of Television and Society." *Human Communication Research* 9, 1982, pp. 3–16.
42. McQuail, D. *Towards a Sociology of Mass Communications.* London: Collier Macmillan, 1969.
43. Mead, G.H. *Mind, Self and Society.* Chicago: University of Chicago Press, 1934.
44. Mendelsohn, H., and H.T. Spetnagel. "Entertainment as a Sociological Enterprise." In

P.H. Tannenbaum (Ed.), *The Entertainment Functions of Television*. Hillsdale, NJ: Lawrence Erlbaum Associates, 1980, pp. 13–29.

45. Messaris, P. "Biases of Self-Reported 'Functions' and 'Gratifications' of Mass Media Use." *Et cetera*, September 1977, pp. 316–329.

46. Messaris, P. Personal communication, 1983.

47. Meyer, T.P., P.J. Traudt, and J.A. Anderson. "Non-Traditional Mass Communication Research Methods: Observational Case Studies of Media Use in Natural Settings." In D. Nimmo (Ed.), *Communication Yearbook 4*. New Brunswick, NJ: Transaction, 1980, pp. 261–275.

48. Michaels, E. "Inhabiting Video." Paper presented at the Annenberg Scholars Meeting ("Creating Meaning: The Literacies of Our Times"), University of Southern California, Los Angeles, 1984.

49. Miles, M.B. "Qualitative Data as an Attractive Nuisance: The Problem of Analysis." *Administrative Science Quarterly* 24, 1979, pp. 590–601.

50. Morley, D. *The Nationwide Audience: Structure and Decoding*. London: British Film Institute, 1980.

51. Morris, M.B. *An Excursion into Creative Sociology*. New York: Columbia University Press, 1977.

52. Pacanowsky, M., and J.A. Anderson. "Cop Talk and Media Use." *Journal of Broadcasting* 26, 1982, pp. 741–756.

53. Palmgreen, P. "Uses and Gratifications: A Theoretical Perspective." In R.N. Bostrom (Ed.), *Communication Yearbook 8*. Beverly Hills, CA: Sage, 1984, pp. 20–55.

54. Pelto, P.J., and G.H. Pelto. *Anthropological Research: The Structure of Inquiry* (Second Edition). Cambridge: Cambridge University Press, 1978.

55. Price, D. de Solla. George B. Sarton Memorial Lecture presented to the American Association for the Advancement of Science, 1983.

56. Radway, J. "Interpretive Communities and Variable Literacies: The Functions of Romance Reading." Paper presented at the Annenberg Scholars Meeting ("Creating Meaning: The Literacies of Our Times"), University of Southern California, Los Angeles, 1984.

57. Reid, L.N., and C. Frazer. "Television at Play." *Journal of Communication* 30 (4), 1980, pp. 66–73.

58. Roe, K., and K. Salomonsson. "The Uses and Effects of Video Viewing Among Swedish Adolescents." Media Panel Report No. 31. Lund, Sweden: University of Lund, Dept. of Sociology (mimeo), 1983.

59. Rosengren, K.E. "Communication Research: One Paradigm, or Four?" *Journal of Communication* 33 (3), 1983, pp. 185–207.

60. Rowland, Jr., W.D. *The Politics of TV Violence: Policy Uses of Communication Research*. Beverly Hills, CA: Sage, 1983.

61. Schatzman, L., and A. Strauss. *Field Research: Strategies for a Natural Sociology*. Englewood Cliffs, NJ: Prentice-Hall, 1973.

62. Scholl, M.K. "Four Young Children Construct Reality: Television Watching in the Home." Unpublished doctoral dissertation, Indiana University, 1981.

63. Schutz, A. *Collected Papers I: The Problem of Social Reality*. The Hague: Martinus Nijhoff, 1962.

64. Schwartz, H., and J. Jacobs. *Qualitative Sociology: A Method to the Madness*. New York: Free Press, 1979.

65. Shweder, R.A. "Anthropology's Romantic Rebellion Against the Enlightenment, or There's More to Thinking Than Reason and Evidence." In R.A. Shweder and R.A. LeVine (Eds.), *Culture Theory: Essays on Mind, Self and Emotion*. Cambridge: Cambridge University Press, 1984, pp. 27–66.

66. Sigman, S. "Why Ethnographers of Communication do Ethnography: Issues in Obser-

vational Methodology." Paper presented at the Speech Communication Association, Louisville, 1982.

67. Streeter, T. "An Alternative Approach to Television Research: Developments in British Cultural Studies at Birmingham." In W.D. Rowland, Jr. and B. Watkins (Eds.), *Interpreting Television: Current Research Perspectives.* Beverly Hills, CA: Sage, 1984, pp. 74–97.

68. Taylor, C. "Interpretation and the Sciences of Man." In F.R. Dallmayr and T.A. McCarthy (Eds.), *Understanding and Social Inquiry.* Notre Dame: University of Notre Dame, 1977, pp. 101–131.

69. Thomas, S. "Learning What People Learn from the Media: Some Problems with Interviewing Techniques." *Mass Comm Review* 8 (2), 1981, pp. 2–10.

70. Toulmin, S.E. "Rules and Their Relevance for Understanding Human Behavior." In T. Mischel (Ed.), *Understanding Other Persons.* Oxford: Basil Blackwell, 1974, pp. 185–215.

71. Turkle, S. *The Second Self: Computers and the Human Spirit.* New York: Simon & Schuster, 1984.

72. Van Maanen, J. *Varieties of Qualitative Research.* Beverly Hills, CA: Sage, 1984.

73. Weick, K.E. "Systematic Observational Methods." In G. Lindzey and E. Aronson (Eds.), *The Handbook of Social Psychology* (Second Edition). Reading, MS: Addison-Wesley, 1968, pp. 357–451.

74. Willis, P. "Notes on Method." In S. Hall, D. Hobson, A. Lowe and P. Willis (Eds.), *Culture, Media, Language.* London: Hutchinson and Co., 1980, pp. 88–95.

75. Wolf, M.A., T.P. Meyer, and C. White. "A Rules-Based Study of Television's Role in the Construction of Social Reality." *Journal of Broadcasting* 26, 1982, pp. 813–829.

76. Worth, S., and J. Adair. *Through Navajo Eyes: An Exploration in Film Communication and Anthropology.* Bloomington: Indiana University Press, 1972.

77. Yarrow, M.R. "Problems of Methods in Parent-Child Research." *Child Development* 34, 1963, pp. 215–226.

78. Zelditch, Jr., M. "Some Methodological Problems of Field Studies." *American Journal of Sociology* 67, 1962, pp. 566–576.

PART I

CHILDREN

Chapter 2

Viewers in Diapers: The Early Development of Television Viewing[1]

Dafna Lemish

Oranim, School of Education of the Kibbutz Movement
University of Haifa

It is very quiet in the sleepy home at 2 o'clock in the morning. A fatigued mother is nursing her newborn in front of an old rerun on television. Sometime later, around 2½ years of age, this wiggling bundle will become a regular television viewer on his or her own (2, 15). How does this happen? By what processes do babies become television consumers? How are they socialized into their media environment? What are the developmental milestones along the way that mark their progress towards such mastery? Those are some of the questions that guided the planning and completion of the study reported here.

Hollenbeck and Slaby suggested three basic reasons why we should expect that television is a factor in the lives of infants: (a) they rely heavily on visual and auditory stimulation in developing social skills, (b) they are exposed to television in their homes, and (c) they are highly receptive to television stimulation (10, p. 41). They note that experimental studies found that "(1) infants as young as 6 months of age will visually attend to and vocally respond to television programming . . . , (2) infants from 6 to 12 months of age are typically exposed to an average of one to two hours of television per day in the home . . . , and (3) infants 15 months of age will imitate a televised model. . . ." (pp. 57–58).

To date, studies of this age group have focused almost exclusively on the development of visual attention to television. Anderson and his colleagues' studies of the reciprocity of attention and comprehension of tele-

[1]The author wishes to acknowledge the contributions of Peter Lemish, Mabel Rice, Aletha Huston, and John Wright to this study. The research upon which this article is based was supported by a grant from the Spencer Foundation to the Center for Research on the Influences of Television on Children (CRITC) and by NICHHD training grant IT32HDO7173.

33

vision provided initial information on amount of attention, as well as a list of the formal features of television that attract young viewers (2,3,4). They noted a dramatic increase in attention to television from 1 to 4 years of age. In the home situation, when the television was on, children increased the percentage of time looking at the screen from 6% at age 1 to 40% at age 2. This is followed by 67% attention at age 3–4, and 70% for 5- to 6-year-olds (4). Babies younger than 30 months were found to be very sporadic in their television viewing. They rarely oriented themselves physically towards the television set, and they monitored the screen unsystematically (4). However, thus far, attention studies have not studied the development of infants' and toddlers' attention in detail. It is apparent, therefore, that an important knowledge gap exists on the development of television viewing at its onset. A description of naturally occurring exposure to television seems to be an important task at hand.

Based on the developmental perspective in psychology, the concern in the study is to understand the manifestations of babies' interactions with television throughout the course of their development. This perspective posits two major groups of explanatory variables which account for any communication development: (a) cognitive abilities, and (b) environmental and experiential factors (16). The focus in this study was on the latter, on those socializing forces in the babies' environment and their daily experiences with television. Babies' cognitive development was assumed to take its natural course through a series of stages appropriate to the age group studied. A similar trend was reported by Carew (7), who found in a developmental study that television occupied less than 1% of a baby's time at 12 months, 2% at 18 months, 3% at 24 months, and 8% at 30 months. While individual cognitive differences were not assessed (except for variability in linguistic skills, which was quite obvious), basic understanding of babies' cognitive development is crucial for placing the data in perspective.

DEVELOPMENT IN THE FIRST 2 YEARS

The developmental theory of Piaget places the baby under 2 years old in the sensori-motor stage. At this time, intelligence is considered to be entirely unreflective, practical perceiving-and-doing (8). "Things are lived rather than thought," objects being a mere extension of the action (6). This action-bound knowledge progresses through stages towards more symbolic representations. Towards the end of the first year (marking the age of the younger viewers in this study) the infant is capable of learning new behaviors by imitation, can anticipate the occurrence of events, and manifests intentional behavior (sub-stage IV, according to Piaget; 8). According to Bruner (6, p. 21) this period marks the transition from the enactive representation to ikonic one: "When a child is finally able to represent the world to himself by an image or spatial schema that is relatively independent of action."

The second year of life is marked by purposeful and active exploration of the real properties and potentialities of objects. The onset of language and the gradual development of the ability to represent the objects constitute the major transition from sensorimotor intelligence to Piaget's preoperational stage (which lasts from around 2 to 6–7 years old), or to Bruner's symbolic representation. By 2 years (roughly estimated) the baby is not so bounded by action anymore. Rather, he or she is more occupied with knowledge, information, and socially shared symbolic systems such as language. This capacity for representation manifests itself also by symbolic play, drawings, mental images, and deferred imitation (8).

Of particular relevance for this study is the development of the object concept: i.e., our belief about the basic nature and behavior of objects as physically distinct entities with existences that are fundamentally independent of our perceptual and motor contact with them (8). Thus, object concept is an acquired concept, linked with other sensorimotor stages of development. In its social manifestations, this cognitive achievement facilitates the process of differentiating self from nonself, persons from nonpersons, and one person from another.

It is toward children in this transitional developmental period that this study was aimed: babies discovering their physical and social world, acquiring symbolic abilities, and mastering language. According to Piaget, growth and development are the consequences of interaction with the world around, of assimilating external stimuli to baby's own internal mental structures and accommodating these structures to newly acquired knowledge (9). Television is both part of the baby's world and a mini-world in its own right. It is there for the baby to interact with. The study reported below attempted to place television within this fascinating framework of development.

METHOD

The observations reported here were collected during a participant-observer study. The object was to study babies' behavior in their natural environment, through a relatively long period of time, with minimal researcher obtrusiveness and with an effort to understand television's role from the viewpoint of the family involved.

Sample

A volunteer sample of 16 families in Lawrence, Kansas participated in this study for a period ranging from 6 to 8 months, between December 1982 and July 1983. From birth listings in area newspapers, a random sample of families was solicited by mail. In addition, posters requesting participation were posted in an infant day care center and a preschool. All respondents were included in the study. Altogether there were eight boys and eight girls in this study. At the beginning their ages ranged from 6½ months to 29½ months; at the end of the study they were from 14½ months to 3 years of age.

The children's families varied in many aspects, including parental income, profession, and education; the presence of siblings; life styles; and television consumption and awareness. Two of the families were of mixed ethnic marriages (i.e., one Afro-American father and one Hindo-African father). In the other 14 families both parents were white Americans (with the exception of one English mother), in their late 20s and mid 30s in all but one case of an older couple in their early 40s. In two families the fathers resided outside the home (one in prison and one in another city) and saw their children on the average of once a week. Individual subject descriptive data are reported in Table 1 and family descriptive data are reported in Table 2.

Table 1.   Description of Subjects and Siblings

	Subject			Sibling	
Subject	Age range (months)	Amount of TV viewing*	Sex	Age (years)	Amount of TV viewing*
A	6½-14½	Low	–	–	–
B	8½-17	Low	–	–	–
C	9 -17	Medium	Male	3	Medium
D	11 -16½	Heavy	–	–	–
E	11 -17	Low	Male	4	Low
F	14 -22	Heavy	–	–	–
G	14 -22	Medium	–	–	–
H	14½-22½	Heavy	–	–	–
I	16½-24	Low	Female	3	Low
J	16 -24	Heavy	–	–	–
K	16 -25	Low	Female	3½	Low
L	21 -27	Medium	Female	13	Heavy
M	22½-27½	Medium	Female	11	Heavy
N	21 -26	Low	–	–	–
O	23 -30½	Low	–	–	–
P	29½-34	Medium	–	–	–

*low – an average of 1 hour or less a day
medium – an average 1-2 hours a day
heavy – an average of more than 2 hours a day

Table 2. Description of Subjects' Family

	Father					Mother				
Subject	Age	Ethnic Background	Education	Occupation	Amount of TV Viewing*	Age	Ethnic Background	Education	Occupation	Amount of TV Viewing*
A	Late 20s	White American	College	Student	Medium	Late 20s	White American	College	Student	Low
B	Mid 30s	"	"	Professional	Low	Mid 30s	"	"	Student	Low
C	Early 30s	"	"	Professional	Low	Early 30s	"	"	Professional	Low
D	Late 20s	White European	"	Student	Medium	Early 30s	"	"	Student	Low
E	Early 30s	Hindu-African	"	Student	Medium	Early 30s	White European	"	–	Low
F	Late 20s	White American	"	Professional	Heavy	Late 20s	White American	"	Professional	Low
G	Early 20s	Afro-American	High School	Prisoner	Unknown	Late 20s	"	"	–	Medium
H	Late 30s	White American	High School	Construction (un-employed)	Heavy	Early 20s	"	"	–	Heavy
I	Mid 30s	"	College	Professional	Low	Late 20s	"	"	–	Low
J	Late 20s	"	High School	Sales	Medium	Late 20s	"	High School	–	Heavy
K	Mid 20s	"	College	Professional	Low	Mid 20s	"	College	–	Low
L	Late 40s	"	High School	Construction	Heavy	Late 30s	"	High School	Professional	Low
M	Mid 30s	"	College	Professional	Medium	Mid 20s	"	College	Sales	Medium
N	Mid 30s	"	College	Professional	Low	Late 20s	"	College	Student	Low
O	Early 30s	"	"	Professional	Medium	Late 20s	"	"	Professional	Low
P	Early 30s	"	"	Student	Heavy	Late 20s	"	"	Professional	Low

*low – an average of 2 hours or less a day
medium – an average of 2-4 hours a day
heavy – average of 4 hours or more a day

37

Data Collection

The 16 families were visited four to five times in their homes. The initial visit included an unstructured, intensive interview about the family characteristics, the total television environment, and the child's personality, development, schedule, and television exposure and behavior. The subsequent observation visits were scheduled about every 6 weeks, during times when the babies' would have been naturally exposed to television. Consequently, these sessions took place at all hours of the day and evening, including weekends. During these visits, the baby's behavior around the operating television set was observed for a period from 1 to 2 hours, and recorded in detail. In addition, at each visit parents were interviewed about their child's viewing behaviors that occurred between visits, and about behaviors observed by the visitor. Most mothers kept viewing logs throughout the study's period in which they recorded their baby's television-related behavior. Two full week diaries of each family member's viewing in 15-minute segments were collected, one at the beginning of the study (winter) and one at the end (summer). Halfway through the study, a screening test of each baby's language development was administered (Brigance). Finally, in the last session, the parents were also asked about their overall reaction to the study and their perception of the role television has in their lives.

THE DEVELOPMENT OF ATTENTION TO TELEVISION

All the babies that participated in this study were exposed to television to some degree. They were present in the room when a variety of programs were broadcast—children's programs, news, sports, situation comedies, soap operas, movies, talk shows, music shows—the whole television fare. Obviously, being in the room with an operating television set is not equivalent to attending to it. It does, however, constitute a necessary condition for viewing television. In addition, these data provide us with significant information on the family's television environment, in general, or the viewing context. Not surprisingly, actual visual attention to television (defined as eyes oriented towards the screen) increased with age, in amount as well as in the variety of content attended to. The following descriptions along the developmental span illustrates this point.

0-6 Months[2]

Babies' acquaintances with television occurred quite early in their lives. In their effort to recall such experiences, parents described the following:

---

[2]The age breakdown emerged from the data themselves. It follows Piaget's sensorimotor substages during the second year.

M:[3]   When she was young—6-8 weeks, she was lying in the playpen and watching the TV. I worried about how it would affect her because her father is a TV addict . . . I'll go out and Father sits on the couch and holds her in his lap. She was paying attention to it. She really was watching football games. All the action and people's voices. (F)

M: He was probably 2-3 months, lying down with the bottle and watching. It was neat. Because we'd move him but his eyes will go straight to the TV. I don't know what it was, but I really thought it was something at the time. When he got more aware of toys and people it changed. (a drop-out subject)

M: When he was an infant in a little seat, I used to put him in front of the TV set for *Sesame Street*. I have pictures of that. I thought the movement and the colors—he'll just sit there and watch at 2-3 months. I thought he enjoyed it then, he'll smile to it. I didn't think he was learning anything, but I thought he was enjoying it. (J)

Similarly, mothers reported immediate reactions to loud voices and sudden noises, such as stopping of nursing and turning of head towards the screen. While parents' interpretations of such behaviors are arguable, there is enough evidence of awareness to at least some auditory cues at a very young age.

6-10 Months

Towards the end of the first year, the attraction to the audio track of television became more apparent. Most of the instances of attention to television were in a similar context—baby was playing or feeding in the room. Certain sounds (e.g., howling wolves, drumming, muppet's voice, Pepsi commercial, laughter) cued him/her to stop an activity and to orient eyes to the screen. In most cases, attention lasted less than half a minute (often a few seconds only), and then the baby resumed his/her activity. Of particular interest as attention attracters at this age were two kinds of programs—commercials and *Sesame Street*. Both types of programs center around a short segment format and specialize in attracting attention through audio and visual means.

---

[3]Abbreviations used in presenting the data are the following:

M – A direct quotation from the mother.
F – A direct quotation from the father.
B – A direct quotation from the baby.
ML – Information copied from mother's television log.
Obs – Data recorded directly during an observation session.

At the end of each example, in parenthesis, appears the code letter of the particular baby studied and his/her age (when the age is not given in the illustration itself). For further information on the baby, the reader is referred to the tables. All names in the body of the illustrations are substituted by the general names: Baby, Mother, Father, Sister, Brother, in order to protect the identity of the participants.

10-18 Months

By the first half of the second year, a few clear patterns of attention have emerged. The attraction to music was one such pattern. A consistent excitement over the *Sesame Street* theme song became evident. Babies would stop whatever they were doing and would run from other rooms to watch, sway, rock, bounce and clap their hands, sing along with the television, and vocalize in excitement. This phenomenon was regularly observed both by me and by the parents, and remained true for all babies once they had become regular *Sesame Street* viewers. In addition, the opening songs of situation comedies (e.g., *Happy Days, One Day at a Time*) and commercials brought a wandering baby from the kitchen or playroom to the television set. Familiarity with some basic aspects of television was already evident in such behavior. Babies knew exactly where the sounds came from, and they had a favorite commercial or song to which they reacted consistently in the same manner.

A second pattern of attention was the interest in particular content. Both mothers' reports and observations revealed growing attachments to some of the *Sesame Street* puppets-muppets (e.g., Big Bird, Ernie and Bert, Grover, Oscar the Grouch). Further, clear personal preferences to one or another were prevalent. Babies as young as 15 months (and certainly by 2 years) were able to point out and name most of these major characters and recognize them in nontelevision contexts as well (e.g., books, toys, stores, posters, or clothing).

Preference to familiar content was observed in other programs. Babies preferred commercials and program bits that included babies and young children, as well as familiar animals such as dogs, cats, and horses. One illustrative example is the following:

> M: Baby sat for 10 minutes looking at herself (home video tape). She got real excited. She does very little of anything for that length of time, definitely never watched television for such a length. She got up, stood very close, 6 inches away from it. She tried to touch the screen, turned around and smiled, and stood there for the rest of it. (B, 12 months)

The data suggest that, by the first half of the second year, babies were not only drawn to television by musical, unusual, or noisy miscellaneous audio cues, but gradually developed a certain selectivity to familiar content, the kind that made some sense to them. This observation seemed to be supported by their verbal references. Babies of this age group were busy pointing to and naming objects on the screen. The strong relationship between television viewing and language development (13) was also manifested by the growing role parents and caregivers played in their babies' attention to television. First, parents simply called the babies' attention to it. More often than not, it was done by providing a name, produced in an exaggerated enthusiastic tone. Such was the case of a 10½ month old baby viewing *Sesame Street*:

Obs: M: There he goes, there is the dog. See the flowers? Where is the boy, Baby? Where is the boy? Oh! Look! There are your favorite ducks and cows! See the cows! Kitten. Little boy. Look at the kittens. Chicks. Look at the little chick, Baby. (A)

Another way was of requesting a label for objects clearly known to the baby:

Obs: F: What's that?
      B: Frog.
      F: And what's that?
      B: Hop, hop, hop.
      F: What's that, Baby?
      B: Ball.
      M: Ball. Three balls. One, two, three. (D, 15 months)

It seems that, close to babies' first birthday, parents start to conceive of television as a potentially useful source of stimuli. Lemish and Rice (13) suggest that parents use television as a talking book. This tendency developed hand in hand with babies' growing interest in television. The brief glances were partially replaced by periods of full concentrated attention. Attention ranged in many cases for the entire length of a commercial, 3–5 minutes of *Sesame Street*, Music TV, and cartoons, or even a few minutes of a nature program on familiar animals. Occasionally, attention lasted as long as 15 minutes of eyes on the screen. Further, by 16 months, two of the babies were reported in their mothers' logs to occasionally watch *Sesame Street* for a straight half hour, seated in front of the television free of other activities.

Second, babies seemed attuned to their parents' own attention and often looked at the screen when their parents seemed engrossed in it. Moreover, babies were seated on Dad's lap or by Mom on the sofa in an attempt to settle them down briefly, so the parent could steal a few quiet moments of a favorite show.

The availability of food was another major attention attractor. Babies provided with a snack or finishing a bottle were very quiet and attentive viewers. The initiative for this combination lay with the parents. For example, mother handed a baby a bottle, placed him in front of the television, and turned it on for him.

M: At 8 a.m. he watches *Sesame Street* with his bottle sitting on his chair. If he just started his bottle, he'll sit for 30 minutes, if already had it— maybe 15 minutes. (J, 16 months)

In sum, during the first half of the second year, babies started noting television more often and for longer stretches of time. Their attention was still affected strongly by the audio track, yet they had already developed some consistently personal tastes for particular content. Seven of the 11 babies studied at this age group were already regular viewers of *Sesame Street*. Clearly, they recognized the music and main figures of this program. In addition, viewing television was an opportunity for these viewers to practice newly acquired words and to interact with parents. There seemed to be no doubt that by this age television had become a part of their lives.

18 Months and Older

From 18 months on, the trends noted thus far became more routinized and evident. Babies up to 2 years continued to be most interested in commercials and vivid music, and most of them viewed *Sesame Street* on a regular basis. By 18 months, the regular *Sesame Street* viewers showed increased interest in numbers and letter sequences, and paid very close attention to them. The short skits and animated bits were next in the development of attention, with the human conversation and "plot of the day" segments being viewed by the full-attention viewers only.

It must be emphasized that this attention trend—from major non-human characters to *Sesame Street* song and other musical and audio special effects, to numbers and letters, animation, and finally to human conversation—was observed and reported for all babies, regardless of the age in which they started to watch *Sesame Street*. Attention to other program categories was significantly lower, with some budding interest in cartoons, *Electric Company*, and action-filled segments of adventure programs (e.g., a car chase on the *Dukes of Hazzard*). Babies started showing signs of disappointment when a favorite segment ended, such as in the following case:

> ML: Baby was watching the *Fall Guy* with us. A helicopter chasing a car segment kept his undivided attention. When it ended he cried in disappointment. (M, 23 months)

Interest in other babies or children who appeared on the television grew even stronger, whether they appeared in commercials, *Sesame Street*, situation comedies, or even the news. Babies' concern over these fellow-beings and other helpless beings was manifested in their behavior and talk:

> M: When TV is on she looks when someone is crying and says—man crying or baby crying. Last night we were watching a man who had been deformed into a monster and he cried and she looked and said—"man crying." That was a time I thought she shouldn't be watching.

F: She seems to be worried when someone cries or gets hurt. (L, 21½ months)

M: Last weekend we were watching *Bugs Bunny* and they had Porky Pig, Petunia and a little baby, and the baby was getting into all kinds of trouble and she was just getting into a fit saying: "No baby. No baby. Do this. Do that. Go away. Be careful," etc. She really got very upset. In fact, it was to the point that I actually had to hold her in my lap and control her and tell her that the baby is fine. And I never thought that will happen—it was only a cartoon. (P, 29½ months)

In addition to the growing interest in television content, babies seemed to be developing new selecting strategy in their viewing behavior.

M: It seems that she is more discriminative now. She knows what she wants to watch and she watches, and what she doesn't watch, she doesn't. Like the morning news—she ignores it. While in the past she'll drift in and out. (F, 19½ months)

Babies were often observed to glance at the television on a regular basis at transition points—between segments, at the beginning and end of programs, and the like. Most transitions of this nature are marked by special music, sound effects, and changes in voices. Following our earlier claim, these phenomena could attract attention in their own right. However, brief glances seemed to be enough for the babies to somehow recognize and maybe even anticipate the nature of the following program, and to make a decision on some level of whether or not to continue watching (11). News broadcasts, talk shows, soap operas, and movies were consistently ignored for long stretches of time, while the first sign of a commercial would get the babies' full attention. From continuous observation of these babies, one could not but appreciate their ability to recognize the closure of a *Sesame Street* segment or a commercial, and to detach themselves from the television to go back to their activity a second or two before the program ended.

Parents continued to play a major role in their babies' viewing habits. They now consciously encouraged viewing—be it *Sesame Street* in the morning, while preparing supper, or the Saturday morning cartoons:

M: I like to put on [television] when fixing dinner because he sits and doesn't pop up all the time. (H, 22 months)

M: We walk in the door, the coats come off, the TV goes on and I go to pick the mail and do all the rest. It's kind of nice, because that's my half hour to get my things done. (P, 29½ months)

Parents continue to interact with their little viewers and reinforce their interest verbally:

Obs: Father turns baby's chair to face television
(Sunday morning religious program for elementary school children).
F: What do you see? You want to watch? (corrects her sitting position). See the cow? See the donkey?
(Father walks to the television, pointing out: Here is a donkey, a pig, and here is the cow. Baby watches. Father goes to the kitchen. Baby follows him.)
F: (From the kitchen) See the animals?
(Baby walks in, walks to the television pointing—touching a puppet.)
B: Who's that?
F: What?
B: Who's that Daddy?
F: I don't know. Oh, I know, it's a lamb. (O, 24½ months)

Most often, babies viewed for longer times as long as parents were around and interacted with them. Six of the 8 babies observed by the age of 2 years old, however, were left to watch alone, and would regularly stay with a *Sesame Street* program for as long as 30–40 minutes of almost full attention. This information was both observed and reported.

Finally, during the second half of the second year, babies started making specific viewing requests. They exhibited viewing habits and recognized that television can be turned on and off at will:

Obs: B: I want to watch *Sesame Street*!
     M: You want to watch *Sesame Street*? O.K. Right on cue. How did you know it's 9 o'clock?
(Mother turns the television on. Baby sits on sofa by the set watching attentively.) (I, 20 months)
     ML: I was watching an afterschool special. Baby came in saying: Turn off TV Mama. I turned the TV off. (N, 25 months)
     M: She watches *Sesame Street* everyday as we walk into the house from day care, about 5:30-6:00. Now it's a habit. So the first thing she asks is to see *Sesame Street*. She comes back and tells me to turn it off when the program is over. (P, 29½ months)

The overall picture emerging from these data is surprising in some ways and not too surprising in others. As expected, based on previous literature, as babies grew older their attention span lengthened and they attended to television more often and for longer stretches at a time. In addition, these data confirm that children come to attend more readily to the following formal features of television—nonverbal auditory features (such as lively or loud music, sound effects, peculiar voices, nonspeech vocalization, audio changes); special effects and pans; high levels of physical activity and dialogue by child characters (11, 1, 2). The babies in this study were therefore much in line with the preschool viewers.

In addition, what is different from the published literature is our conclusion that babies are able to attend to attractive programs (in this case, *Sesame Street* and commercials) at a much younger age and for much longer than we might have expected. Consistent and strong encouragement by parents to watch the program may provide at least a partial explanation of this interest in television. The actual amount of viewing seems to be of less significance than the development of content preferences. A common thread seemed to be the interest in the familiar and the meaningful. An attachment to particular figures and songs, the interest in animals and babies, the almost compulsive need to label familiar objects — all of these behaviors lend support to the hypothesis that more comprehensible programming leads to higher attention (5,4). Newborns' almost reflexive responses to television sounds gradually developed to an active search for familiar content. Clear manifestation of this selective scrutinizing was evident even before the first birthday, while clear and describable preferences were already formed by the second birthday. This evidence lends support to Anderson and his colleagues' attempts to analyze how children learn the codes of television and become increasingly sophisticated in understanding its content (11, 14, 17). According to them, the younger and least experienced viewers' attention "is guided largely by the perceptually salient auditory and visual forms of the medium" (11, p. 40). This form of attention gradually gives way "to perceptual search, a kind of information-getting activity that is instrumental rather than consummatory and that is guided by internally generated goals rather than by external sensory events . . . the shift . . . enables the child to ignore many of the perceptually salient cues and to select for attention those features that are informative, interesting, or pertinent to her reasons for viewing" (11, p. 40). This shift is understood to be a result of both growing familiarity with the medium, its codes, conventions and production techniques (formal features), and developmental changes in the child's cognition. The babies in the study reported here, in their own experiential and cognitive limits, already manifested shades of this shift in those programs that were highly familiar to them. Their attentional sampling at program boundaries suggest that they were at least literate enough to note form codes that are unique to particular appealing bits of programs. This is only a small step towards television literacy, but it is a good start.

There was also support for the hypothesis that changes in bits and scenes recruit attention for those who are not looking, and lose attention for those who are. Huston and Wright (11) suggest three classes of events that could elicit a brief look if the initial decision is not to attend. As have already been reported, all three were clearly observed in this study: (a) very salient events (sirens, screams, crashes); (b) events signaling a change in content (a change from adult to child's voice; change to a familiar puppet's voice; a change to a commercial); and (c) events in the viewing environment (parents' encouragement; availability of alternative activities).

The field of psychology in general has taken a turn recently towards paying more respect to babies' potential to master skills at a much earlier age than has been commonly believed in the past. The case of television viewing, for better or for worse, may provide one additional example of the environment's effect on accelerating the course of development and the role of experience in mastering skills.

THE VIEWING SITUATION

Now that we have established that babies do indeed attend to television, it is of interest to learn of the situation in which this attention occurs and the forms the interaction with television takes.

In general, very little is known about the natural environment in which children and babies in particular view television. Yet, the behavior in these babies while watching television in their home environment highlighted the integrated manner in which television is consumed.

In all cases, television was viewed in the living room or dining room areas while babies engaged in a wide variety of normal everyday activities—playing, eating, changing diapers, interacting with others, drawing, looking at books, climbing on furniture. Babies' viewing positions varied from standing right by the set, sitting close by on the floor, sitting in a favorite spot (e.g., corner of sofa, stool, rocking horse), or sitting in a highchair across the room.

The typical novice-viewer would roam through these activities and occasionally he or she would look up at the television set. If interested, the baby would freeze in position (e.g., in the middle of banging a hammer, or when his or her hand was holding a cracker an inch away from an open mouth) until the "spell" was over, and then the activity was resumed. If interest was great, then the baby would often run right to the television set and watch at an arm's distance from it. Parents typically discouraged this proximity. Often, as the baby was pulled away from the television, he or she would run right back.

This closeness to the set was often accompanied by two touching behaviors: (a) playing with the television knobs; and (b) a seemingly great drive to touch the screen. The regularity of these behaviors with all the babies deserves discussion.

Playing With Television Knobs

Playing with the knobs, remote control, and cable boxes was observed and reported as early as at the age of 8 months old (i.e., as soon as babies were able to pull themselves up to a standing position). At first, playing with the knobs was as playful as many other attempts to explore and manipulate objects in the environment. Thus, babies of the same age were trying out radio and stereo as well as television knobs. Gradually, this behavior became more routinized and purposeful, and attracted more and more parental displeasure:

M: He is real interested in the knobs and things like that, likes to turn it on and off. We don't want him to do it. He thinks it's funny and screams. (C, 9 months)

Obs: Mother turns *Sesame Street* off after Baby lost interest. Baby crawls to television, stands up and turns it on and off. Mother takes him away.

M: Baby has begun to turn the TV on—seems aware of what he's doing. He is into turning it on and off, playing with buttons. It looks like he is doing it purposefully. He does it smiling—but does it. He gets very pleased with himself when he turns it on now. We resort at times to unplugging the TV. (A, 10½ months)

M: She plays with the knobs and with the remote control. She understood at a very young age that this [remote control] made that [television] jump. She doesn't know which button does what, but when she finds one, like the on and off one, she will press it many times. (F, 14 months)

M: Baby gets close to the set, plays with the remote control. He turns the TV off and on and laughs. He knows what he is doing, and thinks it's a lot of fun. (J, 16 months)

All babies in this study turned television on and off, turned volume up and down, switched channels. They all seemed to enjoy it and to know that their parents disapproved of such behavior. Yet, they did it often, seemingly on purpose, perhaps to get parents' attention:

Obs: As we talk, Baby turns the television on, looks at us expecting a reaction, and then he just leaves it.

M: That's exactly what he does. He plays with the knobs and we turn it off and it will go back and forth over 10–20 times at once, 4–5 times a day. It's like a toy, something to manipulate that makes noise. Sometimes I unplug it and he leaves it alone. (K, 17 months)

Except for being a fun activity, it also turned out to be a very important television-learning lesson for these babies. As early as 16 months, and certainly by 2 years, babies were turning television on by instruction, or at will, for the purpose of actually viewing television (and not only for mere fun):

ML: I sang the *Sesame Street* song to Baby and he smiled and walked to the TV and tried to turn it on. (H, 16 months)

M: As soon as we brought the sofa home, he sat on it facing the TV saying—basketball game and then he went to the TV to turn it on. (K, 20½ months)

As this instrumental behavior emerges, other forms of play with the knobs decrease drastically. From around 2 years old, there was almost no incidence observed or recorded of such play. One exception was a 29½-month-old baby who broke the television by turning it on and off vigorously when his mother was on the phone, trying to get her attention!

Touching the Television Screen
The second type of behavior related to proximity to the television set is of even greater significance. Babies seemed compelled to touch characters, faces, animals, and colorful graphic designs on the screen. At first, this touching was quite indiscriminate:

M: When he stands by the TV he pats it like he is trying to feel it. (A, 10½ months)

Obs: While playing with knobs—Baby gets fixed on a black and white segment on the Holocost. Baby puts open left hand on the television screen, moves it away and stares at it (as if expecting the picture to remain on it) and puts it back. Continues to play with volume knob.

M: Sometimes she gets excited and goes up and touches it with both hands and makes loud noises. I haven't noticed that it was anything in particular. (B, 11 months)

Gradually, touching becomes more selective:

M: Baby pats the TV. It could be for lots of reasons—because he knows he isn't supposed to play with the TV and he likes the knobs. Some of it is trying to touch *Sesame Street* figures. Sometimes he tries to get Brother's attention or tease him by being in his way. (C, 12½ months)

M: During evening programs, Baby may stand 2 feet from the TV and dance during commercials, or go right to it and touch it, if it's a face. (F, 14 months)

Obs: Big Bird and Snuffy are on *Sesame Street*. Baby stands next to the TV saying, "kittie," and touching Snuffy with right hand, and then patting him and Big Bird with both hands. (K, 14½ months)

M: Sometimes he watches this cartoon. He likes the dog and tries to touch the screen. When he sees something exciting, he'll go right to it and point or touch it. He tries to give kisses to things, to Kermit for example. (C, 15 months)

ML: The Count was singing about bones. During a closeup of the Count, Baby stood in front of the set and patted it. He then puckered his face into a kissing gesture and tried to kiss the Count. This is a pattern. More than 4–5 times daily. Baby will put his lips to the TV and kiss closeups of puppets, people, and animals. (H, 16 months)

M: Earlier he used to touch the TV indiscriminately, obviously intrigued with the movements and colors. More recently it's more discriminated to figures and animals. With Big Bird today it struck me, because he was greeting him like a friend, running across the room to touch him. (E, 16 months)

Touching out of excitement and familiarity was therefore a common behavior of babies less than a year old and up to a year and a half. The need to touch and explore the screen seemed to be drastically reduced with age and experience with television. Babies must have learned that the screen feels the same regardless of what is on.

Their parents' discouragement probably speeded up this learning. As with other television related behaviors described in this study, this developmental trend from indiscriminate touching to more specific kinds and finally to no touch at all was observed with all babies. The individual differences were manifested in the variability of ages in which the different milestones were reached, and in the frequency of touching. One striking example was that of an 11-month-old baby, a regular *Sesame Street* viewer before her first birthday, whose touching behavior was already in decline:

M: She used to go more towards the TV, and [she had] learned the trick of turning the volume up, and I'll go—"No! No!" and pull her away. And she'll lay just under it, where her shelf of toys is. And she'll occasionally look up at it; or a couple of times pat the TV, like when Bert or Ernie are on. . . . She was fascinated with it [the TV] at the beginning, always going up to touch it. Now I think she [has] almost realized what it is, and that she can't actually reach them, because I noticed that she doesn't play with the volume or with the TV that much anymore. . . . Before she always tried to touch the things (on TV). (D, 11 months)

By 15 months, this baby was completely "weaned" from touching behaviors. On the other hand, another baby who was introduced to television on a regular basis by 18 months, was still touching it at 22 months. Similar to playing with the knobs, almost all touching behaviors disappeared around 2 years of age.

The evidence pertaining to touching objects and figures on the screen can be related to the general development of the "object concept," as was referred to earlier. Babies gradually acquired the understanding that an object or a person is an external entity that exists and moves about in complete independence from self and from his or her own perceptual or motor contact with it (8). The 8- to 12-month-old baby can manually search for hidden objects in familiar places, but will not find them when the place is changed even in front of his eyes. The 12- to 18-month-old baby, on the other hand, learns to search for the object at whatever place the object was most recently seen to disappear. Only by 18 months will the baby start to use visual evidence to imagine or represent an object's hiding places (8). The exposure to television must be somewhat confusing for the baby. Television presents familiar objects without the immediate physical experience of them. This differs greatly from any other object related to in the experiential environment. Hence, all attempts to touch and kiss these objects produce surprising results: The objects can't be actually touched, and their texture is not felt. All television objects feel smooth, like glass. In addition, these objects behave differently: Sometimes they disappear and never come back, while at other times they reappear unexpectedly. In yet other cases, they appear with definite regularity. Finally, at all times, once they have disappeared, no searching strategy can reveal them, including searching behind the "box."

Babies occasionally asked to see an object again that was not on the screen anymore, even one seen days earlier. At other times, they expected to be able to experience an object in usual modes of behavior:

M: Baby gets close and touches the screen and asks to hold things that are on TV. Like she says—"I want to hold that bunny" and I'll say—"No, it's just a picture of TV, it's not real." (I, 22 months)

How do babies cope with such experiences that contradict all other object related lessons? Does the touching behavior facilitate learning about television? Does the disappearance of touching signify certain television literacy, even at a minimal level? Those are relevant questions that need further exploring. Developmentally, touching behavior disappears coincidentally as object-permanency is achieved, and as regularity of experiences with television is established. As in many other television related issues, cognitive development as well as experience with the medium can provide us with initial hints of answers.

The experienced viewer, as has been pointed out earlier, attended for much longer periods of time and moved much less frequently. Often this baby was completely absorbed in the viewing, ignoring other activities around him or her without being affected by the presence of adults (except for level of verbalization). While this "experienced" baby had often outgrown the need to constantly touch the screen, he or she still preferred to view in close proximity to the set. Some of the babies at this stage had well developed viewing habits, such as choice of seating arrangement or eating certain meals while viewing. These habits had been often initiated or encouraged by the parents for babysitting functions.

IMITATION AND LEARNING

Engagement in imitative behavior was an additional aspect of the viewing situation. A separate discussion of this phenomenon is warranted, due to the importance of imitative behavior as an indication of the role television has in the lives of the babies, and for its role as a facilitator of learning.

The first signs of imitative behaviors appeared around 16 months of age. Detailed descriptions can illustrate the richness of the phenomenon. They are organized by babies rather than by the overall chronological age.[4] Simple imitation of television behaviors was apparent in the following examples:

ML: Baby was watching a chocolate commercial at friends' house. She kicked her legs up like the girls did in the commercial. (G, 16 months)

ML: I was watching Donahue in the other room. She heard clapping and started clapping her hands. (G, 21 months)

ML: She was watching a cartoon character cry out and she pretended to cry. (G, 21½ months)

ML: Baby lifted his arms up when two cartoon figures did. (H, 16 months)

ML: Baby watched a small monkey climbing around a fence. He then went to the bottom of the stairs and yanked at the gate trying to climb. (H, 16 months)

ML: Baby watched Cookie Monster stuff cookies into his mouth and imitated putting his hand to open mouth about a half dozen times. (H, 16 months)

ML: Children on the program were clapping out their names. Baby clapped with them. Then he imitated the children running in a circle and started singing and running throughout the downstairs rooms. (H, 22 months)

While the above two babies were clearly imitating television behaviors, the following baby demonstrated an ability for deferred imitation as well as application of the behavior to other circumstances:

---

[4]This was done for two reasons: First, such presentation allows a better understanding of the single baby and his or her style of interaction with television. Secondly, the data produced much more information on imitation for some of the babies. It is probably a reflection of both the variability among babies as well as a mere difference in parents' efforts in completing their daily logs.

Obs: Baby makes an attempt to imitate Mr. Rogers and snaps her fingers at the right places in the song even though Mr. Rogers *did not* do his usual snapping today and even though her attention to the song seemed very minimal. (I, 18 months)

ML: Baby was playing outside acting out a story she'd seen on *Sesame Street* several days earlier. She asked the dog to move so she can look under him. (I, 18½ months)

ML: About 30 minutes after watching people measure on *Sesame Street*, Baby finds a book with people measuring on the cover and then asks for and points to measuring tape so she can measure. She measures herself and several toys. (I, 20½ months)

ML: Baby was watching *Sesame Street* with her mother and sister. She lays down, covers herself up and makes pretend sleeping noises, such as those seen several days before. (I, 20½ months)

ML: Baby imitates in the kitchen ice skating seen 10 minutes earlier on *3-2-1 Contact*. (I, 20½ months)

ML: Baby starts singing the song: "I am you" which she heard earlier on *Sesame Street*. (I, 22 months)

ML: We went to the library the other day – Baby and Sister got so excited reading exit signs enthusiastically – from *Sesame Street*. Also they play waiting for the bus that they have learned from *Sesame Street*. Last night in the bathtub they played "being in the ocean" that they saw on *Mr. Rogers* earlier. (I, 24 months)

Similarly, the following baby was clearly associating television content with his environment and his ability to manipulate it (e.g., asking for milk, playing the piano). He also demonstrated learning a ritual associated with television viewing – going through the *TV Guide*:

Obs: Baby attends to the *Sesame Street* theme song with Sister. He sees a baby with a bottle and goes to the kitchen to ask for milk. (K, 19 months)

ML: A few days ago Baby picked up the *TV Guide*, flipped through the pages, put it back in the drawer and turned the TV on. I think it's something he sees me do. (K, 19 months)

ML: After *Sesame Street* was over, Baby sat at the piano singing "Twinkle Twinkle" and banging his head on the piano shouting: "Never, never." This followed a segment where a puppet composer was trying to make up the "Twinkle Twinkle" song and in frustration saying: "Oh, I'll never get it, never, never." (K, 23 months)

The two babies described below were learning specific physical skills, either by direct imitation (throwing a ball, performing, wrestling) or through the motivation a television stimulus aroused in them (playing baseball):

M: She likes basketball games on TV. I've seen that at home and the babysitter said it too. She goes with her hand like she is throwing the ball. (L, 20 months)

ML: Baby was watching lady sing a song in a variety program. She made the same arm motions as the lady did, pretending to perform. (L, 23½ months)

ML: Baby was watching wrestling with parents. He laughed and jumped up and down like the wrestlers.

ML: Baby was watching a natural history show on snakes with us. After watching the snakes, he crawled all over the living room saying: "Being snake." (M, 24 months)

ML: Baby was watching Mr. Rogers snap his fingers and tried to also. He continued trying to snap his fingers throughout the evening. (M, 24 months)

F: A month ago we watched a baseball game. He was extremely interested, laid beside me for about 20 minutes, completely interested. And the next day he wanted to learn to play, and he's been practicing it everyday since then. (M, 28½ months)

Other common imitative behavior included incidences of laughing, applauding, and yelling on cues provided by the television. Music played an important role in eliciting dancing, rocking, clapping, and singing in babies as young as 11 months swaying in their highchairs, and as old as 2/12 years singing along with words.

The above examples suggest the facilitative potential of imitation for learning from television. As the data suggest, one obvious form of learning was that of expanding vocabulary and practicing discourse (13). But in addition, as we analyze the data we find a variety of cases where babies manifested learning of symbols—letters, numbers, as well as concepts (shapes, relations). This was particularly true for viewers of *Sesame Street* (12). Recognition of letters and numbers, reciting the alphabet and counting, were obviously learned by the babies in this study, both directly from the program and indirectly through parents' and siblings' mediation:

M: She learned how to count from *Sesame Street*, I'm sure, about 3–4 weeks ago. She heard it on *Sesame Street* and we reinforced it. I'll say "1" and she goes: "2-3-4" and I'll say "5" and she says "6." (D, 15 months)

ML: Baby was in other room and overhead David [on TV] counting to 5. She counted by herself to 10 correctly. I had no idea Baby can count to 10. It was a big surprise. (I, 18½ months)

ML: Baby eats her toast in different letters and makes an x with her diaper pins. She learned it from *Sesame Street*. (I, 20 months)

ML: Several hours after a *Sesame Street* segment on the letter B was over, Baby went around making B sounds. (I, 20½ months)

Similarly, there was clear evidence of learning concepts:

ML: After a *Sesame Street* skit that called objects small and big, Baby went around calling objects small or big. She continued doing that for a week. (I, 21 months)

M: Today on *Sesame Street* they were doing something about opening and closing things. And, after that, he went to the kitchen and did it with all the cupboards saying: "open-close, open-close, open-close." (M, 22½ months)

ML: Baby brought three sticks and said: "Three sticks." Then he put them in a shape of a triangle and said: "look Mommy, a triangle!" He must have learned it from *Sesame Street*. (M, 24 months)

All parents reinforced this kind of learning, to one degree or another, using *Sesame Street* as a catalyst. They often admitted to their own surprise at how receptive their babies were to learning, and that through their experience with television they learned to expect more out of them.

SUMMARY

The purpose of this study was to discover and describe the process through which babies become television consumers. The overall picture emerging out of the home observations is of babies engaged in a normal variety of everyday activities. Age, experience with television, individual differences, the presence of siblings, parents' attitude and behavior—all affected the nature of the viewing situation. Nevertheless, television viewing in 15 out of the 16 homes was an integrated phenomenon in the routines of a typical day. The data presented in the above pages leave no room for doubt: babies do attend to television, they do comprehend some of its messages, and they are capable of learning, and applying knowledge.

Two overriding themes escorted the above discussions: (a) the role of *Sesame Street* in the viewing diet of babies; and (b) the interrelationships between television viewing and language. Although these issues have been specifically addressed elsewhere (13, 12), a brief reference is warranted due to their importance.

Sesame Street

Without doubt, *Sesame Street* was the most common, regular, and important program viewed by the babies in this study. It played a significant role in the lives of these young ones in many areas—in the amount and regularity of the exposure to it, in structuring their day, in providing objects for attachments, in creating and reinforcing viewing habits, in fostering a cheerful mood, and in manifestation of direct learning. In addition, of all programs babies were exposed to, *Sesame Street* came the closest to their comprehension and attention level (although even *Sesame Street* is targeted at an older age group). As a result, manifestations of both attention to and comprehension of parts of the programs were clearly on a different level than any other program (excluding attention to commercials). The significance of *Sesame Street* for babies' development as television viewers in general is intriguing: What does it teach them about the role of television in a person's life? What kind of expectations from television does it develop in them? What kind of formal features of television does the program make known to the baby? What kind of content preferences does it foster? The questions are many, and the answers are yet to be studied.

Television Viewing and Language
Television viewing in this study was embedded in a rich verbal interaction that has strong parallels with mother–child book reading routines. Babies were engaged through a variety of ways in an attempt to name or to discover the names of objects, characters, animals, or other things seen on the screen. They asked questions that reveal their attempts to understand what they were viewing. In addition, those babies with relatively advanced linguistic skills often described content seen on television with their own interpretation and expansions. These linguistic outputs provide us with valuable information on what attracts babies' attention, how comprehensible television is to them, how they process television messages, and the like. Analyzed in an integrated manner with the general context of the viewing situation as well as the individual baby's characteristics in mind, language becomes a major platform for our understanding of babies' interaction with the world of television.

Validity Considerations
The study, however, is not without its limitations. The 16 babies studied are not a representative sample. If anything, they represent families with a higher educational background and with more media awareness than one might expect from a representative sample. Few of the mothers admitted that their motivation for participation in the study resulted from their concern over their husbands' addiction to television. They hinted at their hope that my involvement with the family might enlighten them. Some parents participated more actively than others, providing detailed logs, calling on the phone to share an experience, and confiding in great detail all their secret television habits. Others were more restrained. As a

result, more information became available on some of the babies than the others. Babies occasionally performed for me voluntarily, and at other times were more interested in me than in the television. Overall, however, parents confirmed my judgment that in most cases babies were their usual selves during my visits. No novel television-related behaviors were discovered in my presence. Neither does this report discuss issues that were not regularly observed and reported. The length of the study and the moderate level of intensity of the contact with the families allowed for the development of a friendly-trusting relationship, without slipping into too much closeness. There was almost no case of contradiction between parents' reports and observation notes. The two sources consistently complemented each other. In part this reflects the training and supervision the parents received in filling their role as "informants" on their babies' behavior.

This study is only one step towards a better understanding of young children's television viewing. Many questions remained unanswered, many issues untouched. Clearly, babies are indeed television viewers. They develop a certain grasp of television as an object and as a source of messages before they learn to use the potty. By 2½, they are already regular viewers with clear habits and expectations. Television is by all means a part of the modern baby's everyday life, an environment within an environment. The significance of this observation is yet to be understood.

REFERENCES

1. Alwitt, L.F., D.R. Anderson, E.P. Lorch, and S.R. Levin. "Preschool Children's Visual Attention to Attributes of Television." *Human Communication Research, 7*, 1980, pp. 52–67.
2. Anderson, D.R., and S.R. Levin. "Young Children's Attention to *Sesame Street.*" *Child Development, 47*, 1976, pp. 806–811.
3. Anderson, D.R., E.P. Lorch, D.E. Field, and J. Sanders. "The Effects of TV Program Comprehensibility on Preschool Children's Visual Attention to Television." *Child Development, 52*, 1981, pp. 151–157.
4. Anderson, D.R., and E.P. Lorch. "Looking at Television: Action or Reaction?" In J. Bryant and D.R. Anderson (Eds.), *Children's Understanding of Television: Research on Attention and Comprehension.* New York: Academic Press, 1983, pp. 1–33.
5. Anderson, D.R., and R. Smith. "Young Children's TV Viewing: The Problems of Cognitive Continuity." In F.J. Morrison, C. Lord, and D. Keating (Eds.), *Applied Developmental Psychology, Volume 1.* New York: Academic Press, 1984, pp. 115–163.
6. Bruner, J.S. "On Cognitive Growth." In J.S. Bruner, R.R. Oliver, and P.M. Greenfield (Eds.), *Studies in Cognitive Growth.* New York: Wiley, 1966.
7. Carew, J. "Experience and the Development of Intelligence in Young Children at Home and in Day Care." *Monographs of the Society for Research in Child Development, 45(187),* 1980, pp. 1–89.
8. Flavell, J.H. *Cognitive Development.* Englewood Cliffs, N.J.: Prentice-Hall, 1977.

9. Gruber, H.E., and J.J. Voueche. *The Essential Piaget.* New York: Basic Books, 1977, pp. xvii–xi.

10. Hollenbeck, A.R., and R.G. Slaby. "Infant Visual and Vocal Responses to Television." *Child Development,* 50, 1979, pp. 41–45.

11. Huston, A.C., and J.C. Wright. "Children's Processing of Television: The Informative Function of Formal Features." In J. Bryant and D.R. Anderson (Eds.), *Children's Understanding of Television: Research on Attention and Comprehension.* New York: Academic Press, 1983, pp. 35–68.

12. Lemish, D. "The Pampered *Sesame Street* Viewer." Under review, 1984.

13. Lemish, D., and M. Rice. "Toddlers, Talk and Television: Observations in the Home." Paper presented to the International Communication Association, San Francisco, May, 1984.

14. Rice, M.L., A.C. Huston, and J.C. Wright. "The Forms and Codes of Television: Effects on Children's Attention, Comprehension, and Social Behavior." In D. Pearl, C. Bouthilet, and J. Lazar (Eds.), *Television and Behavior: Ten Years of Scientific Progress and Implications for the Eighties.* Washington, DC: U.S. Government Printing Office, 1982, pp. 24–38.

15. Schramm, W., J. Lyle and E.B. Parker. *Television in the Lives of Our Children.* Palo Alto, CA: Stanford University Press, 1961.

16. Wartella, E. "The Developmental Perspective." In E. Wartella, (Ed.), *Children Communicating: Media and the Development of Thought, Speech, Understanding.* Beverly Hills, CA: Sage, 1979, pp. 7–19.

17. Wright, J.C., and A.C. Huston. "The Forms of Television: Nature and Development of Television Literacy in Children." In H. Kelly and H. Gardner (Eds.), *Viewing Children Through Television.* San Francisco: Jossey Bass, 1981, pp. 73–80.

Chapter 3

How Children Negotiate Television

Michelle A. Wolf

Department of Broadcast Communication Arts
San Francisco State University

The initial objective of this study was to create and test naturalistic research methods to determine if they are useful for understanding how
children make sense of television. A key assumption here is that the dominant, traditional procedures used to explore relationships between children's developing cognitive abilities and televised programming are
obsolete. This is not simply because more traditional research methods
are naive responses to phenomena, but because it seems that, as methods, they yield results that are severely limited in the face of the range of
objectives which potentially guide inquiries into human processes.

This chapter begins with an overview of a variety of procedures that
were developed and applied during a 10-month period in which 107 children were observed in a natural setting. Following this, a more elaborate
account of the field work is given, which involved three distinct phases:
becoming acquainted with the children, helping the children to create
their own television programs, and examining the children's perceptions
of televised programming.

In the next section of this chapter, three types of television conventions
(production/nonverbal, other nonverbal, narrative/verbal) are defined,
and examples of each are provided. Then the research procedures used to
assess the children's understanding of television conventions, and the
steps taken to analyze the data, are presented. Finally, after delineating
the results of this research, the study as a whole is summarized and discussed so that major findings and implications are highlighted.

OVERVIEW OF RESEARCH METHODS

One primary researcher and seven trained research assistants informally
observed and interviewed 107 children (63 males, 44 females) who were

enrolled in a day care/summer camp facility. We spent a total of 10 succes-sive months (December 1981 to September 1982) with children between the ages of 4 and 12 years. The size of the group was inconsistent from day to day, with approximately 40 to 85 children present during a typical visit. While most were from white, Protestant, middle- and upper-middle class families, about twenty percent of the children were from black or Mexican-American families with low incomes.

The research site occupied roughly four acres of partly wooded grounds in the southwest part of Austin, Texas, a city with a popula-tion of approximately 350,000 persons at the time of the study. On the grounds were a basketball court and football field, two shaded play-ground areas with swing sets and a treehouse, and three small buildings which were used for indoor activities. The largest building provided a space of 18 by 20 feet, and was equipped with a 24-inch color television set that received signals from two of the three local network affiliates. Only one of the signals was clear. In addition, a large swimming pool was filled and used from May to September.

Since attendance at the facility was relatively high, we interacted with small groups of individual children. Because the children were free to come and go as they pleased, our contact time with individuals was not constant; we spent more time with some children than with others. The amount of time each assistant spent in the field varied as well. One partic-ipated for 7 months, five were each involved for 5 months, and one assist-ant was involved in the study for 4 months. Each visit lasted about 3 to 4 hours, and at least one researcher/assistant (but usually two or three) was at the site for about 10 hours per week.

During the school months the children engaged in "free play"; they roamed about in a self-directed manner, guided only by instructions to stay within the grounds and to avoid any activities that might result in harm to others. While the summer program was more structured, all chil-dren had 3 hours of "free time" per day. These hours were divided into "quiet time" and "swim time." During both periods, the children were permitted, but never required, to visit the television room or to engage in other optional activities. The last of three major research phases occurred during the summer months. Each phase is detailed in the section that follows.

DESCRIPTION OF THE THREE PHASES OF FIELD RESEARCH

The study was initially designed in two major parts, but an important transition stage emerged during the field work. The first phase went on for about 5 months and involved making regular visits to the facility. We functioned primarily as observers for the first 3 weeks, and attempted to become acquainted with as many children as was possible. Attention was paid to behaviors as a whole, and notes were made of both general observations and any situations in which mediated content appeared to be integrated into individual and group activities. Observations and insights were recorded each day, and we met two or three times per week to share our experiences and compare our notes.

After the first 3 weeks of relatively distanced observation, children began to make efforts to incorporate us into their day-to-day activities, and their invitations to play quickly became expectations. This marked the beginning of a 2-month period in which we were integrated into the daily activities but not fully considered as members of the group.

Such acceptance was the goal during the weeks to come, and by March 1982 we began to make even more forceful efforts to become active members of the group. We took part in "juice time" and brought our own treasures in to share with the children, striving to remove any barriers that obstructed the path toward a more complete acceptance. We also began to make occasional visits to the television room to watch afternoon programs with our friends.

Several incidents underscored the fact that such acceptance had occurred by early April. For example, although we always drove our own automobiles to the facility, children would often ask us when our parents were coming to pick us up at the end of the day. And when we were "caught" observing but not participating in a given event, we would be scolded by one or more of the children. At this point, it was time to initiate more directed television viewing experiences, and we looked for a natural entry point to introduce video tapes and playback equipment. This point emerged one day when we were watching a late afternoon television show with a small group of children. As the program ended, a young boy (C.5)[1] proclaimed that he could make better television shows. He was quickly challenged to the task by a friend, who offered to bring his parent's camera and video recorder so that C. could demonstrate his video skills.

It was not a problem that the boy's parents would not loan their equipment, because we had already made plans to use our own. We brought a half-inch VHS format package that included a camera and tape deck. This marked the onset of an unexpected phase of the research, that of making our own television shows. One child suggested that we think of ideas for good television stories and share them with one another. We recorded the stories on audio-tape as we went along. From this point on, all spatially confined interactions were audio-recorded and later transcribed.

Some children chose to work on their stories with their friends; others

---

[1] "C" refers to the child's first initial; "5" refers to his age in years.

developed their ideas alone. Within a few days, there were six group stories and sixteen individual stories. Nine of the stories told by individual children were never completed. The children selected four group stories to be "test" programs, basing their decisions on an interest in stories that were both markedly different from one another and would involve a relatively large number of participants. Those who created individual stories preferred to observe the group processes before pursuing their own ideas.

We proceeded to produce the shows, one by one. As a group, we decided to establish some procedural rules so that we would not become preoccupied with any one program idea. Each production would take no more than 2 days. Before beginning the video-taping, those who developed stories gave explicit plot descriptions, focusing on how their ideas should look on the television screen. For example, if someone first told a story in which a person was having a dream, she might say: "You see the girl in bed, and she's tossing around like she can't sleep."

After the second versions were described to the satisfaction of all involved, the children selected actors and actresses and again reviewed the plot. Productions began the following day, and children brought in whatever props they felt were important and could be secured in time for the taping. Each show was shot scene-by-scene, a temporal method that was determined by the children to be the most efficient and logical way to proceed. Before each scene, participants were again reminded of the general sequence of events and were told to speak and act in an unrehearsed, spontaneous manner. As one of the rules was that no scene could be shot more than two times, some scenes were taped twice. This generally happened because someone forgot what to do or when children were overtaken by an event and began to laugh. All decisions about how and what to record were made by children, and all camera work was done by one or more of the story creators. Basic instructions and a brief practice period were provided just before shooting began.

The four productions were completed just as the school year ended. At this point, the final phase of research was discussed. The summer program began after 1 week, and most of the children from the original sample, along with a number of new faces, were enrolled. We spent the first 2 weeks of the camp session in the same informal way we had approached the group in December when we started the field work. However, because we had already been accepted by such a large number of children, the process of integration at this point in time was much less time-consuming.

Shortly after the summer session convened in early June, a girl from the school program asked if we would bring the videotapes and recorder in again so that we could watch programs that "were better" than those on the afternoon network schedule. We spent the remaining months watching television together and talking about our perceptions. As a group, the children decided what their video preferences were, and the research assistants obtained samples of the requested programs and brought them to the summer camp.

Along with the playback equipment, we had a remote freeze frame/slow-fast motion device that was connected and set out to be used by anyone who wished to control the media content for more careful examination. This directed "viewing" was the formal beginning of the final phase of the study, an ongoing focus on how the children made sense of production and narrative conventions of television. The conventions of interest are summarized in the pages that follow.

TELEVISION CONVENTIONS

Production / Nonverbal Conventions

In order to isolate a manageable list of production conventions for the study, the primary researcher and three assistants each spent roughly 6 hours talking to the children about programs that they most often watched on television. Two episodes of each of the ten most mentioned shows were video-taped, and the content was analyzed with a focus on production devices. These conventions were noted and discussed by the researcher and assistants. Formal definitions and descriptions of the production conventions, and intended effects associated with each one, were collected from two sources (6, 10). The specific conventions isolated for study are described as follows, in terms of the definitions and explanations that the researchers synthesized from the two sources noted above.

Some of the production conventions of interest are similar in that they are basic, relatively simple *camera shots* which are secured during production. Examples of this type of convention are close up shots, which are used to intensify and emphasize detail, and zooms, in which the camera pulls forward to enlarge the object of focus.

Some production conventions involve *picturization*, the process of structuring shot sequences by way of using transitions or editing. Three types of transition devices—cut, dissolve, and fade—were considered in this study. While a cut is an instant change from one shot to another, a dissolve is a more gradual transition in which two images temporarily overlap. Fade transitions occur when the screen gradually goes to black (fade out) or when an image gradually appears on the screen (fade in). Considering editing devices, two post-production techniques of interest involve the sequencing and pacing of discrete shots. The first is the use of establishing shots to denote a primary locale; the second involves editing

a succession of shots together in order to indicate passage of time, stream of consciousness, or events leading to a climactic scene.

Other production conventions can be subsumed under the heading of *special effects* in that they are presumed to work because they are unusual. More specifically, there are three basic types of special effects shots: electronic (image combination or manipulation), optical (visual scenic devices, optical distortions), and mechanical (simulated). The special effects shots most often found in the programs viewed by the children in the sample are superimposition, split screen, and process shots. Superimposition requires image combination and is a form of double exposure in which an image from one camera is electronically placed over an image from another camera; both are simultaneously projected on the screen. With split screen, each half of the screen contains a different picture, depicting different views on a single event or simultaneously portraying widely separated events. Process shots are composed when moving background projections are photographed with an actual scene in the foreground (often used in police action scenes).

In addition to camera shots, picturization, and special effects, various *audio effects* are used in television to somehow alter the content by adding to, deleting from, or otherwise changing the sound track so that it differs from what was actually recorded during the initial production. Sound dubbing and voice-over were the two audio techniques that were most often used in the programs we viewed with the children. With sound dubbing, sound is added, often to indicate some type of offscreen action. This technique is also used to help establish time and locale (e.g., cricket sounds may be used to denote night and country settings) and to intensify action on the screen. Voice-overs are heard over the action on the screen; the sources of such voices are not depicted on the television screen.

Other Nonverbal Conventions
Another major area of nonverbal content focus during the viewing sessions with the children was on the many wordless messages expressed by characters in the programs. Knapp (5) developed a classification system to define a broad range of nonverbal human communication behaviors. His seven major categories and subdivisions were adapted for the study presented here, and are summarized as follows.

One area of interest was *body motion*, or the use of gestures, facial expressions, eye behaviors, and postures to convey information without using the spoken word. Knapp also refers to *physical characteristics*, or nonverbal cues which are not bound to movement, in the sense that they generally remain constant during human interaction. Some examples of physical characteristics are body shape, odors, hair and skin color, and height.

Touching behaviors and *paralanguage* are two additional nonverbal conventions of relevance to this study. Touching behaviors occur when one or more persons have actual physical contact with another or other persons. Some of the many examples of touching behaviors are stroking, hitting, and greeting. Paralanguage, on the other hand, is a term used to refer to how something is said, and involves voice qualities and vocalizations (7). While voice qualities are simply such features as pitch, rhythm, and articulation, vocalizations can be subdivided according to three types. These are vocal characteristics (e.g., laughing, crying, hiccuping), vocal qualifiers (e.g., intensity, pitch height), and vocal segregates (e.g., um, uh, uh huh) (7).

Three additional nonverbal conventions, *proxemics, artifacts,* and *environmental factors,* were considered in the study reported here. Proxemics refers to how spatial relationships function for people in both formal and informal settings, as in the arrangement of chairs in a room. In contrast to proxemics, artifacts are important in terms of how objects are manipulated by persons in communication situations. That is, in some instances, artifacts such as wigs or other beauty aids may function as nonverbal stimuli for communication. Knapp concludes his classification system by noting that environmental factors are elements that impinge upon but are not directly a part of human relationships. Examples in this case are room furnishings, traces of human action such as orange peels or cigarette butts, and the like.

Narrative / Verbal Conventions

The narrative conventions examined in this study are the words, verbal exchanges, and methods of verbal organization commonly used to introduce, establish, and/or develop plots. The specific conventions of focus were adapted from Applebee's analysis of how children come to understand the concept of "story" (1). From his studies of what he calls the interaction of children and stories, he delineates four areas in which children develop cognitive skills which help them to understand stories in an adult-like manner.

To begin, Applebee argues that children gradually acquire abilities that help them to grasp the concept of a conventional story framework. In addition, children become progressively more able to use organizational elements to deal with various levels of complexity in stories. A third area of consideration involves children's notions of fantasy versus reality story elements, and the fourth area Applebee explores is centered on how children respond to and evaluate stories. Each area of skill development is explained in more detail in the pages that follow.

Conventional Story Framework

Considerations of how a sense of conventional story framework develops center on children's growing familiarity with five basic story elements: beginning, development of plot, climax (shift in events), resolution, and ending. Applebee notes some phases of this process, beginning with a stage he calls "prelanguage." At this point, children are aware of and can play with language, have a sense of vocal techniques and devices, and appreciate the sound of language. At about 2 years of age, children develop simplistic concepts of story structure, as evidenced by their own loosely and informally organized stories.

By the time children are 5, they introduce common characters into their stories and tell stories which, according to Applebee, are characterized by common patterns or trends. One such feature involves the use of a beginning with a title or formal opening phrase (e.g., "Once upon a time"). This is usually accompanied by a relatively formal ending, such as "They all lived happily ever after" or, more simply, "The End" or "That's it." At this point, children also seem to have a weak hold on the reality level of their stories, which are usually told in the past tense.

By the time children are 6 or 7 years of age, their understanding of character types and story structures become more well defined. Children are also more flexible and will deal with "what if" changes in the stories they create, indicating that they are beginning to make a more clear separation between fact and fiction. During this stage of development, children appear to realize that some parts of their stories are not real, but they may be unsure about the reality basis of other story elements.

Organization and Complexity

Children's use of organizational elements and the complexity of their own stories are also areas to consider when examining how a sense of narrative form develops. Complexity is partly a function of how many story elements must be controlled and coordinated, and involves awareness of story linkages and bonds, concepts, movement, and abstract bonds. Stories told by younger children tend to have few internal links and to be organized in terms of immediate perception. With development, children begin to use concrete or factual bonds, which are later replaced by more abstract, logical connecting devices. Finally, children's stories become true narratives; each incident grows from previous events and elaborates a new aspect of the incident. These narratives are also characterized by consistent forward movement, with cores based on either abstract (conceptual) or concrete (perceptual) bonds.

Fantasy and Reality Dimensions

According to Applebee, children's stories undergo developmental shifts in terms of both the amount of fantasy employed and the ways that fantasy is used as a resource to create stories. For example, children in his study tended to use different techniques to distance themselves when their stories contained threatening behaviors which were contrary to their previously learned, culturally accepted values and norms. Three techniques most often employed to control the fantasy/reality dimensions of their stories involved focusing on realistic characters, consistently using past tense, and stressing behaviors of characters other than themselves.

In addition to the consistent use of such distancing techniques, Applebee discovered some common themes in the stories told by the children in his study. For example, children under 6 years of age were more likely to deal with developmental problems such as abandonment by a parent or fighting among siblings, friends, and family members. Their stories also generally focused on everyday occurrences, with topics that were not personally disturbing, and were predictable in that problems introduced were resolved according to generally accepted expectations. These younger children also told stories of adventure, using distancing techniques to remove themselves from the violence, naughty behaviors, and other activities that were relatively difficult for them to accept as their own.

This study extends beyond Applebee's considerations of theme and distancing, in that the fantasy/reality dimension is also explored in light of children's understanding of the various levels of fantasy commonly found in televised programs. The specific levels considered are as follows:

1. content that is totally based upon real world events (e.g., on-the-scene coverage of a news story).
2. content that is relatively unrealistic, but is pre-planned and rehearsed and features actresses and actors engaged in fictionalized (often stereotypical) situations (e.g., characters and events from popular programs such as *Happy Days*).
3. content with real people who are somehow altered or "disguised" and/or content with people engaged in superhuman or humanly impossible behaviors (e.g., *The Incredible Hulk* [man as creature] or *The Muppets* [people as animals, creatures, etc.]).
4. content that is clearly not real (e.g., fantasy/animated programs, cartoon characters).

The verbal and nonverbal conventions previously delineated are obviously related to these levels of fantasy and reality. For example, one can talk about levels of "production reality" by focusing on differences in perceptions of and reactions to depictions of real snake versus an artificial but

realistic-looking snake versus an animated, clearly unrealistic snake. Such distinctions were the core of many of our discussions with the children during the data collection phase of the study.

Responses to Stories

Developing a concept of story also involves children's responses to narratives in terms of how they discuss televised situations and characters and how they evaluate mediated content. Applebee suggests that adolescence brings a "new concern with analyzing the parts of a story, and with forming generalizations about its meaning" (1, p. 108). He believes that it is not until adolescence that the ability to explain why items that have been categorized belong to one group versus another. Applebee argues that the best way to study children's responses to stories is to elicit conversation in the "expressing mode." He refers to Britton's (2) summary of the significance of this sort of conversation:

> The language remains "expressive" throughout, in the sense that it is relaxed, self presenting, self-revealing, addressed to a few intimate companions; in the sense that it moves easily from general comment to narration of particular experiences and back again; and in the special sense that in making comments the speakers do not aim at accurate, explicit reference (as one might in an argument or sociological report) and in relating experience they do not aim at a polished performance (as a raconteur or a novelist would) (1, p. 7; 2, p. 96).

This qualitative study of children's perceptions of mediated content was designed so that responses were elicited in a relaxed atmosphere much like the one described above by Britton. In addition, Applebee's distinctions between pre- and post-adolescence skills were examined. The research methods developed to explore how children negotiate television are detailed in the pages that follow.

PROCEDURES FOR ASSESSING UNDERSTANDING OF TELEVISION CONVENTIONS AND ANALYZING DATA

During the earliest viewing experiences, one major goal was to create an environment in which commenting about and openly discussing mediated content were encouraged. Children were shown how to use the remote device for advancing, reversing, and pausing the videotapes. In short, ongoing responses were not only acceptable, but were natural behaviors in the face of television.

Discussions were stimulated by both the children and the researchers. The question-asking procedures were based on a model previously developed by the primary researcher and two colleagues (9). The model consists of a series of structured steps, each designed to direct children to a different level of thinking by generating responses to free-flowing questions. The questions determine the types of responses offered by the children, who are led to progress sequentially in formulating generalizations, explanations, and predictive inferences. Each of these processes is central to a different stage of the model, and the type of thinking process employed is a function of the questions posed to the children. All viewing sessions were recorded on audio-tape and later transcribed for analysis.

Data reduction and analysis involved two general steps. To begin, data from the three phases of research were summarized and organized. After this, all information gathered in the field was further condensed and transferred to index cards which were grouped according to areas of research interest about which results statements were made. Each step is more carefully explained in the pages that follow.

Step One: Initial Data Summaries
Data reduction procedures were first organized according to the three phases of field research described earlier in this chapter. The first data set was based on the earliest informal months of relatively random interaction with the children enrolled in the after school care program. Data from the period in which the children created stories to make into television programs were examined next, followed by a focus on the information gathered during the more directed summer viewing experiences.

Considering the early, informal observational phase of the research, the daily field notes of all involved researchers and notes from their discussions of their ongoing experiences were organized and then matched according to corresponding visits. Observations from each day were compared, and perceptions of individual researchers were discussed. Since the daily visits had already been reviewed in an ongoing manner, inconsistencies in perceptions were rare and could be easily explained. In fact, "inconsistencies" were generally products of different levels of researchers' involvements (e.g., observations of children playing a game versus notes from someone actually playing the same game).

Summaries of significant daily events and profiles of individual children were developed. Profiles included references to all available data for each child, and contained information concerning demographics, home and school environments and experiences, personal and social behaviors at the day care facility, and performance on standard tests of cognitive developmental level that were administered after the last day of qualitative data collection (3, 4). Pictures and other creative efforts, when available, were attached to each profile.

After completing the summaries, data for each day and child were again reduced to the most essential elements. Notes for each day were synthesized so that, in most cases, they occupied the space of a single page of 8" x 11" sheet of paper. Profiles were organized in a similar manner, and then divided into two groups according to sex. Profiles in each group were ordered successively by age and assigned a number, with lower numbers representing younger children. Numbers were used to facilitate subsequent data analysis.

Considering the second phase of the research, when the children created their own stories and television programs, transcripts from all audio- and video-tapes were examined. Each story was coded according to Applebee's four areas of concern, beginning with his notion of a conventional story framework. Here, the absence or presence and nature of the following basic story elements were recorded: beginning, development of plot, climax or shift in events, resolution, and ending. After this, use of tense, reality of plot elements, and character types were noted. The stories were then characterized in terms of how they were organized and levels of detail, so that their structural complexity could be examined. Remarks on transitions, concepts, and general plot progressions were also made.

Stories were also explored in terms of fantasy and reality dimensions, with Applebee's points about the amount and nature of fantasy, distancing techniques, and theme serving to guide the analytical procedures. Finally, the children's responses to the stories (when initially told in aural form and after being video-taped) were logged in summary form.

Data analysis for the final, more directed viewing phase of the research involved a few general procedures. To begin, the content of each program and advertisement presented to the children, which had already been coded according to existing production and narrative conventions, was summarized and recorded on separate sheets of paper. Data from all audio- and video-tapes of interactions with children during this viewing phase (which had also been transcribed after each visit to the facility) were summarized. Each summary included notes on all references to the conventions of interest, as defined earlier in this chapter.

Step Two: Final Procedures for Data Reduction and Analysis
Once the data were organized according to the procedures delineated in Step One, they were further reduced and classified and then transferred to 4" x 6" index cards. Each card contained three different types of information: a child, a particular research interest (e.g., the child's perceptions of a single production convention from a television program), and one or more cognitive skills related to the child and the research interest. Each index card essentially represented one or more researcher's observations of a child using cognitive skills to negotiate mediated content. The cognitive abilities noted were grouped into one or more of the following catego-

ries: coding processes, language acquisition, memory, social-cognitive development.

The index cards were then grouped in terms of research areas of interest, and subdivided according to the more specific points of focus within each general interest area. In addition, index cards containing information about research methods that evolved during the study, and miscellaneous insights which had been noted during the field research, were summarized and organized into relevant groups. These procedures were followed so that the statements of results could be developed in a systematic manner.

RESULTS

The results of this qualitative study are organized according to the three research phases reported earlier in this chapter. Some procedures are included as "results" because they were in fact the outcomes of our ongoing exploration for appropriate methods and sensitive measures to use during the final research phase, when we sought to assess how the children made sense of mediated content. Each of the three phases is considered in the pages that follow.

Phase One: Approaching a Child's Frame of Reference

The first weeks of the study involved exploring a variety of ways to best position ourselves in order to deal more directly with our questions about how the children processed mediated content. With general goals in mind, we followed the leads which evolved from our interactions with the children. Rather than pursue any specific research agenda, we spent several months making connections that were close and secure enough to allow children to express themselves freely to us and to others in our presence. We responded in kind.

At this point, we recorded our perceptions of how the children tended to group themselves in terms of both peer associations and collective activities. For the first half of their daily visits to the day care facility, the boys generally organized themselves in the outdoor playing field or the adjacent basketball court, both on the northwest side of the grounds. Most of the girls gathered on the southwest part of the facility, on a small hill scattered with several swing sets, a treehouse (built by the children with our help), and a few small buildings which the children called "houses." One of the houses contained the old, color, 24-inch console television set with poor signal reception.

This sort of segregation usually changed after the juice break, when the children were likely to engage in activities involving both sexes. Brought together by the break, they generally moved on to the football field, which served as the base for most activities requiring ample space. Playing along with the children, we began to learn their names and to note individual communication styles (e.g., outgoing, reticent, nervous, and the like). We also looked for clear friendship patterns and observed the roles that characterized those relationships. At this point, we also paid special attention to uses of verbal and nonverbal modes of communication and to any references to or observable behavioral linkages with television.

In small groups, the girls often played "dress up" and "house" and talked about grocery shopping and their desires to purchase beauty products and clothing. They frequently made references to, or pretended they were attending, a dance class, and they openly shared their thoughts about wanting or having boyfriends. We regularly noticed them pretending the treehouse was a real home, but they did not seem to take on clear social roles which differed from their own.

When alone, the boys usually played sports-related games with the program director, an ex-pro football player, and one of the research assistants named Jeff. Jeff used these games to develop descriptions of and insights into the boys' comments and behaviors during their activities. All but three of the boys had favorite sporting events, teams, and players. As a group, they were most fond of football and could discuss both players and aspects of the game. They did, however, pay attention to other televised sports as well.

One day, while resting after a strenuous workout, B. (M 9) referred to the Leonard–Flinch boxing match he had seen on Home Box Office. "Sugar Ray was just being nice to him at first," he said. When asked how he knew this, he replied, "The slow motion showed him kinda just not really trying. . . . It looks like film, when they go real slow." B. went on to describe how Sugar Ray got mad and "really killed him."

This clear example of awareness of slow motion as a device or tool used in television is just one of many insights elicited by informal talks about sports. On another occasion, a 7-year-old boy (B.) mentioned a wrestling match. He referred to a late night television program generally advertised or promoted as "professional" or "studio" wrestling. B. argued that the matches were "fixed," noting that the manipulation involved "either guys faking it" or "some tricky camera stuff where they get a close shot so it's all you can see, while there are the wrestlers setting up a fake shot or fall." Agreeing that he had similar notions about such matches, J. (M 7) added that "even on really real fights, those camera guys get close and at different places." To clarify, J. explained that he was referring to shooting the event "at different angles to get exciting views."

When the boys and girls played together, Jeff often devised new things to do, as in January when he introduced a group exercise called the "blind walk." Jeff explained that to more clearly understand any abstract concepts the children might try to convey (e.g., concerning televised pictures, complex plots, and so on), we would need some exposure to their grasp of interpretive, expressive language on a more basic level. Our goal, then, was to identify certain codes or terms used by the children to communicate abstract ideas.

The children were initially so taken by the novelty of the experience that our efforts to instigate discussion were in vain. Rather than force unnatural responses to questions, we decided to wait and play the game again in a week or so. The next day, however, I was able to share with some of the children some of their feelings about the "blind walk" as they invited me to join them as they ate their snacks. It was the first time such a gesture was made, and the invitation marked the beginning of a transition from a relatively uninvolved observer to a participant observer for myself and the research assistants.

"Didn't you get some juice?" asked B. (F 7) as she motioned for me to join her and her friends. I asked her if the others might mind my barging in on their discussion, but she ignored the question as she explained that they were talking about the walk we had taken on the previous day. The children, who ranged from 5 to 8 years of age, were surprisingly adept at making the abstract concrete so that others could share their experiences during the walk. Initial feelings of hesitation, for example, were likened to "tippy toeing in the woods where your friend caught poison ivy" or "walking on water." They agreed that it became easier to "be blind" as they went along, that "the water began to be more like cement, or at least a diving board." Only J. (F 7) was unable to verbally express herself. But when I imagined how I would have felt by standing with closed eyes and teetering on the lawn, she joined me in her own way, projecting the shakiness that her test of trust evoked.

The transition to participant observer was easy for the research assistants as well; by February we were all actively involved with some children during every visit to the day care program. On one rainy day that brought everyone indoors to watch the only clearly received television station, Luis (a research assistant) talked with some children about programs they would have preferred to see at that time. He noticed that seven of the more calm and mature (but not necessarily older) children tended to mention programs like *Barney Miller*, *All in the Family*, and *M*A*S*H*, while the others favored *The Greatest American Hero*, *The Dukes of Hazzard*, and *The Fall Guy*. In short, there was a positive correlation between those with more low key activity levels and serious outlooks on life and the viewing of social comedy-type content. Conversely, those who tended to be silly and engage in more aggressive play preferred fantasy-oriented, action-packed adventure programs. The distinction seems to center on the sort of processing the programs require for full enjoyment. While adult-oriented shows are more heavily grounded on verbal puns and include moral statements of a more serious nature, *The Fall Guy* is based on such attention-grabbers as fast-paced action and aggressive behaviors. These preference patterns were consistent only for children who fell on the more extreme ends of these behavioral continua.

With time, the children made comments and gestures which indicated that any "observer" roles on the part of the researchers had become obsolete. In early March, for example, K. (F 5) asked me when my mother usually came to pick me up. When an assistant missed a few consecutive days of attendance, children were likely to be concerned, as when J. (F 8) worried that Luis was ill.

During this period of more intense interaction, we noticed that most children were quite materialistic and would often try to "out have" one another. The most wealthy were likely to openly flaunt their possessions, as when J. (F 9) would hold her diamond-ringed finger in the air with a smile, being careful not to soil her "Calvin Kleins." She obviously delighted in discussing her designer labels with at least six other affluent girls, who ranged from 5 to 10 years of age. Those with the most obvious symbols of "the good life" tended to cluster together and be more overt in their references to the latest fashions, beauty products, and even places to dine. We heard them describe dinners or "dress" outfits to one another, right down to the colors of their pumps, which in one case were presented as being similar to those worn by Brooke Shields when she appeared on a televised talk show. When asked how they made their purchasing decision, these girls most often mentioned their mothers, popular fashion magazines, and television or movie stars as their information sources.

The wealthier boys had very different symbols of prosperity, including television sets, computerized games (e.g., Atari), and other samples of the latest toys and games designed to please those who could afford them. These boys were more likely to integrate themselves into activities with their peers, and rarely brought treasures in for display.

The others were not left out of this showcase. They brought small toys and games, as well as miscellaneous candies and other edibles which they had received as gifts or purchased with their allowances. They were most likely to cite television as the source of their consumer information. During such exchanges, we were included in the discussion and offered tastes of goodies, and children often asked for our opinions of their things.

By early April we could describe each child in terms of language and interpersonal communication skills, use of nonverbal gestures, family composition, and other characteristics such as level of maturity vis à vis community and world events and other phenomena which were beyond the child's immediate environment. We also formulated general impressions of the children's home lives, based on information provided by them directly and on our own regular encounters with their parents or caretakers, who came to pick them up each day.

In late April several weeks of rainy weather drew us together in large groups in front of the television. With few exceptions, the boys insisted on watching *Gilligan's Island*, while the girls cast a conflicting vote for *Wonder Woman*. These were the only two programs we could see on the old television set. The disagreements about program preferences were useful for stimulating talk about the "whys" of such choices. One 6-year-old boy responded to my question of why Wonder Woman was so unacceptable by enacting an exaggerated demonstration of his perceptions of her. Focusing on her feminine qualities, he pretended to toss his hair over his shoulder as he gazed at me with penetrating, almost sexy, eyes. In defense of the show, a 6-year-old girl responded by engaging in dramatic support of *Wonder Woman*, reinforcing her behavioral argument with comments that indicated she placed the heroine in a position of reverence. Such expressions came easily to the children.

The process of continuously becoming more intimate with the children serves as a metaphor for the many interactional shifts that evolved during the early months of the study. Our ability to understand their verbal expressions in light of what we came to know they perceived and thought in a cognitive sense (i.e., what they *said* versus what they *knew*) was markedly enhanced as the days and weeks passed. We engaged in the ongoing development of procedures which enhanced the children's opportunities for self expression. These methods extended well beyond posing simple questions and accepting immediate responses. We engaged in dramatic play and enjoyed role-taking activities, and we shared our personal experiences in story (often as "fiction") form. On several occasions we acted out behaviors of family members and friends, as well as our perceptions of people we had seen on television. We also played games with words, such as reciting tongue twisters of poems, and we read stories to one another and shared ghost tales on dark and rainy days. Almost every week we climbed into the big television set we made from a large cardboard refrigerator box, and we pretended we really were on television. By May we were ready to begin to focus more directly on the children's perceptions of television, and, as researchers, we decided to wait for an opportunity to make a smooth transition to watching television.

Our chance to do this came more quickly than we expected. During the first week of May, a young boy's criticism of the poor quality of our late afternoon television offerings served as a perfect opportunity to introduce video playback equipment so that we could start considering prime time televised content. The comment also led to an unexpected research phase, that of creating our own programs.

Phase Two: Making Television Shows

The young boy's negative evaluation of the afternoon television fare was challenged: "Do you think you could do better?" He and several other children were convinced they could create better shows, and, after the necessary equipment was secured, the children began to develop their ideas for television programs. The following day we waited for children to approach us with ideas so that no one would feel pressured by our requests. We heard a total of 22 stories. Six were the products of small groups of friends, seven were developed by individuals, and nine were told in incomplete form by individual children. Most of the incomplete stories were interrupted when parents came to take their children home.

Distinctions between the stories were not necessarily clustered in relationship to age. In fact, almost all with the developed plots were at least partly a function of the language abilities of the story tellers. When less verbal children were encouraged to tell parts of their stories by dramatically acting out their ideas, plot details and sophistication were much more evident. Such dramatic play also functioned, so that, when telling the story a second time, the words they needed to express their thoughts came more quickly and easily.

The ways in which the 22 stories were organized can be explained by referring to Applebee's notions of how organizational abilities develop. He believes that the work of Vygotsky can be used to analyze narrative form:

> If we treat the plots of stories as a series of elements or incidents, each of which has a series of attributes (characters, actions, settings, themes), we can use this previous work in concept development to provide a highly suggestive model for our analysis of narrative form. . . . six basic types of structures were found, bearing a remarkable resemblance to Vygotsky's (1962) stages in concept development and showing the same developmental order (1, p. 7).

As depicted in Figure 1, the stages are labeled heaps, sequences, primitive narratives, unfocused chains, focused chains, and narratives.

The six structural types represent the developing awareness of story linkages and bonds, concepts, movement, and abstract bonds. The most simple structural type, *heaps*, includes stories with few internal links and organization that parallels immediate perception. In the case of *sequences*, bonds exist in concrete or factual (rather than abstract or logical) form, and time sequence is arbitrary. *Primitive narratives* are the products of thinking in "collections," in that structures are based on complementary

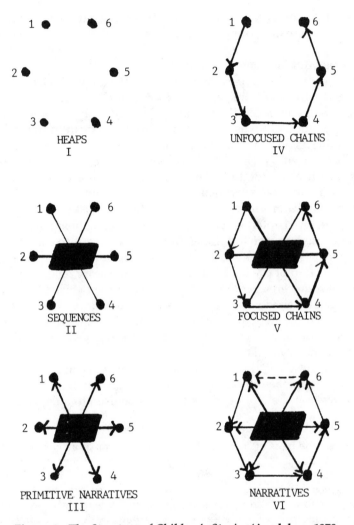

Figure 1. *The Structure of Children's Stories* **(Applebee, 1978, p. 58).**

(as opposed to similar) elements which are grouped into sets around which stories are developed. In the case of *unfocused chains*, each element shares a concrete attribute with the next, but defining attributes shift inconsistently. "Pseudo concepts" emerge in *focused chains*, in that stories are perceptually (rather than conceptually) based. Such stories often take the form of "The Continuing Adventures of" an individual or groups of people. Finally, children construct *true narratives*, developing each incident from previous events so as to elaborate a new aspect of the incident.

Narratives are characterized by consistent forward movement with cores that are either based on abstract (conceptual) or concrete (perceptual) bonds.

None of the 22 children's stories was arranged in a heap, sequence, or primitive narrative form. Only one story, created by a 7-year-old girl, was organized as an unfocused chain, with related elements but no center or clear direction. Three stories were focused chains with "continuing adventure" themes, and the remaining 18 stories were fully developed narratives.

Considering some story elements, several trends are apparent. Nineteen stories had formal beginnings, and 12 of the 13 completed stories had formal endings. The storyteller was included as a major character in 12 stories, and all but one story had some fantasy element in the form of a character and/or in relation to the plot. Only two children would not accept their creations as make-believe, and every story included at least one conventional character type, often in the context of a good-versus-evil scenario. Only two children were inflexible with their stories, rejecting possibilities for change. This was apparently a function of the fact that both of these stories were reports of actual dreams the children had. These were also the same two children who would not accept their ideas as make-believe.

Four of the six group stories were video-taped by the children, who maximized the capacities of the camera by using fades, zooms, close-ups, cuts, and various angles to realize their ideas. They also made admirable use of establishing shots, taking great care to set each scene. Although the verbal content was not rehearsed, dialogue was carefully planned and flowed nicely in light of the limited preparation time. Further, the children obviously considered nonverbal aspects of their program ideas, and nearly all of the nonverbal elements included in Knapp's typology regularly appeared in the programs.

All of the stories created by the children indicate the existence of a relatively firm grasp of the concept of narrative. While the group stories differ in plot, design, and detail from the creations of the other children, all 22 stories (even those that were never completed) are more sophisticated than one might expect from reading the traditional literature (e.g., the work of Piaget) on cognitive developmental abilities. The significance of these points is developed more fully at the end of this chapter.

Phase Three: Making Sense of Television

Before long, several children asked us to bring the video machine and tapes of television programs, and we decided to first talk to the children to see if they had program preferences which differed from those of the previous group. We met privately with individual children, and all but two boys mentioned *The Fall Guy, The Dukes of Hazzard,* and/or *Magnum P.I.* as their favored shows. Only one girl requested a program from this group; the girls were more apt to mention one or more of the following: *Too Close for Comfort, Diff'rent Strokes, That's Incredible, Joanie Loves Chachi,* and *Facts of Life.* Almost all requests had been previously taped, and samples of the rest, as well as a few that were not mentioned, were collected for potential screening during the summer.

From the remaining portion of May until early September of 1982, we went to the grounds about three times per week to watch television with assorted groups and individual children. The results of these interactions are arranged into three areas, including "Narrative Conventions," "Production Conventions," and "Other Nonverbal Conventions." For these sections, most of the data were collected during the summer program, however, data collected during the school year from day care participants are used as examples when appropriate.

Narrative / Nonverbal Conventions: Sense of "Script" or "Schema"
Nearly all of children revealed schematically- or script-based expectations they had developed from their past television experiences. These perceptions occurred with regard to characters as well as plots. For example, when B. (M 4) commented on *The Greatest American Hero* (hereafter, *GAH*) by noting that "good guys always be brave," K. (M 10) agreed, adding: "You know that he's always going to win." D. (M 11) quickly corrected him by saying, "Not always," and explaining his comment in this way: "Well, like if there are two crooks, you don't know which one he's [the Hero] going after, and what he's going to do. . . . All you'd know was that the good guys are going to win. You don't know exactly how, or just what's going to happen, but you know how it'll all turn out." B.'s reply revealed some of his own expectations with regard to the *GAH*: "Because he always crashes into things, and lots 'a times he cries . . . and he falls onto the ground and goes through fires."

Those present clearly knew they should not expect injuries to result from such escapades because, as J. (M 5) pointed out, "He has powers." J. (M 9) added to this, mentioning his "special suit," and S. (M 11) summed the whole thing up when he offered "It's show biz" as the bottom line.

When making their own commercials one day,[2] other kinds of expectations indicated the children could distinguish between advertisements designed with different points of selling intent. In the following excerpts,

---

[2]In June, we brought in a cardboard box used to pack a refrigerator. With the children, we made a giant television set with a screen and knobs drawn in crayon and magic marker. We often used the set to "play TV," especially when the children were reticent or had trouble expressing themselves.

some note differences between selling programs, products, events, and shopping malls, while others present different ideas about commercial appeals.

P. (M 6):   Oh yeah . . . commercials, there is such a thing as a commercial of a movie[3] like the "Fall Guy." They show us a little bit of the fall guy, what's going to happen next, and then they show.

J. (M 9):   Commercials try to get you to buy something, because they make it look real good and . . . and, and then they try to make you think that the other people are so great.

C. (M 6):   They get you to know where things are, like a carnival, so you can go and get things and play.

B. (F 5):   In Corpus they showed a commercial that showed where something is . . . some mall . . . a Greenhouse Mall.

T. (M 6):   They prob'ly don't like it, but to me they're so I can get up and go to the bathroom.

G. (F 5):   They show you how to work things and then you want . . . and get them . . . at a store.

Fact versus Fiction

With a few exceptions, the children knew what was and was not real on television. Differences between children were manifested in their various attempts to explain what "nonreal" things actually were. Such distinctions were more apparent in the context of production (rather than narrative) conventions.

When television characters were invested with super-human powers, children were quick to respond to questions addressing those powers, as when J. (M 4) said of the Greatest American Hero: "He just has it, uh, they given him powers just for the story, so he can do what he has to. We couldn't do that, and my dad neither." In the same discussion, S. (F 9) said that real people do have powers. She was, however, referring to a different kind of powers: "Well, no sir, some people do too have powers. Not like him, but something like ES something, where they can 'see' things we don't."

Another challenge to the general consensus about the reality of powers versus the use of powers as a narrative device was more semantic in nature. Ten-year-old K. corrected a question about getting hurt by saying the following:

Well, the question that he [another boy] answered, if you get hurt, if you run into a wall like he does [GAH] . . . I'd say 'no', because if I . . . if you fly,

---

[3]P. actually did understand the differences between HBO/theater movies and television shows. He simply preferred to use the term "movie" to refer to both.

you have to have a suit you wouldn't get hurt. . . . And anyhow, one time he ran into a train and got amnesia.

Others focused on the reality of televised social conventions, as B. (F 6) referred to a remark on *Three's Company*. "Janet really wouldn't be really in love with him already. It wouldn't happen so fast, but they don't have much time." Here, her point is also indicative of her awareness of one of the limitations of televised narratives, the scheduling constraint of conforming to a half- or 1-hour time slot.

Considering advertisements, most children grasped the level of reality at which the selling techniques were operating. Some conceptualized the fiction in advertisements as tricks, while others perceived such deception to be more akin to lies. When making his own commercial, J. (M 4) suggested that he claim that the pillow he wanted to sell was "rip-proof." In his words, "Oh, let's see. You know how it rips? You could tell them it was rip-proof, cause any pillow could rip." When questioned about this assertion, he conceded that "TV, on TV their words don't lie like that; but in the pictures you always can't see all the things. . . parts . . . and stuff."

Cartoons, of course, stimulated much discussion about what was and was not real. For example, at one point it seemed that E. (F 4) actually believed cartoon dogs could talk. It later became clear that by "talk" she meant "dog talk" (or "bark"), rather than human verbalization. During the same session, M. (M 5) argued that "everything on television is make-believe, except on some news and things."

Cartoon plots were perceived as artificial, in the sense that they were overly simplistic, much like other types of televised content. When watching a situation comedy one day, J. (M 7) had something to say about a girl who asked a boy for a date: "She just wouldn't. 'Least no one I know would . . . maybe when we get older, like it's all right for men. But he's too little to go on a date 'cause they'd be embarrassed. . . . Well, it *could* happen, but most times it really prob'ly wouldn't." A few days later, S. (M 6) referred to lines spoken by a retarded man on a very realistic program by saying: "There's prob'ly something wrong with him, I'm not sure what. But regular people wouldn't say that." The boy's limited real world experiences prevented him from identifying the man's handicap, but he was accurate in his presupposition of what a "normal" man would say in the televised situation.

Responses to Narratives
Considering the detail, comprehensiveness, and accuracy with which children told their friends about the programs they have seen, some clear differences did emerge. Many were related to linguistic abilities. In other cases, the absence of any obvious developmental stage (Piagetian) dis-

tinctions indicated that other variables were probably more salient and useful for accounting for such variation. Since some of the videotaped shows we saw had been aired only a short time before the summer program began, there were numerous times when we could observe children in the process of recalling things they had previously seen on television. When this happened, we often stopped the picture and asked children to recall the content.

Overall, the children were more adept at recounting stories that were more recently seen. While younger children were more likely to provide summaries that were less elaborate and more poorly organized, the summaries were significantly more detailed with prodding and the provision of alternative opportunities to "talk" (e.g., acting out, coloring, and the like). However, the key determinants of ability to recall fully developed plots and characters in a well organized manner were neither age nor level of cognitive development as measured by standard tests. While no general statements of this kind can be advanced as descriptive of any "groups" of children, a few points repeatedly emerged as characteristic of some of the children's abilities to recall the content of televised programs. These factors, of course, were operating in a much broader context, and should not be misconstrued as isolated "predictors" of memory skills vis a vis television. They are as follows:

1. As time since exposure elapses, ability to remember content decreases.
2. Memory is enhanced when situations presented on television are reality-based and have been personally or vicariously experienced.
3. Memory is enhanced when situations are novel and violate expectations.
4. Repeated exposure to content enhances memory.
5. Watching previously viewed content with significant others enhances memory.
6. Memory is enhanced when programs are preferred ("favorites").
7. Memory of half-hour prime time programs is more accurate in comparison to memory of hour long prime time programs.
8. Prime time programs in the early part of the evening hours are better remembered than are programs in the later hours of the evening schedule.

When recalling and/or evaluating stories and characters in both programs and advertisements, children's initial comments were nearly always brief. Younger children were most likely to respond to questions of why they like something by replying: "It was funny." They expressed dislikes equally as simply: "It was dumb." "It was silly." But when encouraged to provide reasons or examples of things like "funniness" or "dumbness," only a very few had difficulty developing the terms they used. Some did this verbally, as in these explanations of perceptions of the *GAH*:

J. (M 5):   It has lots of flying in it, and it looks like a lot of fun. . . . will sometimes make him look funny, too!

S. (M 9):   I like the action; it has lots of exciting action, like in chases and catching criminals and just having adventures.

P. (M 6):   It's pretty exciting and can scare me for a minute sometimes, even when I can tell what will go on . . . like 'cause when he went into the bridge and crashed right into the train.

C. (M 6):   I like the powers, and sometimes wish they could really be real. That would be really funny, but maybe bad and might could cause some trouble for some people.

At other times, likes and dislikes centered on the degree to which televised content was relevant to the children. The comments that follow provide support for this contention:

E. (F 5):   Well, it's about a guy who, every show, when it's on, who keeps getting into messes. And it's mostly boys, and I like girls 'cause they do stuff like me.

S. (F 9):   I just don't really care too much about shows that only have things like who got caught with whose husband and who is in what kind of mess now.

L. (M 6):   I wouldn't buy one, but my mom would 'cause she cuts lots of stuff up. Someone who cuts a lot of stuff up would like it, but not me, so I don't like the commercial too much and it wouldn't make me buy it. Nope.

In other cases, more often with less linguistically sophisticated children, verbal elaborations of likes and dislikes were poorly developed when first offered. However, with appropriate nonverbal opportunities to communicate, their ideas were clearer. For example, one 4-year-old girl demonstrated her concept of "funny" by taking dolls we had previously made from yarn and scraps of fabric and manipulating them so that they acted out her sense of what "funny" was. She then placed this in the particular context of the television show at hand. In other cases, evaluations and descriptions of televised content were focused on nonverbal elements. Some of these are considered in the pages that follow.

Production / Nonverbal Conventions

Data and results concerning understanding of production conventions are organized according to four areas. These points of focus are: (a) sense of story (script, schema); (b) fantasy versus reality; (c) camera shots/ operations, picturization, and special effects; and (d) audio effects.

Sense of Story (Script, Schema)

Many children understood that production conventions are often used to foreshadow events and provide information about plots and characters. This was illustrated one day while we were watching a series of programs on a 2-hour video-tape. Following the usual pattern of coming to (or leaving) the television room whenever it was convenient or desired, I interrupted *The Fall Guy*. I asked the children if they knew how much of the program we had missed, and D. (M 5) quickly replied:

> This is the beginning and it's going to show what happened. . . . I know 'cause it happens every time. It says "Part II" and after the start we'll see some things that happened last time so if you didn't see it you can see what happened, you know, what you missed from the last show.

To this, M. (M 7) added:

> Yeah, it's abbreviated. It will show you the title again, like maybe you came in late or weren't paying attention. See, it says "License to Kill, Part II" but it didn't write it. They make it easier in case maybe you had to do something last week, or when it was starting today.

Children were also aware of how locations are established, indicating they knew these shots are often used to introduce scenes and provide a context for the story. This is clear from J.'s (F 6) comment: "They're in Honolulu, I think, at least Hawaii or a place just like it. See, you can tell by the trees and things, and the girls with those skirts and necklaces. . . . I had never been there, but, so, that's where it is, but maybe not the whole show, maybe just this part." They also knew that establishing shots are not necessarily real. For example, when J. (M 4) compared a commercial set in Africa to a scene from *Raiders of the Lost Ark*, L. (F 5) responded to the question of whether or not they had to travel to Africa to make the commercial in this way: "No, that's just background. I don't, uh, really know exactly how, but I think they put some kinda pictures in back." Her reference is obviously to a technique called "chroma key" in which action is shot in front of artificial background pictures.

It was also clear that children observed how production conventions are used to schematically organize stories in that scene and location changes are often conveyed nonverbally. An interesting example of this occurred when one child exclaimed, "Did you see that?!" during *Happy Days*. No one present understood his point of reference, so C. (M 6) rewound the tape to point out the "X things," referring to an extremely brief transition frame composed of small "X-shaped" markings. In his words, "It's changing scenes! That's how they get to the next picture. They changed the picture!" Several episodes of *Happy Days* were unique in the use of such devices, as other children were careful to note:

J. (M 5): It's a checkerboard. It's what they use when they change from room to room. It has a little thing like this [freezes the frame and walks to television set to point].

B. (M 7): Sometimes, if they have the checkerboard in the middle of the, uh, scene, in the same room, that means "later that day." We could actually be seeing this and be back in that same room in the kitchen and we would know it was later that day. . . . later on, but the same day as before.

In addition to location, children identified character types by how they were introduced and depicted on television. Nonverbal cues helped them to do this, as when we were watching a movie with a classic good-versus-evil theme:

S. (F 5): See, he's all black. Well, the clothes, they're black. That's how you can tell he is bad, like those other guys, the girl too, all black. It means we won't like them.

D. (F 7): So, then, do the good ones have to be all, uh, white? Never mind, dumb thing to ask. They don't have to all be white, or be all white. But, you know they will be light, lighter than the bad ones. That's how you can tell, one way to tell. There's lots of other ways.

Another signal of events to come involves presenting certain program elements at strategic points such as just before a commercial break. Children easily recognized this technique, as when this 6-year-old boy commented during *The Fall Guy*: "Guess what we're gonna see after that ad; something very exciting's gonna happen. I can tell. First, after the commercials, we'll see Salem and a car and a truck, because we just saw the window to the car and the truck. And Salem, 'cause he's the main character, and it looks like him in the mirror."

Still other devices that are schematic in nature because they contribute to the development of a sense of story were recognized by the children. One episode of *Happy Days* revolved around an attraction that Fonzie had for a nun. K. (M 6) made the point that we would probably see some signal from God to the nun, and said the way we would know this was as follows: "The nun does something for Jesus and Jesus is God. So God'll make the lightning, or something, happen. It could be a good thing she does, or if someone does something bad. [Question from another child: Do you think it really is God?] Yeah, prob'ly, but only TV God."

J.   (M 5):   Movies look plain, but cartoons look funny. Your hair [points
to my hair], it moves. Cartoon's hair don't. It's like a "man-
kin's" in a store; it is hard.

At one point, some children were trying to make distinctions much like
the one last quoted above, but they were having difficulty expressing
their ideas. We all took paper and crayons and proceeded to draw real
people and cartoon people. Details in the real versus cartoon people
were clear (e.g., distinctions in hair, absence or presence of seams on
clothing, etc.). Further, children's subsequent verbal explanations of
their thoughts were enhanced by the drawing activity. Making pictures of
their ideas stimulated their ability to articulate them; the art work functioned as a visual counterpart to a different mode of expression.

Camera Shots / Operations, Picturization, and Special Effects
The children consistently voiced their opinions of how "things" on television were "done." The more technically accurate responses could often
be traced to situations in which the device at hand had previously been
explained by some third party. The source of explanation was not always
another person, however, as some children learned *about* television *from*
television or some other media source. This was true for G. (M 4), who
knew how the Hulk was made-up to look real because he had seen the
process demonstrated on a talk show.

In addition to explanations from other sources, some children called
on their own unique past experiences and applied them to television so it
would be meaningful. With regard to camera shots, for example, B. (M 6)
solved one production dilemma for the television program he created by
deciding to use two cameras:

Okay, so the buffalo comes out of the cave, and we have pictures of the
cave. Now we go outside, so we have to move outside. If we stop the camera
and walk and then start there'll be a blank space. No!! I'll just have another
person with a camera; we'll have two cameras.

Although B. did not know that editing would allow him to remove the
"blank" spot, his idea of using two cameras implies an awareness of the
need for editing to finish off a production. The concept of editing came
more directly to him later on, but his lack of technical production experience prevented him from understanding the concept in a clear manner:
"There must be something. On TV I think they must have machines, so
they can make the tape and later on use 'em to make the picture be
smoother. But I don't know how . . . some kind of machines, I bet."

Children also referred to camera operations while in the process of seeing them on the television screen. While talking about how "they make people die" on camera, several methods were offered as explanations:

A. (M 8): They have blanks in their guns and they use tomato juice, or catsup or anything red like blood. You know, how they always have their hand right there [gets up and points to the screen], well, they can do it. You know, they always have something in their hand.

B. (M 9): Well, they could just stop the screen . . . and make it look sweaty. They could stop and get some fake blood in there, then go back down to the position they were in, but put the camera in a different place.

S. (F 6): Yeah, it's trick camera. Well, a real camera, but you know for TV they can make it do things, kinda tricky 'cause we never see them, how they do it. We jus' see what they do, after they do. I think, but I didn't never have a camera, or really see the kind they got on TV.

When speaking about other visual aspects of television, the children referred to lighting techniques in conjunction with camera shots. This exchange grew out of a boy's question about a particular scene:

B. (M 7): Hey, why does the man have his face in the black and in the red? Why can't you see the rest of his face? . . . Maybe he's against the wall and you can't really see it looks like this.

B. (M 6): There's a black wall.

B. (M 7): [Answering his own question] I know why. Because the camera is at a certain angle so you don't see the dark door in the background and you hear weird music. At this angle it's going to cut off half his face. . . . The light would be this way [gestures] so that you could see the whole thing . . . and you could shoot it straight on, ahead, and it will look that way.

When talking about how their own ideas for television shows could be produced, children also indicated some awareness of lighting effects. In this case, B. (F 6) decided that special lights would be needed to accurately depict a snake that was a part of her program idea:

Make a paper snake and someone can be behind the rock and move it out. You know, you can't see the person behind the rock, so it looks like the snake is really moving. It'll have to be a big one, 'bout right here [indicates a snake that is about two feet long]. We'll have to make it light, out of light paper, for night time, so you can see it in the dark. Maybe use a light, light brown, and like little things like that on each side [makes jagged gestures] . . . zig zags. Hmm, I'm not too sure, but, oh yeah! We could . . . or, we could use some special lights and put the camera over here, at an angle, so they can't tell it's fake. Yeah, that's best, if we can get lights and put 'em right, and make the camera at an angle, then with the lights and camera just right they could never tell the snake is just paper.

In other cases, comments about camera usage were directed toward pictures that move more quickly or slowly than one would expect. During a chase scene, L. (F 6) correctly assessed one technique when she pointed out: "They can't really go that fast. The man is speeding them up, by his camera or something else." Again, while the children did not always know just how effects were produced, they did recognize that some kind of manipulation had taken place.

In addition to variations in speed, a number of special effects were the focus of children's observations and assessments. J. (M 6), for example, made this comment about superimposed pictures used to make a transition:

You can see them on one side, see there [uses the remote device to rewind and freeze a few frames]. You can still see them kissing! A picture on top of a picture! I seen that before, I can't remember when, on this same show but a different program. You know why they use it? I'll tell you. It's for, uh, to change to the next picture . . . so to see what's happening on both.

Perceptions and opinions of other children varied greatly, but recognition of special effects was not unusual during the course of viewing. Other examples of insights are as follows:

D. (M 10): It looks like 3-D. They have these special goggles, and they make a special picture with the cameras, so it looks like everything is coming at you . . . three dimensional.

B. (M 5): Use the camera to make it look better and they'd buy it. How to get people to buy it, the camera and people using it can make it look different from this, like some of those special pictures where the two are on top of each other . . . or use two different pictures on the sides of the picture, uh, screen, so we can see both ones at the same time.

L. (F 7): Or do it like when there's stuff in the back, pictures, and they're moving and from a different place. But we're just like we really are, here, only in front [reference here is to process shots].

M. (M 7): He's seeing things in his mind. . . . See that little picture? It's like a picture of ideas in his mind. You can tell, see? They're just showing it to the people watching TV, but not the people on the show.

Audio Effects

In addition to the perceptions discussed thus far, there were many references to audio devices on television programs. Children spoke not only of audio conventions per se, but also of the presumed functions of such techniques. Here are some examples of things they noticed during different viewing sessions:

P. (F 7): That's the guy offstage sayin', "Will Draino let you hurt your pipes?" It's like he has the answer to her problem, that she doesn't know.

J. (M 6): He's not talking in his normal voice, you can tell so easy, because he's drunk! Or maybe someone we can't see makes him sound so drunk. Otherwise he wouldn't really run his words over like he is.

C. (M 8): You know, the music before the commercial, that exciting music. It means something exciting will happen next, or very soon, on the show.

N. (F 5): They are trying to keep something from Larry. They're just trying to make it funny. She doesn't want to be embarrassed. That's what makes it so funny, 'cause Janet's trying to tell Jack to be quiet. She's whispering and talking at the same time. Or, that's how they make it sound to the people who's watching.

J. (M 5): It's bad music . . . warning music . . . danger music.

D. (F 6): Did you hear that guy talking? Well, he, uh, wasn't on the commercial. He's out somewhere where we can't see him, but we can listen. He's said that what she's gonna buy is good.

J. (M 5): Hear that? It comes from behind from somewhere we can't see 'cause it wasn't, there was nothin' on the TV that can make that noise. It was maybe a record, maybe.

Sometimes the children disagreed about the source of some audio effects. On one occasion, there were different ideas about the source of an off-stage "clap-track." While B. (F 6) thought some people "on the sides of the stage make noise," her friend D (F 5) believed it was "from people down in front of the camera." J. (M 7) corrected both of them: "There's two kinds of boxes, two kinds of little machines. One is for clapping—they have different rates of clapping—and one's for laughing. They have different rates . . . and I think they recorded it."

Cartoons were not excluded as objects of thoughts about the audio content of televised programming. For example, in reference to the feminine-sounding voice of a frog prince, M. (M 5) said: "They probably didn't have a boy to talk." The use of a female voice for the prince in this cartoon was puzzling, even to the researchers. We could not think of any implicit or connotative intentions that would logically explain why a woman was used to speak for a man. When the scene ended, however, J.

(M 5) stopped the tape and offered his own version of a gruff voice that he felt was closer to how the frog should have sounded. But he was careful to point out that frogs cannot really talk, and that the voice was just for television.

DISCUSSION

The goal of developing appropriate research procedures for assessing children's perceptions of television was met during the early months of the study. The information concerning the children's peer associations, verbal and nonverbal communication styles, program preferences, and family environments proved to be invaluable. Our exposure to, for example, the children's nonverbal and interpretive skills, which grew out of the "blind walk," was important when analyzing data collected at later points in time.

Another aspect of the early phase which was helpful for understanding the children's personalities was that we could actually see relationships between the children as individuals and their uses of televised content. The fact that the calmer, more mature children with relatively serious outlooks on life preferred adult-oriented fare with verbal puns and moral lessons was helpful for determining some of the factors that apparently draw children to particular types of programming. That is, the relationship between personality and content preferences is at least partly a function of the nature of cognitive processing required to appreciate the specific content at hand. Furthermore, our observations of the children's orientations to material objects and sources of consumer information provided a framework from which we could better assess their responses to programs and commercials during the more directed summer viewing sessions.

The research methods that evolved essentially grew out of our natural responses to situations at hand; we were continuously confronted with "puzzles" to be solved. Our flexibility allowed us to experiment with our guesses of how to solve the puzzles and then adapt our efforts to achieve maximal results. This necessary flexibility means that the methods we developed cannot be presented here in the form of the step-by-step explanations found in reports of more traditional studies. It is impossible to duplicate the procedures used in this study because they emerged in vivo, as parts of a holistic process. A *process* cannot be reduced to a series of discrete components or units. However, the qualitative procedures reported here are certainly useful to others as ideas to explore, as skeletons to be fleshed out with the unique phenomena that comprise all human encounters.

The goal of getting a sense of how the children negotiated television was also achieved. When the children created their own television ideas, they expressed them in relatively sophisticated narrative form. Neither age nor cognitive developmental level, as measured by the Piagetian and Cartoon Conservation scales, were good predictors of the children's ability to comprehend such story elements as complexity and organization. But their sense of the form and content of televised stories was evident when they were in the act of processing media content.

The children readily recognized traditional ways in which programs on television begin and end, and they had clear notions of plot structures in terms of development, climax, or shift in events, and resolution of events. They also had well developed ideas about the extent to which elements of television content were realistic. The major differences between the children's senses of reality were grounded in the various ways that they articulated or otherwise communicated what was and was not real on television.

Considering how the children responded to television, the methods were such that we could observe signs of memory processes as the children were engaged in the act of remembering particular features of programming. While discrete predictors of memory skills could not be isolated, several factors consistently emerged as contributors to the children's ability to remember meaningful programming, or content that included events and experiences with which they could readily identify. They were also relatively adept at remembering details from favored shows, and they indicated strong memory abilities when exposed to elements which were surprising or novel. In short, the factors that apparently facilitated memory of televised content were both varied and complex. Such processes frustrate simple, linear, schematic explanations.

With respect to evaluating television, the children were most apt to be brief in their initial reactions. When encouraged to elaborate their perceptions, however, the children enjoyed exploring the factors involved in how they responded to television. Likes and dislikes often centered on the extent to which the children could personally relate to programs, but also extended to appreciation of such narrative devices as the use of humor, suspense, and the like.

In addition to understanding television's narrative conventions, the children in this study regularly indicated sophisticated perceptions of production conventions. They knew how devices are used to introduce, refer back to, and foreshadow events. If they missed portions of programs, they could make sense of the available nonverbal cues that referred to elements which were missed. The children also had clear notions of how most of the production techniques in the programs they saw functioned so as to structure stories. In fact, at times they even noted production devices that the researchers had missed. This was true in the case of a *Happy Days* episode in which "X things" and "checkerboards" were used to indicate scene changes. As one little girl pointed out: "It's changing the picture, see! It's not just a design, you know."

The children were also aware of the significance of nonverbal aspects of characters and people on television, and often talked about things like clothing, gestures, and facial expressions, indicating their awareness that such elements are both intentional and meaningful. Based on these elements, and interpersonal interactions, the children easily made distinctions between good and bad guys. In doing so, it was clear that the children also knew that these elements are not necessary characteristics of good or bad persons, but are exaggerations.

As with narrative conventions, differences in how the children made sense of the fantasy/reality dimensions of production conventions were not in terms of whether elements were or were not real, but were grounded in how the production devices were created. For example, while there were several different notions of how animated shows were made, the children did have a concept of animation as being aesthetically distinct from other types of media fare.

Considering camera shots/operations, picturization, and special effects, the children's remarks were often surprisingly sophisticated. Time and again, they expressed their awareness of the use of multiple cameras and angles, editing, lighting, slow and fast motion, superimposition, process shots, and numerous other production devices. They also referred to audio effects used on television shows, recognizing that voices they heard were not often delivered by "invisible" persons, and that words could be slurred by manipulating the sound track. They also made distinctions between such elements as "sad" versus "happy" music, and were quick to recognize the implications of what one boy called "danger music." In his words: "Oh no! It won't be good. That song means bad things are gonna happen. If you want, we can close our eyes. You do it and I'll watch and tell."

The results of this study can be used to support the argument that traditional studies of cognitive abilities are constrained by the use of research methods that are rigid and not process-oriented. In this study, not only was it impossible to use results of traditional tests of cognitive skills to place the children in distinct, qualitatively different stages, but test scores were useless for explaining how the children varied in performing complex cognitive tasks. Furthermore, the traditional tendency to rely on verbal indices of cognitions was repeatedly shown to pose serious limitations on one's ability to understand children's thought patterns. As such, the utility of traditional methods and cognitive developmental theory is an area that requires additional critical attention.

This study is limited to some extent by the sample of children in that minority groups were not fully represented; the children tended to be from more rural than urban home environments. However, the goal here is not to make generalizations about all children. It is to be able to talk about *these* children in the context of knowing them as they revealed themselves through the course of this study. Given the parameters delineated with respect to the sample and procedures, however, it is likely that the findings presented do reflect patterns of behaviors that exist in other situations. Future research should be pursued with this point in mind, and should be designed so that the naturalistic methods developed, applied in the field, and presented in this chapter are refined and used in studies of children from different environmental, familial, and developmental backgrounds.

REFERENCES

1. Applebee, A. *The Child's Concept of Story.* Chicago: University of Chicago Press, 1978.
2. Britton, J.N. "Talking to Learn." In D. Barnes, H. Rosen, and The London Association of Teachers of English (Eds.), *Language, the Learner, and the School.* Harmondsworth, England: Penguin Books, 1969, pp. 79–115.
3. DeAvila, E.A. *Cartoon Conservation Scales.* Corte Madera, CA.: Linguametrics Group, 1976.
4. Goldschmid, M.L., and P.M. Bentler. *Concept Assessment Kit: Conservation, form A.* San Diego: Educational and Industrial Testing Service, 1968.
5. Knapp, M. *Nonverbal Communication in Human Interaction* (2nd Ed.). New York: Holt, Rinehart and Winston, 1978.
6. Nash, C., and V. Oakey. *The Television Writer's Handbook: What to Write, How to Write It, Where to Sell It.* New York: Barnes & Noble, 1978.
7. Trager, G.L. "Paralanguage: A First Approximation." *Studies in Linguistics, 13,* 1958, pp. 1–12.
8. Vygotsky, L.S. *Thought and Language.* Cambridge, MA: M.I.T. Press, 1962.
9. Wolf, M.A., R. Abelman, and A. Hexamer. "Children's Understanding of Television: Some Methodological Considerations and a Question-Asking Model for Receivership Skills." In M. Burgoon (Ed.), *Communication Yearbook 5.* New York: Transaction Books, 1982, pp. 405–431.
10. Zettl, H. *Television Production Handbook* (3rd Ed.). Belmont, CA: Wadsworth Publishing Company, 1976.

Chapter 4

Mothers' Comments to Their Children About the Relationship Between Television and Reality

Paul Messaris

Annenberg School of Communications
University of Pennsylvania

It is often pointed out that a child's way of responding to television may be influenced by his or her real social environment (15, pp. 426–427; 17; 25). For example, Wright has argued that "The impact of the mass media must be evaluated in relation to the total complex of social relationships within which the audience members function before, during, and after their exposure to the medium" (32, p. 154). There is a wealth of evidence which suggests that parents, in particular, may play an important role with regard to children in the processes which Wright is talking about. Patterns of parental behavior (or the behavior of other influential adults) have been shown to be linked to children's retention of televised information (2; 5; 6; 30), as well as to children's behavioral responses to the medium (e.g., 3; 7, p. 323; 11; 12; 16; 20, p. 238; 21, p. 312; 27). There is also some evidence—although not always direct—of parental influence on children's perceptions of the relationship between television and reality (10; 21, p. 296; 24). Encouraged by such findings, several investigators have conducted detailed examinations of the family viewing environment and of the kinds of parent–child interactions occasioned by television (e.g., 1; 4; 18; 19; 23; 28; 29). This paper describes some of the findings of one such investigation. The focus here is on what mothers tell their children about the relationship between television and reality.

In principle, one can distinguish among several issues with which a child might have to grapple in the process of developing a "mature" understanding of the relationship between television and reality. Perhaps the most elementary point to be learned is that the image on the screen is a representation of events occurring elsewhere (i.e., not at that point in space and time). Presumably, an implicit understanding of this point comes early in any viewer's developing relationship with the medium, although even a "mature" viewer may sometimes respond to events on the screen as if they were actually occurring in the viewer's own space/time frame. (Indeed, it can be claimed that some fictional genres, such as horror movies, depend upon such a response.) It should be clear that even this elementary point may involve several complications, since the television image may correspond to events which are actually happening (while they are being shown) in some other place (e.g., some parts of the news), fictional events set in real or imagined locations, or even events with no necessary space/time referent (e.g., some kinds of advertising).

To a certain extent, the complications mentioned above also figure in a second major issue with which a developing viewer must inevitably come to grips, namely, the distinction between reality and fiction. This distinction is obviously not a simple matter of either/or. There are several senses in which something that a child sees on television may be "fictional." For example, at a minimum one might distinguish among the following: a fictional recreation of events that actually occurred (e.g., a "docudrama"), a fictional program about events that *could* occur (e.g., a realistic crime drama), and fiction that could not occur in real life (e.g., a movie about Superman). It should be clear, however, that further distinctions could readily be made (e.g., cartoon vs. "live-action" versions of Superman). Perhaps more than any other medium, television presents the child with a very wide range of "mixtures" of reality and fiction, and a "mature" appreciation of the relationship between these two elements may, in some instances, be a matter of considerable delicacy.

Even when a viewer has a relatively secure grasp of the concept of fiction, there is at least one other aspect of the relationship between television and reality that may be problematic. Regardless of degree of ficticity, a television program may be more or less *accurate* or *representative* as a portrait of corresponding real-life events. For example, a "docudrama" may contain inaccuracies and oversimplifications, while a science-fiction program may be quite "realistic" in its portrayal of the psychology of human behavior. A viewer's ability to make discriminations of this sort is probably much more a matter of real-life experience than of familiarity with the medium itself, and we might expect this issue to be of continuing relevance to a viewer well beyond the point at which the more formal conventions of the medium had been mastered.

This paper explores the ways in which the kinds of issues discussed above are handled in television-related conversations between mothers and their children. The underlying concern, as already implied, is to develop a more detailed understanding of how such conversations might contribute to the child's developing relationship with the medium. The paper is based on the findings of a more broadly focused, exploratory study of television-related mother–child discussions. The study entailed a series of 119 interviews with mothers of pre-school and school-age children. The interviewees were white residents of a city in the Eastern U.S. and were recruited on a volunteer basis through a local parent–teacher association in a public school (chosen for its relatively broad social-class representation and for the presence of a pre-school program which made it possible to include mothers of younger children in the study). The average number of children in the interviewees' families was 2.4, and the average age of the oldest child was 11 years, with a range from early childhood through middle adolescence.

The interviews consisted primarily of open-ended questions about some 30 general types of television-related mother–child interaction. The mothers were asked to indicate which of these types of interaction were regular occurrences in their families, and to give detailed examples for each type which did occur. All interviews were conducted by one of four trained graduate students. The typical duration of these interviews was 30–45 minutes, and they were tape-recorded. Quotations in the text below are all given verbatim from transcripts of these tapes. This paper is based on the mothers' responses to the following set of questions: "Do your children ever ask you if something they have seen on TV is true, if that's the way things really happen?" "Do you ever tell your children that something on TV is just like real life?" "Do you ever tell your children that something on TV is unrealistic, that things wouldn't happen that way in real life?" (Each of these questions was followed by several probes, aimed at eliciting concrete examples with various particulars.)

The mothers' open-ended responses—many of them quite detailed and lengthy—to these questions were analyzed with regard to the specific kinds of issues which mothers described dealing with. In broad terms, three kinds of issues account for the bulk of the cases described by these mothers. First—and most predictably—mothers of younger children described a variety of situations in which their children had to be told that some things that happen on television are make-believe and/or could not happen in real life. Second, mother described having to make a more complex point, namely, that some "realistic" things shown on television (i.e., things that *could potentially* happen in real life) are in fact very improbable. Interestingly enough, the kinds of things mothers typically mentioned in this category were portrayals of exaggerated morality, wealth, good fortune, etc., rather than their opposites. Finally the third kind of issue mentioned by these mothers is, in a sense, the complement of the one above: Many mothers described having to point out to their children that television's portrayals of immorality, poverty, bad fortune, etc., disturbing though they may be, are often accurate pictures of reality. Each of these three issues will now be examined in greater detail.

MOTHER'S COMMENTS ABOUT FICTION AND FANTASY

The first of the three types of discussion described above occurred, as might be expected, almost exclusively among families with very young children, who, according to the mothers interviewed, would have to be taught at some point that certain occurrences witnessed on the television screen were "pretend," "make-believe," etc. In other words, maternal commentary of this sort can be seen as part of the child's socialization to the concept of "fiction" (as an explicit cultural category, rather than as an implicit aspect of the child's own behavior). The following examples from the interviews will illustrate this kind of discussion:

> When someone gets hurt on TV, I'll have to explain that the person isn't hurt, that it's only make-believe, it's just a story, you know, 'cause they [two girls, age 2 and 5] get really concerned when they see someone on TV get hurt. It used to happen a lot when *Emergency* was on the air. She's a very sensitive child [a 7-ear-old]. Even in cartoons, it's, eh, what the heck was the name of that show . . . with the dogs . . . oh, *The Lady and the Tramp*. I remember specifically she got so upset, and she starts to cry. And we have to explain to her that it's only pretend.

Related to the above are cases in which a mother has to point out the artificiality of various kinds of "fantasy" material on television. For example, mothers mentioned having to point out that real people or animals cannot recover from accidents in the manner typcial of certain cartoons (e.g., "With the cartoons, with *Tom and Jerry*, when they get violent or whatever, we'll say, 'You know, well they can do that 'cause they're cartoons and they're really only pieces of paper that are drawings, but you [two boys, ages 2 and 5] can't do that, 'cause you would really get hurt if you rode your bike into the wall, or whatever' "); that monsters, witches, and other inhabitants of the world of television (and films shown on it) do not exist in reality (e.g., "The first time she [a 4-year-old] really got scared, I think, when she was watching *The Wizard of Oz* and seen the witch, and she got scared, and I told her it was all pretend—you know—and I explained to her, 'You know what lady that does the commercial with the coffee? That's her with her make-up off' "); or that real-life people cannot fly or perform other kinds of feats exhibited by Superman, the Hulk, etc. (e.g., "A lot of times I've seen them [two boys, ages 3 and 4] do a thing, like, they pull up a chair to the sofa, and they get up on the sofa and then they're going to jump off the sofa onto the chair or vice versa. And I try to tell them, 'Don't do this because, it's not really real,' you know what I mean?...And I'd try to explain to them that when Superman and Spiderman do this jumping and flying around, it's not really real. They'll get hurt this way.")

Two things should be noted about these kinds of discussions. The first is that there is some indication in the interviews that children's initial reaction to the kind of comment quoted above is to conclude that all aspects of television are "pretend" or "make-believe." For example, one mother reminisced about the following incident, which had happened when her children were between the ages of 2-3 and 6-7:

> I remember during the Viet Nam war getting very upset: We were watching television, the news, while we were eating dinner. And they were showing the children and women dead in the village and I–I started crying, and I couldn't eat my dinner. And the kids got very upset. It wasn't the thing to watch at dinnertime, actually . . . I explained to them that everything that you see on television isn't make-believe. The news is real. And . . . it hit cold to them that this was real that they were looking at. And it upset them terribly.

In other words, as has been suggested elsewhere (13), children's *explicit* conceptions about the relationship between television and reality may begin with a complete distinction between the two, and then progress to differentiation within television content and differential assignment of truth-value.

The second point to be made about the kinds of discussions described in this section is that they appear to entail, not information enrichment for its own sake, but, rather, very direct protection against various threats to a child's world, threats which in this case take one of three forms: distress at the misery of a person or animal on the screen, unrealistic expectations about one's own abilities or prospects (the ability to survive accidents or to fly), or unrealistic fears about the environment (presence of witches or other fantastic creatures). As will be shown below, this characteristic, i.e., the "protective" nature of the mothers' comments, is a typical feature of all of the categories of discussions described here, and is apparently the common thread binding together most forms of mother–child discussions about television and reality.

MOTHERS' DISCONFIRMATIONS OF THINGS TOO GOOD TO BE TRUE

Most of the reported discussions about the representativeness of "realistic" televised portrayals (i.e., things that *could* conceivably happen in reality) revolved around one of two broad issues: first, children's use of television as the basis for positive expectations about self and immediate environment which mothers had to contradict; and, second, children's use of television as a source of negative images about the world outside the home, and mothers' validation of these images. With regard to the first of these, children were typically described as having acquired from television expectations of material welfare and harmonious social circumstances which, in their mothers' views, real life was unlikely to satisfy. Children's expressions of such beliefs, then, were cited as the occasions for mothers' denials of the representativeness of the television portrayals in question. For example:

> Q: Do you ever tell your children that something on TV is unrealistic? A: Um, yes. You know, like people, uh, falling into millions of dollars, you know. All of a sudden they become so rich and then they live happily ever after. I mean—but that's so far fetched. You have to make your own life, your own fortune. You know, you have to work for it. That's what I try to explain to them [a 5-year-old girl and a 12-year-old boy]. I want them to know the value of a dollar. I explain to them [three children, ages 3 to 6] that, you know, television is not all real. It's make-believe and it's made to look like everything's, you know, sunshine and roses, but it's not.

An interesting instance of a television series which apparently gave rise to many such discussions among the families in this study was *The Brady Bunch*, which was available to children in daily reruns at the time of the study. Many of the mothers described mother–child disagreements based on children's responses to this series (cf. 14). The situation typically described was that children would complain to their mothers about not being as well-provided-for—materially as well as in terms of style and parental guidance—as the Brady children. For example: "They [three children, ages 7 to 14] think the Brady Bunch has it terrific. They want to be part of that family. There's no question about it." "He's [a 12-year-old boy] told me that a few times that *Mrs. Brady* wouldn't do it like that, you know, or *she* wouldn't say this." "Both my own and children in school seem to feel that that is—at that age, at the sixth, seventh, and eighth grade level—they seem to feel that that's reality and what they're living in is somehow a mistake and it's going to go away and they're going to get the Brady Bunch moving into their living room." The mother who gave the last example also reported that her children asked her: "How come *you* don't solve things like Mrs. Brady?" The mothers' responses to such circumstances are predictable:

> The Brady Bunch especially, they—it's just sort of, wh—everything's perfect. Their family's perfect, and . . . I point that out to them [two girls, ages 3 and 5] a lot. That's like with TV commercials, I'm always saying, "You know, that's not real." I've tried when he [a 13-year-old] was younger to suggest that not everyone lives glamorously and gloriously and, uh, he sees that now, but I think at one point he must have felt very deprived because he wasn't living in that house like the Brady Bunch [unintelligible] great deal of material, uh, ah, wealth, there.

The whole program of the Brady Bunch, um, being portrayed as this super-fantastic family and everything is always solved in the nicest way so that the least number of feelings are hurt . . . and my usual comment to this is, "Well, you know, they've got a whole team of writers . . . and, you know, there's great brains working on this for a whole week, and you're [a 15-year-old female and a 17-year-old male] asking me in 30 seconds to solve your problems."

I would say, you know, things don't work out like the Bradys all the time, you know, everybody doesn't always end up *being* happy, and, yes, you are gonna be sent to your room, and, I just can't see that they're such goody two-shoes, because no father and mother can go all day without hollering and kicking and screaming and sending you to your room. Things don't always work that way. There is not always a happy ending [a 7-year-old boy and a 10-year-old girl].

The general thrust of such maternal commentary, then, is that a child should consider televised images of material or social circumstances which are superior to his or her own as unrepresentative of real life – and, therefore, inappropriate to one's expectations or aspirations. There is some suggestion in the interviews that the outcome of this kind of commentary may be a general resistance, on children's part, to the use of television in a normative sense, as in the following case, in which a mother's exhortations to her children are countered by the same mechanism used defensively by the mothers in the previous examples:

The Brady Bunch: They watch that every single day. I mean, I'm getting tired of seeing the same reruns. . . . And . . . the kids are so respectful of their parents, and they're . . . most of the time they're so well behaved that I show them [a 5-year-old girl and a 12-year-old boy]. I say, "Look! Look at that. Look what they're doing. Look at how they talk to their parents. That's the way you should be." (Q: And how do they respond to that?) "Oh, it's only on television. They don't really act like that."

MOTHERS' CONFIRMATIONS OF BAD ASPECTS OF REALITY

Not all maternal commentary about the representativeness of televised portrayals is aimed at discrediting these portrayals, however. A frequent situation described by respondents in this study involved confirmation of the representativeness of things seen on television; but the characterizations or events of which this was true tended to be qualitatively very different from those described above. What mothers appear to encourage their children to believe tend to be images of things remote from their home and, more importantly, they tend to be images not of enviable situations but of deprivation, suffering, and evil. What remains constant in these comments, though, is the protective intent which one can also quite readily read into the comments described earlier. In this instance, however, this intent tends to be more explicit. In one version of this kind of comment, mothers would confirm the representativeness of various kinds of dangers that a child could stumble upon in the outside world. For example:

> When they started with the drug business. A lot of programs dealt with that. You see kids taking overdoses, being dragged out of apartments, you know, or a police story, uh, uh, they arrange some kind of, I don't know, whatever. You know. . . . And they [three children, ages 3–12] would say, "Is that what really happens if you took those or if you did that?" and I'll say, "Yes, indeed."
>
> We watched, uh, *Prisoner in Cell Block H*. Well, I started to watch it with the kids, [three children, ages 8–11] trying to teach them, you know, "This is the way it can be if you're a bad girl or a bad boy," you know, and now we've really gotten hooked on the thing, you know, and every now and then they'll ask me, you know, if that's really true or, you know, "Do they really do that to people?"
>
> On *Eight is Enough*, one of the girls snuck out of the house to go to a disco (and got in trouble), and they [a 7-year-old boy and a 10-year-old girl] said, "Mom, does that really happen?" and I said, "Yes, I know it happens, because I did it, and the unfortunate thing is I got caught, and I really got in a lot of trouble."

Also of cautionary intent, or consequence—one would hope—is the following case of a mother who had just watched *M*A*S*H* with her children (three, ages 13, 14, and 24) before the interview: "We just watched *M*A*S*H* and the first segment dealt with, you know, really the horrors of war. You know, it wasn't a comedy show tonight, and I think it's probably my favorite episode, and, you know, I made the point that, 'Hey, you know, this is what war is really about.' " The spirit which seems to be behind such comments is made explicit in the following statement:

> You know, a lot of people will say, "Well, I don't want my children to watch that because it's violent." I think that, you know, that might be made into a good point in so far as it'll make some people more leery when they go out on the street, you know, more careful, and rather than turning them into violent people . . . you know, especially when we're in a big metropolitan area.

However, not all comments of this kind can be said to have such an explicitly cautionary tone. Indeed, in many instances the thrust of the comment appears to be simply that the outside world is a vile place, rather than the sources of any specific menace to the child. For example:

We were watching *Lassie*. And the man, uh, stole the dog or something, and she [a 7-year-old] was asking me a lot of questions about it. "Do people really do things like that?" And I had to explain to her that everybody isn't nice and everybody doesn't sit down and talk to their kids and some people are mean and this is the way it is.

I say, "This is what it's really like out there, kids, [a 7-year-old boy and a 10-year-old girl] it's terrible. You know, we are—how can humans be this way? But that's human nature. But yes, these things happen, and we just hope that maybe sometime there will be a better place to live in."

Ironically, in view of the Brady Bunch examples discussed earlier, several mothers also reported confirmations of portrayals of child abuse:

They had a special on child abuse and, uh, I let them watch it, you know, and—I mean, this really sounds terrible but, like, I told her, [a 10-year-old] I said, "You are really lucky, 'cause there are parents that treat their children like that." You know, so I mean, I have done things like that, which probably sounds cruel to you.

I believe she's [a 6-year-old] been exposed to child abuse type things, you know . . . so anyway, I'll have to tell her that things like that do happen, and for some children things really are this way.

CONCLUSIONS

It is commonly believed that the development of the child's sense of the relationship between television and reality is simply a matter of increasing differentiation between these two realms—in other words, that what is involved is a movement from the complete lack of a television-reality distinction (thought to be characteristic of younger children) to a firm sense of total separation between the two. This process is often thought to result from children's acquisition of increasing knowledge (technical, artistic, etc.) about the workings of various media, a knowledge which is thought to lead to a tendency to see images as artificial creations of an intentional agency (see, e.g., 8; 9; 26; 31).

With regard to these assumptions (which are probably the standard assumptions on these issues), the findings of the present study suggest that following: First, while there may be certain respects in which a child's "maturation" as a viewer does indeed entail an increasingly firm sense of distinction between television and reality, the evidence of mothe⋅ ⁻hild discussions of these issues indicates that the problem of the relaʔ between television and reality may persist well into children' cence, rather than ceasing to be an issue at the point at which tʰ tificiality of the medium's images is no longer a matter of coˑ 22). Furthermore, it may well be that mother's comments abⁿ and reality are often a source of encouragement, not discouragement, of a child's tendencies to treat what he or she sees on the screen as though they were faithful images of the real world. Finally, mother–child discussions about the relationship between television and reality appear to be occasioned predominantly by images which a mother or child finds threatening in various ways, rather than by any concern with the workings of the medium in a technical or artistic sense.

As for the more specific consequences of mothers' comments to older children about television and reality, the patterns described in this study suggest the following: On the one hand, mothers' denials of the representativeness of certain images to which a child might aspire (wealth, happiness, etc.) may lead to a more general rejection, on the child's part, of those aspects of television which might conceivably be taken as guides or goals for one's own behavior or characteristics. On the other hand, mothers' confirmations of images of evil and suffering may encourage children to treat television as a window on an unpleasant and forbidding outside world.

In addition to the specific substantive implications summarized above, this study may also be seen as having more general methodological implications for research on television-related family interactions. A fundamental assumption of studies such as this is that being an audience member entails a certain kind of creativity—specifically, the creativity exercised when one adjusts one's interpretation of a message to one's evolving perception of reality. A related assumption of this kind of study is that the construction of meaning is in part a social process—a matter of interpersonal calibration of interpretations among members of a social network. Although these assumptions are shared widely enough to make them appear relatively uncontroversial, they nonetheless bear repetition—if only because of the prevalence, both in research and in public perception, of an opposite view of the audience member, as passive and isolated. Both of these assumptions find expression in the design of this study—in the decision to investigate problematic features of the television-reality relationship as these emerge in the interaction between mother and child; and in the decision to treat the mothers as informants capable of identifying these problematic features and articulating intent. However, interviews with mothers are obviously not the only possible method for addressing the issues investigated here. When the study was being designed, two other methods were considered: interviews with children, and direct observations of families watching television. (Use of a more structured instrument, such as a questionnaire, was considered inappropriate for an exploratory study such as this). Consequently, it may be useful to conclude this paper with a retrospective assessment of the relative merits of these methods as ways of approaching the study of television-related family interactions.

As part of the process of composing this study's interview schedule (which, as noted earlier, encompassed many more questions than the ones discussed in this paper), a small number of interviews were conducted with preschoolers and elementary-school-age children. These interviews made it clear that younger children (including those in the first few grades of school) could not be relied on to provide the detailed retrospective accounts that this study required. Although older children were able to do so, constraints of time and resources precluded the use of more than one method of data collection, and the decision was therefore made not to base the study on interviews with children. The decision not to rely on observations was less obvious. A small number of observations conducted in the planning phase of the study suggested that it would be possible, even in as short a period as one evening per family, to obtain useful data on television-related interaction. Family viewing in the presence of a visitor did not appear to be remarkable enough (for the families studied) to lead to any conscious disruption in patterns of family life. However, these observations also suggested very strongly that, in order to get the kind of extensive coverage of varieties of family discussion that this study was after, much longer observation periods would be required. (A subsequent study, based entirely on observations of families watching television, supported this conclusion—see 23.) Since time limitations precluded repeated visits to families, this method, too, was ruled out.

The method chosen—interviews with mothers—had several advantages which should be obvious in light of the points made above: The mothers were able to provide detailed accounts of incidents occurring months or even years before. They were able to select those incidents which their own experience suggested were potentially important. And they were able to do all this in much less time than would have been required even for a short observation session. Thus, the study was able to encompass a sample or satisfactory size. However, as with all methods relying on self-report, the use of these interviews raises certain questions. One must ask to what extent one is willing to trust the memory of these informants: to what extent their responses might have been affected by considerations of social desirability; and how the study's results might have been affected by the fact that it was the informants who chose which interactions were important enough to report.

With regard to the first of these questions, the findings of this stud˙ ˎ encouraging. Even in written transcription, the mothers' account gest that the particular area of family life which this study was cor with is a source of readily-accessible memories. (This impreˊ

comes even stronger when one listens to the interviews on tape.) This conclusion should not be surprising: A child's cognitive development is clearly a topic of such salience to a mother that one should expect ready recall of incidents related to this development. Regarding the second question mentioned above, however, the experience of the interviewers who participated in this study suggests that there is, indeed, some cause for concern. Specifically, the interviewers reported that in several instances the mothers who were being interviewed required some reassurance that it would not be "held against them" to show an interest in television. The concern rarely arose explicitly—but it is clearly present in nuance and tone of voice on the tapes, and considerable tact was required on the part of the interviewers to make it clear that this was *not* a study based on a negative view of the medium. The lesson here may be that the most publicized research findings concerning television have indeed conditioned the public to expect all academic researchers to disapprove of people's use of the medium. As a consequence, research along the lines of this study may inevitably encounter some degree of resistance.

The final question mentioned above has to do with the implications of allowing mothers to select which types of television-related interactions will be recorded. This element of the study described here would be absent from a study based on observations. However, how one regards the implications of this selectivity depends on one's theoretical premises. If one views family members as active creators of shared meaning, the reliance on the informant as a guide to the important aspects of this process might actually be a matter of choice. From such a perspective, interviewing would always be necessary, even in a study which drew its basic data from observations. In conclusion, then, it may be useful to reiterate a point that may be quite apparent, namely, that the methods discussed here are usually not substitutes for one another. Given adequate resources, a study would do well to include all three.

REFERENCES

1. Anderson, J.A., Traudt, P.J., Acker, S.R., Meyer, T.P., and Donohue, T.R. "An Ethnological Approach to a Study of Televiewing in Family Settings." Paper presented to the Western Speech Communication Association, Los Angeles, 1979.
2. Ball, S., and Bogatz, G.A. *The First Year of Sesame Street.* Princeton, NJ: Educational Testing Service, 1970.
3. Brown, J.R., and Linne, O. "The Family as a Mediator of Televison's Effects." In R. Brown, (Ed.), *Children and Television.* Beverly Hills, CA: Sage, 1976, pp. 184–198.
4. Bryce, J. "Family Styles and TV Use." Paper presented to the Conference on Culture and Communication, Philadelphia, April 9–11, 1981.
5. Corder-Bolz, C.R. "Mediation: The Role of Significant Others." *Journal of Communication*, 30(3), 1980, pp. 106–118.

6. Corder-Bolz, C.R., and O'Bryant, S.L. "Teacher vs. Program." *Journal of Communication,* 28(1), 1978, pp. 97–103.

7. Dominick, J.R., and Greenberg, B.S. "Attitudes Toward Violence: The Interaction of Television Exposure, Family Attitudes, and Social Class." In G.A. Comstock and E.A. Rubinstein, (Eds.), *Television and Social Behavior, Vol. 3.* Washington, DC: U.S. Government Printing Office, 1972, pp. 314–335.

8. Dysinger, W., and Ruckmick, C.A. *The Emotional Responses of Children to the Motion Picture Situation.* New York: Macmillan, 1933.

9. Friedson, E. "Adult Discount: An Aspect of Children's Changing Taste." *Child Development,* 24, 1953, pp. 39–49.

10. Greenberg, B.S., and Reeves, B. "Children and the Perceived Reality of Television." *Journal of Social Issues,* 32, 1976, p. 86–97.

11. Grusec, J.E. "Effects of Co-observer Evaluations on Imitation." *Developmental Psychology,* 8(1), 1973, p. 141.

12. Hicks, D.J. "Effects of Co-observer's Sanctions and Adult Presence on Imitative Aggression." *Child Development,* 39, 1968, pp. 303–309.

13. Jaglom, L., and Gardner, H. "Decoding the Worlds of Television." *Studies in Visual Communication,* 7(1), 1981, pp. 33–47.

14. Kerr, D. "Family Discussions about Depictions of Families on Television." Paper presented to the Conference on Culture and Communication, Temple University, Philadelphia, 1981.

15. Klapper, H. "Childhood Socialization and Television." *Public Opinion Quarterly,* 42(3), 1978.

16. Korzenny, F., Greenberg, B.S., and Atkin, C.K. "Styles of Parental Disciplinary Practices as a Mediator of Children's Learning from Antisocial Disciplinary Portrayals." In D. Nimmo, (Ed.), *Communication Yearbook 3.* New Brunswick, NJ: Transaction Books, 1979, pp. 283–293.

17. Leifer, A.D., Gordon, N.J., and Graves, S.B. "Children's Television: More than Mere Entertainment." *Harvard Educational Review,* 44, 1974, pp. 213–245.

18. Lull, J. "Family Communication Patterns and the Social Uses of Television." *Communication Research,* 7, 1980a, pp. 319–334.

19. Lull, J. "The Social Uses of Television." *Human Communication Research,* 6, 1980b, pp. 197–209.

20. McLeod, J.M., Atkin, C.K., and Chaffee, S.H. "Adolescents, Parents, and Television Use: Adolescent Self-report from Maryland and Wisconsin Samples." In G.A. Comstock and E.A. Rubinstein (Eds.), *Television and Social Behavior, Vol. 3.* Washington, DC: U.S. Government Printing Office, 1972a, pp. 173–238.

21. McLeod, J.M., Atkin, C.K., and Chaffee, S.H. "Adolescents, Parents, and Televison Use: Self-report and Other-report Measures from the Wisconsin Sample." In G.A. Comstock and E.A. Rubinstein (Eds.), *Television and Social Behavior, Vol. 3.* Washington, DC: U.S. Government Printing Office, 1972b, pp. 239–313.

22. Messaris, P. "The Film Audience's Awareness of the Production Process." *Journal of the University Film Association,* 33(4), 1981, pp. 53–56.

23. Messaris, P. "Family Conversations about Television." *Journal of Family Issues,* 4(2), 1983, pp. 293–308.

24. Messaris, P., and Kerr, D. "Television-related Mother–Child Interaction and Children's Perceptions of TV Characters." *Journalism Quarterly.* In press.

25. Messaris, P., and Sarett, C. "On the Consequences of Television-related Parent–Child Interaction." *Human Communication Research,* 7, 1981, pp. 226–244.

26. Pallenik, M. "A Gunman in Town!" *Studies in the Anthropology of Visual Communcation,* 3, 1976, pp. 38–51.

27. Prasad, V.K., Rao, T.R., and Sheikh, A.A. "Mother vs. Commercial." *Journal of Communication*, 28(1), 1978, pp. 91–96.
28. Reid, L.N. "The Impact of Family Group Interacton on Children's Understanding of Television Advertising." *Journal of Advertising*, 8(3), 1979, pp. 13–19.
29. Reid, L.N., and Frazer, C.F. "Television at Play." *Journal of Communication*, 30(4), 1980, pp. 66–73.
30. Salomon, G. "Effects of Encouraging Israeli Mothers to Co-observe 'Sesame Street' with their Children." *Child Development*, 48, 1977, pp. 1146–1151.
31. Worth, S., and Gross, L. "Symbolic Strategies." *Journal of Communication*, 24(4), 1974, pp. 27–39.
32. Wright, C.R. *Mass Communication: A Sociological Perspective.* 2d ed. New York: Random House, 1974.

Chapter 5

Commentary On Qualitative Research and Children's Mediated Communication

Ellen Wartella

Institute of Communications Research
University of Illinois

In a social history of symbolic interactionism, Paul Rock (25) characterizes this school of sociology as one which resides in an oral tradition. He argues that its major proponents (George Herbert Mead, Robert Park, W. I. Thomas, and others of the University of Chicago school of sociology in the early part of this century) tended to shun academic publications, to resist the practice of precisely formulating the research questions, methods, and accumulated findings which arise from the tradition's commitment to naturalistic inquiry. Rock, a sympathetic biographer of interactionism, however, is bothered by the tendency for adherents to ignore their own historical roots. Rock (25, p. 45) writes:

> A sociology which forgets its past may be committed to the continuous rediscovery of old ideas. When the provenance of thought is unknown, authorship can be claimed by those who lack any proper title to it. Old issues are proclaimed innovations, only to recede again into the limbo from which they were retrieved.

Rock's commentary about the lack of historical awareness among symbolic interactionists may be equally relevant to scholars of mass communication research on youth. Our memories are short, and, as has been pointed out (29), the literature on media effects on children tends to be discontinuous during the 20th century. Scholars who were active in studying film effects on children through the late 1930s tended to be ignored (with a few notable exceptions) by those who studied radio effects, a dominant topic of research from the mid 1930s to late 1940s. Most clearly, the research on children and television has been isolated intellectually since the early 1950s, with scholars in this domain tending to forget the history of research on children and media from earlier in this century. But it is not just that the scholarship on media's influence on youth has lacked an historical appreciation of the work in the field; rather, there have been ruptures and discontinuities in the particular traditions within the domain of children and media research. Rock's commentary on the interactionist school in general is equally and particularly pertinent to the qualitative, naturalistic tradition of inquiry into media and children. My point here is simple: qualitative research on media effects on youth is *not* an innovation of the current "ferment" in the field of mass communication. Rather, such qualitative research has an old and distinguished history in American mass communication studies of media and youth. Indeed, such studies may mark the root methods for studying the influence of media on children and families. Paradoxically, the studies of media and children compiled in this volume are relatively novel in the literature on television's influences on youth.

My goal in this commentary is to recover the historical roots of naturalistic inquiry into media's effects on youth, to locate the current volume's selections within this tradition, and to comment on these three studies and their contribution to contemporary understanding of media's roles in children's lives.

THE TRADITION OF QUALITATIVE RESEARCH ON MEDIA AND YOUTH

Fifteen years ago, Roger Brown (5) commented that an adequate history of communication research in the United States had not been written. His comments are still true today. Within the past few years, several scholars in the field have reflected on the history of American communication research and found the "received history" of basic texts such as DeFleur and Ball-Rokeach (9) and Klapper (17) inaccurate descriptions of either the nature of theorizing about mass communication effects or the traditions of scholarship present in American research (e.g., 15, 26, 27, 29). Important in these critiques is the basic charge that American research on media has had a rich and varied tradition well beyond the traditional history's focus on quantitative empirical studies of the influence of media on individuals. Indeed, the "received histories" have quite inadequately represented the history of American research on children and media, which has largely been conducted by people outside of the Lazarsfeld school. While I do not intend to reiterate the criticism of American communication research history, I would like to be more specific in charting some of the early roots of research on children and media. Again, with the caveat that an adequate social history of this research domain has yet to be written, a few comments about the early history of media and youth research can be useful.

First, there have been qualitative studies of media's influence on youth before the recent work on television and families. Indeed, these early studies reside at the University of Chicago in the first several decades of this century. Just as symbolic interactionism as an American sociological traditon began there, American communications research in general and research on media and youth in particular can be traced to the Chicago program on communication (22, 27).

One of the classic studies utilizing life history methods, Thrasher's 1928 study of *The Gang, A Study of 1,313 Gangs in Chicago* included a detailed analysis of the influence of media, particularly movies and dime novels, on the boys in the gang. Thrasher, for instance, wrote that "the movies provide a cheap and easy escape from reality, and they furnish the gang boy with patterns for his play and his exploits" (28, p. 102).

Thrashers's study was later followed by two other important early studies, Blumer's *Movies and Conduct* (2) and Blumer and Hauser's *Movies, Delinquency and Crime* (4), both of which are volumes in the Payne Fund studies investigating the influence of movies on children and adolescents. In these Payne Fund studies, a young Herbert Blumer focused his symbolic interactionist perspective on media. Blumer subsequently became a major proponent and theorist in symbolic interactionism (3). Earlier, through the Payne Fund research, he utilized life history methods as well as naturalistic observations to write presciently about media effects on youth. In *Movies, Delinquency and Crime,* he concluded the following about the effects of film on audience behavior:

> It is evident that motion pictures may exert influences in diametrically opposed directions. The movies may help to dispose of or lead to delinquency and crime or they may fortify conventional behavior. How are these conflicting influences to be explained? Two conditions determine the nature and direction of the effects of motion pictures on the behavior of a given person: first, the diversity and wide range of themes depicted on the screen; and second, the social milieu, the attitudes and interests of the observer (4, pp. 201–202).

Furthermore, in *Movies and Conduct* Blumer identifies the major findings of his studies of movies' influence on youth as follows: they influence children's play; serve as a source for considerable imitation ("forms of beautification, mannerisms, poses, ways of courtship, and ways of lovemaking, especially are copied"—2, p. 193); influence fantasy and daydreaming of adolescents; influence viewers' emotions; and provide people with "schemes of life," fixed images and stereotype conceptions of different peoples and modes of conduct (2, p. 194). These conclusions, I might add, sound very similar to contemporary discussions of television's influence—that television influences children's knowledge, attitudes, and behavior is clear—and that such influences are conditional depending on the exact children and their interpretations of the content also are clear.

Thrasher, Blumer and Hauser are clearly major symbolic interactionists of the Chicago tradition. These media and youth studies are cited as part of that tradition. But they also form the roots of a tradition in American research on children and media. These studies and their progenitors out of the University of Chicago such as Fenton (11) and Mitchell (20) may have been major agenda setters for subsequent research on media and youth during this century.

Several features of the Chicago school concern with communication are worth noting. The school is that community of intellectual thought and academic research that has its roots in the Department of Sociology at the University of Chicago, beginning in 1892; however, as Rock has noted, the sociological tradition of the school can be traced to Simmel's formal sociology and American pragmatist epistemology (25, p. 28). One of its major characteristics was a commitment to social reform through the scientific study of social problems. Thus, the scholars of the Chicago school fused pragmatism with the "new" scientific research methods to examine the role of mass media in creating and recreating American culture and traditional values. As Pecora (22) has noted, seven of the twelve Payne Fund volumes were written by University of Chicago faculty or former students, and the Payne Fund studies represented a major attempt to bring together the work of social scientists to definitively examine the influence of movies on youth. They were much like the 1972 Surgeon General's Committee on Television and Violence in that they were a well-organized, funded attempt to attack scientifically a social problem which generated significant public and industry debate. The University of Chicago's commitment to scientific research on visible social problems of the day may have encouraged scholarly attention to questions of media's impact on youth, a commitment not foreign to current scholars of media effects on children.

A second feature of the University of Chicago program in communication is that it encompassed *both* qualitative and quantitative research on media and youth. For instance, in addition to Thrasher and Blumer and Hauser, the school also held the roots of a tradition of experimental and survey statistical research. For instance, the 1933 Peterson and Thurstone (23) controlled experimental studies of the influence of movies on changing children's attitudes toward ethnic groups were conducted at the University of Chicago. Similarly, Dale's (7) highly quantitative content analysis of the themes of motion pictures utilzied some of the earliest methods in content analysis which had been developed by another University of Chicago graduate, Harold Lasswell. The survey research techniques for studying children's attendance at motion pictures conducted in 1929 by Mitchell (20) for her Ph.D. at the University of Chicago were replicated as a Payne Fund study by Dale (6) in 1935. Lastly, a highly influential work in the radio literature is the 1938 dissertation by DeBoer (8), which combined experimental studies of children's emotional reactions to radio with naturalistic observations of children's listening behaviors. Thus, both qualitative and quantitative methods are part of the American research tradition on studies of children and media from the first third of this century, and these roots are firmly planted at Chicago.

As Denzin (10) has pointed out, although naturalistic inquiry has existed alongside quantitative methods for research in sociology, such qualitative methods have never been as popular as the latter. As well, in mass communication research, the field has been overwhelmingly quantitative in orientation. This is clearly seen in the research on television and children since the early 1950s. Although there have been a few qualitative pieces in this literature, e.g., Friedson's 1952 University of Chicago dissertation and subsequent articles (12, 13, 14), it is only in the past 5 years and recent work by Lull (19), Reid (24), James and McCain (16), Lemish and Rice (18), and Alexander, Ryan, and Munoz (1) that we see a growing interest in qualitative studies. Thus, the current volume signals an important recovery of the tradition of qualitative research on studies of media and youth.

THE CURRENT VOLUME

The three studies reported here involve both naturalistic observations of children in school settings (Wolf) and at home within the family (Lemish), as well as a life history technique of interviews with mothers about the course of their experiences and interactions with their children and television (Messaris). While the methods they employ are old ones, the problems these studies address are very contemporary. Lemish asks: What is the nature of infants' early socialization to television? Wolf examines in rich, interpretive detail how elementary school children negotiate and come to understand the medium. And Messaris examines through the mothers' own self-reports how they aid their children's understanding of the reality/fantasy of television portrayals. In each case, the studies provide provocative insights into how children use and make sense of the medium of television. Moreover, one theme which runs across the studies is their attention to the questions of children's abilities to distinguish the fantasy and reality of televison content. As might be expected, the studies raise more questions about the latter than they may answer.

Lemish analyzes the early development of television viewing among babies between 6½ months and 3 years of age. She observed these children in 16 families during 6 to 8 months of in-home observations. Her findings are astonishing: "Babies do attend to television, they do comprehend some of its messages, and they are capable of learning and applying knowledge." Lemish provides particularly strong evidence and detail of the nature of babies' interactions with the TV: from toddlers walking up and touching the television set, talking back to *Sesame Street* characters, asking to have the set turned on, reiterating (outside of the viewing context) language they have heard from television, to imitating TV action. Television is a rich stimulus in the infant/toddler environment. Moreover, it is quite clear from Lemish's work that it is difficult for late 20th century American children to grow up without being exposed to *Sesame Street*. The ritualistic nature of the communicative environment provided by *Sesame Street* is clearly in evidence in this research. The children Lemish observed are early and enthusiastic *Sesame Street* viewers. These are children younger than the target age group for the program. American mothers, moveover, seem to have faith in the goodness of *Sesame Street*; they allow, and often encourage, their babies to watch it. As Lemish rightfully asks: What is the significance of having a generation of children who first encounter television (and it might be added, much of the world) through *Sesame Street*? Although the long-term influences of such a phenomenon are not at all clear, Lemish has documented an important cultural ritual in contemporary American life.

The import of this study is major: Lemish challenges much of the research on children and television which has underestimated the the importance of early television viewing. Most of the contemporary research on children and television has been conducted on grade school children, with 5-year-olds considered "young viewers." Clearly, to understand how children are socialized into TV watching, we must attend to much younger age groups. Secondly, Lemish's rich contextualized accounts of children's verbal interactions with television challenges contemporary disclaimers of the lack of television's impact and role in language development. Like a "talking picture book," television is used by babies and their mothers to explore the children's linguistic abilities and to teach children language. This is a particularly challenging finding. Finally, Lemish's work is well grounded in contemporary developmental critiques of the underestimation of infant abilities of the Piagetian paradigm. Like other current research on infants (21), Lemish's work points out that we must not underestimate the abilities of the very young child.

Wolf, too, argues that contemporary research on children's comprehension of television and understanding of medium production conventions has underestimated the competencies of school-aged children. Her evidence comes from extensive interviews and observations of 107 children, aged 4 to 12, enrolled in a day care/summer camp facility and observed over a 10 month period. The study reported here is intriguing on several points. Methodologically, Wolf demonstrates the enormous task of collation, transcription, interpretation, and analysis entailed by such expansive observational work. Theoretically, like Lemish's study, Wolf's naturalistic methods and interpretation of children's understandings of television challenge contemporary descriptions of deficits in the elementary school aged children's abilities. For instance, Wolf argues that even children younger than middle childhood demonstrated relatively sophisticated understanding of the narrative forms of television stories: "The children readily recognized traditional ways in which programs on television begin and end, and they had clear notions of plot structures in terms of development, climax or shift in events, and resolution of events." She found evidence, for instance, of detailed analysis of production conventions: a 9-year-old understanding "slow motion" or the use of different kinds of music to signify "danger," "sad," or "happy" events in the action. Again, by contextualizing how children talk about television, and by concretizing children's understanding of television productions through their production of their own TV shows, Wolf provides evidence of how the children she observed work at making sense of television. Her analysis is suggestive of the nature of chilren's development of genre preferences in television use: she argues, for instance, that the "calmer, more mature children with relatively serious outlooks on life preferred adult-oriented fare with verbal puns and moral lessons." It would seem that individual differences in personality characteristics and interpretive skills influence the nature of children's program preferences, understanding of television's conventions, and content.

While Wolf and Lemish highlight the possible underestimation of young children's abilities to make sense of television in the current literature, Messaris focuses his attention on the processes of parent–child interaction about television which may aid the child's interpretation. Moreover, he complicates the issue of "viewer sophistication" by providing evidence that in at least one domain, that of how children distinguish reality and fantasy, the developmental task of interpreting the fantasy nature of television persists into adolescence. Messaris argues here that, even after young children cease to be confused by the verisimilitude of television's images and portrayals of "real people," they are still puzzled by the faithfulness of how television portrays American culture. Messaris sees the mothers he interviews (119 mothers of pre-school and school aged children) as encouraging children's acceptance of the reality of television. Certainly, questions of the representativeness of television images are topics of discussion between the mothers and children. Moreover, he finds the discussions "occasioned predominantly by images which a mother or child finds threatening in various ways, rather than by any concern with the workings of the medium in a technical or artistic sense." This latter point is particularly insightful, since most of the current literature—certainly the quantitative empirical literature—has examined the issue of children's understandings of the reality/fantasy of television from the perspective of children's abilities to distinguish the constructed, technical nature of the medium. Messaris offers a deeper analysis of the ways in which different social groups (in particular working class vs. middle class parents) construct different meanings from the cultural content of television. Moreover, the methodological note at the end of this chapter suggests that mother/child discussions about television are not necessarily a site of tension and debate between parents and children. The mothers interviewed here were conscious of their child's developing understanding of television, had "readily accessible" memories of their discussions with their children, and were interested, in a seemingly positive way, in their children's use of television. Again, this study affirms the central role of television as a medium of communication—and one encouraged by parents—in children's lives. Messaris' caveat to researchers is important: the mothers he interviewed were anxious we not hold against them their interest in television.

Indeed, all three studies reported here suggest that, as academic researchers of children and television, we need to be more cognizant of the frames of reference for television adopted by the chidren and parents we are studying. These studies impress the reader by the very naturalness, ordinariness, and matter of factness of television's role in children's lives. More than any statements to this effect, these rich descriptions of how babies and children incorporate television into their lives demonstrate television's role in the ecology of childhood. From the "pampered" *Sesame Street* viewer to the young adolescent examining the nature of middle class wealth through television's portrayals, television is embedded in the lives of American children. As with all good interactionist accounts, such elaboration of the commonplace of social life is a central feature of the strength of naturalistic observation.

But such rich, interpretive accounts are not without their costs. Sometimes the evidence complicates our understanding of a phenomenon as well as clarifies it. Such, I suggest, is the case here. One inconsistency across these studies is in the theoretical treatment of the issue of children's abilities to interpret fantasy and reality on television. Wolf, for instance, claims that young (seemingly 6- through 9-year-old) children are much more adept at this than the quantitative literature suggests. She argues that the verbal measures employed by the scholars of television comprehension studies underestimate the children's cognitive abilities and ignore children's frames of reference for approaching television. Messaris, on the other hand, interprets the discussions between mothers and children about the representativeness of television portrayals as another indicator of the ongoing developmental task of children's growing understanding of the nature of television's reality. He argues that even adolescent children are puzzled by what is "real" and what is not. Certainly, the two authors are providing *different sorts of evidence* for their claims about when and how children distinguish the real from the unreal. But their evidence is not directly comparable. To reconcile their seemingly inconsistent claims requires both empirical evidence of the range of fantasy/reality distinctions children make throughout childhood, and conceptual clarity in categorizing the evidence. This is not to argue that the current studies are either misleading or wrong-headed in their interpretations. Rather, it suggests that no method of study is without its problems.

One last note in this regard: I've said very little about the nature of doing qualitative research. This is intentional. I think these studies and others in this volume discuss and demonstrate the worth of the method. Clearly, some of the insights offered here into children's use of and interactions with television could not have been acquired by other methods. For instance, the Lemish work with babies is not amenable to the more traditional interview methods typically employed to understand older children's interpretations of television content. My hope is that this volume signals a recovery of a qualitative research tradition in studies of media and youth; such a research tradition has much to offer our understanding of the role of mediated communication in children's lives.

REFERENCES

1. Alexander, A., M.S. Ryan, and P. Munoz. "Creating a Learning Context: Investigations on the Interaction of Siblings During Television Viewing." *Critical Studies in Mass Communication,* 1(4), 1984, pp. 345–364.
2. Blumer, H. *Movies and Conduct.* New York: Macmillan, 1933.
3. Blumer, H. *Symbolic Interactionism.* Englewood Cliffs, NJ: Prentice-Hall, 1969.
4. Blumer, H., and P.M. Hauser. *Movies, Delinquency and Crime.* New York: Macmillan, 1933.
5. Brown, R. "Approaches to Historical Development of Mass Media Studies." In J. Tunstall (Ed.), *Media Sociology: A Reader.* Urbana: University of Illinois Press, 1970, pp 41–57.
6. Dale, E. *Children's Attendance at Motion Pictures.* New York: Macmillan, 1935.
7. Dale, E. *Content of Motion Pictures.* New York: Macmillan, 1935.
8. DeBoer, J.J. "The Emotional Responses of Children to Radio Drama." Unpublished Ph.D. dissertation, University of Chicago, 1938.
9. DeFleur, M., and S. Ball-Rokeach. *Theories of Mass Communication.* New York: David McKay, 1975.
10. Denzin, N. *Sociological Methods.* New York: McGraw Hill, 1978.
11. Fenton, F. "The Influence of Newspaper Presentations Upon the Growth of Crime and

Other Anti-Social Activity." Unpublished Ph.D. dissertation, University of Chicago, 1911.

12. Friedson, E. "An Audience and Its Taste." Unpublished Ph.D. dissertation, University of Chicago, 1952.

13. Friedson, E. "Adult Discount: An Aspect of Children's Changing Taste." *Child Development* 24(1), 1953, pp. 39–49.

14. Friedson, E. "Consumption of Mass Media by Polish-American Children." *Quarterly of Film, Radio and Television* 19, 1954, pp. 92–101.

15. Gerbner, G. "The Importance of Being Critical—In One's Own Fashion." *Journal of Communication* 33(3), 1983, pp. 355–362.

16. James, N.C., and T. McCain. "Television Games Preschool Children Play." *Journal of Broadcasting*. 26, 1982, pp. 783–800.

17. Klapper, J.T., *The Effects of Mass Communication*. Glencoe, IL: Free Press, 1960.

18. Lemish, D., and M. Rice. "Toddlers, Television and Talk: Observation in the Home." Paper presented at the International Communication Association annual convention, San Francisco, 1984.

19. Lull, J. "How Families Select Television Programs: A Mass Observational Study." *Journal of Broadcasting*, 26, 1982, pp. 802–812.

20. Mitchell, A.M. *Children and Movies*. Chicago: University of Chicago Press, 1929.

21. Osofsky, J.D. *Handbook of Infant Development*. New York: John Wiley and Sons, 1979.

22. Pecora, N. "Children, Mass Media and the University of Chicago, 1892–1940." Paper presented to the Conference on Culture and Communications, Philadelphia, 1983.

23. Peterson, R.C., and L.K. Thurstone. *Motion Pictures and the Social Attitudes of Children*. New York: Macmillan, 1933.

24. Reid, L. "The Impact of Family Group Interaction on Children's Understanding of Television Advertising." *Journal of Advertising* 8, 1979, pp. 13–19.

25. Rock, P. *The Making of Symbolic Interactionism*. Totowa, NJ: Rowman and Littlefield, 1979.

26. Rowland, W. *The Politics of TV Violence*. Beverly Hills, CA: Sage, 1983.

27. Rowland, W. "Recreating the Past: Problems in Rewriting the Early History of American Communication Research." Paper presented to the International Association for Mass Communication Research conference, Prague, Czechoslovakia, 1984.

28. Thrasher, F.M. *The Gang: A Study of 1,313 Gangs in Chicago*. Chicago: University of Chicago Press, 1928.

29. Wartella, E., and B. Reeves. "Historical Trends in Research on Children and Media: 1900–1960." *Journal of Communication* 35, 1985, in press.

PART II

THE FAMILY

Chapter 6

Family Time and Television Use[1]

Jennifer W. Bryce

Faculty of Health Sciences
American University of Beirut

The concept of an "active audience" (3) raises a set of complex questions about the processes of selection of, and attention to, television content. An active audience selects and attends to television based on its personal history and past experience of the medium, the immediate social context of viewing, and the meaning web in which all behavior is embedded. An active audience brings to reception a personal competence in television use which has been developed and negotiated in daily interaction, most often in family settings. Despite recent increases in the amount of time spent by mothers and children in nonfamily settings (7), the preponderance of television viewing can still be assumed to take place at home. The accomplishment of family viewing involves a set of meanings, rules and practices which form the context for media interpretation. This chapter explores some of the ways that this competence is developed and maintained in families through their uses of time, and suggests that television viewing behavior is an embedded reflection of the family's organization and orientation to its social milieu.

Attendance is a temporal issue, and can be investigated through at least two levels. First, there is the place of television in the family's round of daily activities: where does television fit in among members' obligations to school and work, among their other leisure activities, and among the logistical necessities of daily family life? Inseparable from this first level of exposure to television is the question of values. The use of time reflects personal or family priorities at a basic behavioral level.

---

[1]The ethnographic portion of the research reported on in this chapter was supported by the Spencer Foundation and conducted through the Elbenwood Center for the Study of the Family as Educator at Teachers College, Columbia University. The interview and videotape study of family time was supported by the Agricultural Extension Service of the University of New Hampshire.

At a second level, there is the issue of attendance to television once the machine has been turned on. Previous studies have used eye gaze (e.g., 1,2) as a measure of attention to television, and the early study by Bechtel, Achelpol, and Akers (5) used video cameras in homes to investigate attentional styles. It has been suggested that the factors which influence attention to television can be grouped into three broad categories: person-related factors, stimulus-related factors, and environment-related factors (10, pp. 264–265). Most of the research attention has been focused on stimulus-related factors, investigating the role of different structural and content features on children's attention to and learning from television. The concept of an active audience, however, strongly implies that more focused research efforts should address the environment-related factors which influence attention to television, and particularly the immediate social context of viewing and the creation of television-related meanings. If, as has been suggested, family viewing "is no more casual and spontaneous than the family dinner," and "is accomplished by competent actors with great improvisational skill," and if it is the family practices surrounding media use which form its interpretive context (4), we need to know more about how these practices are realized in the course of everyday life. This requires laying open the mundane and unremarkable interactions which constitute family living, and examining their meaning and prescriptive value for family members.

The study of attendance to television must begin with an investigation of the overall structuring of time by families. There has been suprisingly little previous research in this area, perhaps because the concept of time is so slippery and ever present, and because naturalistic investigations of families are both time consuming and forbiddingly invasive. Kantor and Lehr (13), in their seminal theoretical work on the family, have identified time as one of the basic dimensions of family organization. They have suggested that families organize their experiences in the past, present, and future, and provide emphasis and integration among these three realms. In addition, they suggest that, through the process of "clocking," families regulate "the sequence, frequency, duration, and pace of immediately experienced events from moment to moment, hour to hour, and day to day" (p. 82). Included here are the family's synchronization of their activities, their setting of priorities, and their organization of time to meet family goals. Television viewing, like all other family activities, cannot escape the power of the family's organization of time, and Kantor and Lehr's concepts of orienting, clocking, and synchronization provide useful tools in the analysis of the relationship between family time and television use.

Significant contributions to an understanding of the family's use of time and television viewing have been made by researchers of the overall

use of time in families (e.g., 18, 19). However, such studies have traditionally resulted in summaries of the time allocated to various tasks, with
little attention directed to the dynamic process through which families
construct their individual days. In an effort to remedy this, Berk and Berk
(6) supplemented daily time use diaries with interviews and additional
information on the respondent's classification of an activity as "work" or
"leisure," other participants in an activity, and their feelings about the activity. Unfortunately, little specific information about the process of attendance to television was included in the report, and television was
often grouped with other "leisure" activities in the analyses. Time use
studies, then, have documented primarily the amount of time the television set is operated in homes, but very little about the nature of that
viewing or how it comes to occur.

The relationship between the family's uses of time and television,
then, raises many questions which have not yet been addressed. The
sequencing of viewing, its place in the mesh of family activities, reflects a
choice, an organization, a negotiation process about which very little is
known. Within the whole fabric of a family's experience, television is accorded a particular place through some as yet unidentified process. It is
the question of the temporal placement of television within the frame of
family life which I address in this chapter. This focus includes not only
some of the environment-related factors which can influence exposure
and attention, but some of the person-related factors as well, as family living establishes the meaning frame through which individual experience
is filtered (16).

Ethnographic research is by definition processual, with data collection
and analysis proceeding concurrently and reflexively. This chapter
moves chronologically through this process—beginning with the development of a set of questions and reporting on efforts to answer them
through observation, participation, and interviews. The first section of
the chapter describes an ethnographic study of three families. The second
section presents further efforts to answer the questions raised in the ethnography through the use of interviews and microanalysis of videotaped
samples of children's behavior. The third section addresses the theoretical implications of the work and possible directions for further study. The
goal of the chapter is both to suggest that television use is inextricably
embedded in the web of social meanings and practices that constitute
family life, and to lay open the circular process of naturalistic inquiry.

As with all research, there are some types of questions which cannot be
adequately addressed within the chosen methodological frame. For example, at no point should the data presented be taken to document individual learning from television—learning outcomes and cognitive styles
are beyond the reach of this research endeavor. The discussions which

follow should also not be taken to suggest typologies of family styles – the goal is to delineate a process and the inevitability of the relationship between family temporal organization and television use, not to identify a limited number of styles through which this process can be realized. In short, the reader is asked to "honor the perspective of the social construction" of the work (3, p. 12), and to keep firmly in mind that the research is directed at the discovery of the meanings of actions and events for the actors rather than a generalizable accounting of the patterns of all families.

AN ETHNOGRAPHIC LOOK AT FAMILY TIME AND TELEVISION

In 1971 and 1980, I conducted an ethnographic study of three families and television. The purpose of the research was to investigate the family's role in creating a meaning context for viewing. A full description of this research is available elsewhere (8, 9), and the basic characteristics of the three families are available in Table 1. I lived with each of the families for approximately 1 month, in two cases moving into the household and in the third living next door and spending most of the family's waking hours with them. I returned to each family for 1 week approximately 6 months after the initial period of data collection, to see whether their patterns of activities and television use changed with the seasons. Further contact

Table 1.   Summary of Characteristics of Participant Families in Ethnography

Characteristics	Family		
(at time of study)	Andrews	Brady	Chapman
Race	White	White	White
Religion	Protestant	Protestant	Jewish
Number of Children	Four	Three	Six
Apparently Stable Marriage	Yes	Yes	Yes
First Marriage for Both Spouses	Yes	Yes	Yes
Number of Non-Kin Household Members	None	None	One
Educational Level of Mother	One year beyond high school	One year beyond high school	Masters degree
Educational Level of Father	High school	High school	M.D.
Approximate Income	$25,000	$20,000	Above $70,000
Housing	Own home	Rent home	Own home
Number of Television Sets	Two	One	Four
Researcher Resided	In home	Next door	In home

was necessary with the families to check my analyses with them and to discuss and review the written products of the research.[2]

Before entering the "field," or moving in with the first family, I was sensitized to the issue of "time" and its potential significance for television use by the work of the family theorists and other researchers mentioned above. I was prepared, therefore, to collect information on the daily activities of all household members and the scheduled commitments of family members outside the household. Thus armed, I moved in with the Andrews family.

The members of the Andrews family lead heavily scheduled lives, and I was immediately immersed in a cycle of activities and planning. The four children were ferried from baseball practice to summer craft sessions to tennis lessons to church outings. My record of activities for the family shows a linearity (completion of one activity, followed by another, rather than numerous concurrent activities) and regularity (a tendency to have similar daily and weekly schedules), even though the initial data were collected during the month of July, when family members reported that they were less scheduled than during the school year. Within a week of moving in with the Andrewses, I was incorporated into the schedule—on the fifth morning, for example, I was asked to drive one child to her tennis lesson at 8:30, pick another up downtown at 9:00, and meet the family to look at a possible camper at 9:30.

Television was awarded only a minor place in this routine. Family members would sit in the kitchen with the newspaper, and programs of particular interest would be discussed and viewing would be planned. These planned programs were then awarded a slot in the round of activities. Unplanned viewing occurred in the gaps in the family's day—while waiting for the school bus, immediately after getting up and before breakfast was ready, or after a day's activities and before bed.

All this, of course, was entered into the data record, but assumed no special significance and stimulated no particular theoretical interest at this time. That was to come later, after my stay with the Brady family.

I moved directly from the Andrews family, with their "clock" orientation, into the Brady family, where one activity flowed into another, planning of time was minimal, and activities outside the home rarely included those which required a prompt arrival. I was initially disoriented and struck by the variation in temporal organization between these two families of basically similar demographic characteristics. While both families were likely to be similarly affected by the reported effects of young chil-

---

[2]Numerous audiotapes were made of family conversations, both in the presence of television and at other times. Samples of these tapes were then transcribed and used for analyses of family verbal interaction. The notation '/' means that the speaker was interrupted.

dren on parental time use (6, 14), these demands were handled differently. I was particularly interested in the differences in the two families in the temporal placement of television in their lives. This aspect of the family's use of television, which had not initially seemed theoretically significant, was thrown into high relief by what Glaser and Straus (11) have called the "constant comparative method."

In the Brady home, the television was turned on immediately in the morning and remained on until another activity was formally initiated (school, leaving the house, cleaning your room, etc.). Even then, the television was either left on, to be turned off by the mother, or one of the parents would expressly demand that the children turn it off. When the competing activity lost its fascination, or was completed, or when a child returned to the house, the television was immediately turned on again and remained on until the sequence was repeated or until the last family member went to bed (in fact, the father often fell asleep in his chair in front of the operating set). Rather than activities forming the frame and television the filler, as in the Andrews family, television was itself the frame and other activities were temporally oriented around it. Baths were scheduled for "at the end of this show," and bedtimes were established in relationship to specific television content. When the parents went out, I was told that the children could stay up "until the end of *Little House on the Prairie*," and the established time for school leave-taking was "after the second commercial." As the mother said, "You know that the second commercial means it's time to go. Now come on!"

My structured sheets for the recordings of activities could not accommodate the temporal organization of the Brady family. Activities were initiated and then quickly abandoned, more than one thing was done at once, and the activity shifts did not occur in relation to planned schedules, despite the group's reliance on TV as a clock. While members of the Andrews family engaged in joint efforts to organize themselves for time-specific activities, and any lapse in these preparations was corrected immediately, in the Brady family, efforts to meet deadlines were a tug-of-war between the mother and her children, usually resulting in conflicts and always in delay. Andrews rules for time use were clear and mutually enforced. Brady rules regarding time were endlessly negotiable, and had to be reestablished for individual events.

My curiosity was aroused. It seemed that the interaction between family time and television use was an important aspect of "getting organized for TV watching," and that exposure to television in these families varied enormously as a function of their "clocking" processes. I turned back to my data from the Andrews family, and began posing questions to them relating to time. For example, what about while TV watching—was there any evidence that "watching TV" had different meanings for members of the two families, and was this reflected in its placement in the temporal order of family activities?

One clear difference between the families was what their members did *while* watching TV. In the Andrews family, viewing was primarily an exclusive activity. On several observed occasions, attempts to engage in another activity while viewing were actively discouraged. For example, one evening when the Andrews family was watching a baseball game, 8-year-old Norman began to get out his building blocks and spread them on the floor in front of the television. Norman had earlier stated that he was excited about watching the game, and his mother's response to this apparent change of heart was: "If you're going to watch this game, don't spread that stuff all over." In the Brady family, doing something else while watching TV was the norm. Their ample playroom was used only as a storeroom for toys. A chosen game or toy would be brought to the living room floor, to be played with in front of the television. Toys no longer of interest would be left there until a parental prompt reminded the child to return them to the playroom. Dad Brady had "his" table beside his reclining chair in front of the TV, where his books and papers were kept to be perused while viewing. For the Brady family, watching TV was often a part of the contextual background of family life rather than an activity in and of itself.

These differences raised questions about the nature of attention afforded television in the two households. Observations, both immediate in the Brady instance and retrospective for the Andrewses, suggested that the Andrews children watched with much more intensity, or visual attention, than the Brady children. In trying to write this into an analytical memorandum to myself, however, I had difficulty in talking about attention. How can you document that one child watches more closely than another, and what kind of behavioral evidence can be drawn on to support such statements? I decided to use eye gaze as an index of attention to assist in substantiating my observations. Each child's eye gaze direction was recorded at 5-second intervals for 30-minute periods while they were viewing a variety of television programs in the absence of overt competing activities. I began with the Brady children, and then arranged to return to the Andrews household to collect comparable data as well as observe more critically their behavior while viewing.

A sample analysis of the eye gaze data did indicate behavioral differences between the two sets of children. Every time one of the Andrews children looked at the screen during the 120 minutes they were observed, it held their attention for an average of 82.25 seconds. Every time one of the Brady boys glanced at the screen during the 240 minutes of recorded observation, it held their gaze for an average of only 28.85 seconds. This rough index supported the observations I was making at a grosser behavioral level—the Andrews children watched with more visual involvement than the Brady children.

As a participant in the lives of these families, I found my own watching being shaped by those around me. In the Andrews family, for example, trying to initiate or maintain a conversation on a topic not related to the television content being viewed was difficult if not impossible, and in fact efforts to do so, both by me and other family members, were considered so obvious a breach of the rules that they were squashed with what, at other times, would be unacceptable rudeness. The following excerpt shows the youngest Andrews child attempting, and failing, to gain the attention that I and the other members of the family were according to television:

> Eight-year-old Norman is playing with a homemade airplane made from sticks, a rubberband, and paper on the living room floor. His three sisters, mother, and I are watching the long-awaited *Miss Universe Pageant* in the same room. Suddenly Norman's airplane breaks.
> Norman: "I can't shoot it anymore."
> (pause, 2 seconds)
> Sister 1: "Oh her dress is pretty."
> Norman: "Hey! Um, you know I ripped all my/
> Sister 2 : "Be quiet!"
> Norman: "I ripped all my"/
> Sister 3 : " we don't care."
> Norman: "I ripped all my xxx off. This, this stick was from my mobile."
> (pause, 7 seconds)

This type of interaction continues throughout the 23 minutes of audiotaped interaction, with Norman making a total of 26 attempts to initiate a conversation not related to the Pageant, of which 16 were ignored by the viewers, four explicitly rejected, and two responded to by suggestions that Norman leave the room. In the last 2 minutes of recorded dialogue, however, Norman offers three "appropriate" (i.e. Pageant-related) comments which are not refused or rejected by his family, suggesting that he may still be in the process of learning Andrews-appropriate viewing rules.

In the Brady family, non-TV-related interruptions were permitted by viewers sporadically, and more frequently than in the Andrews home. The procedure for making a conversational bid was systematic. The individual would first "test the waters" by offering a brief verbal bid (e.g., "Hey, Dad?"). If the attempt was considered intrusive by another viewer, in general it was openly rejected immediately. If this opening gambit was ignored or not met with a clear statement to be quiet, attempts continued and the conversation was allowed to flower. After the first opportunity for rejection, later attempts to halt such non-TV-related verbalizations met with little success.

So far, what I seemed to be seeing were different temporal organizations in these two families, which permeated not only their exposure to television but all aspects of their lives. Of course, both families provided numerous examples of behaviors which were not strictly in accordance with this construction. What I am drawing on here is the preponderance of each family's behavior. Taken as a whole, two different sets of temporal and attentional rules were being maintained in these families through their everyday interactions, both in front of the TV set and in other contexts.

My interest in the issue of family time was not heightened to the point where I wanted to talk to the families about it. Edward Hall's *Beyond Culture* (12), in which he discusses the concepts of monochronic and polychronic time as explanatory terms for what he maintains are widely divergent ways of handling time and space on the cultural level, provided an apt framework for trying to talk about time in concrete and everyday language. He suggests that:

> Monochronic time (M-time) and Polychronic time (P-time) represent two variant solutions to the use of both time and space as organizing frames for activities . . . M-time emphasizes schedules, segmentation, and promptness. P-time systems are characterized by several things happening at once. They stress involvement of people and completion of transactions rather than adherence to present schedules (p. 14).

A rereading of this work seemed to provide a conceptual framework for what I was seeing, and provided guidelines for open-ended interviews about time with each of the families. Operationalized at the level of family life, the two concepts suggest several continua along which families vary: (a) the way a family's daily activities are organized in time—their degree of linearity and the amount of sequencing involved, (b) the amount of planning and scheduling by the family, and (c) the relative emphasis on process or completion which is evident in each group (see Figure 1). These specific behaviors and the attitudes associated with them were the focus of my talks about time with the families.

Combining the interview and observation data, it seemed that the Andrewses and Bradys could be roughly understood as monochronic and polychronic microcultures, respectively. Members of the Andrews family, as I said above, led highly scheduled lives. Each day was an ordered round of scheduled activities, and both parents explicitly told their children that they should do *one* thing at a time, and finish it, before moving on to another. Just prior to the period of research, the father reported

Figure 1. Hall's (1976) Temporal Characteristics of Cultures as Applied to Families and Family Viewing Behavior

Monochronic	Polychronic
Family Temporal Behavior	
Linear and sequential organization of activities	Multiple concurrent activities
High planning and scheduling	Low planning and scheduling
High emphasis on clocks and calendars	Low emphasis on clocks and calendars
Closure oriented	Process oriented
High emphasis on promptness	Difficulty in meeting preset schedules
Family Viewing Behavior	
High planning and scheduling of television viewing	Little or no planning or scheduling of television viewing
Television watched between other activities	Television serves as "clock" for other activities
Television viewing as singular activity	Television viewing as one of several concurrent activities
Close visual attention to television	Intermittent or sporadic attention to television

feeling that his children were "wasting too much time." He gave each child time cards identical to those he used to record the hours of his employees, and had them keep a complete record of their activities for several weeks. Planning and scheduling were emphasized in this household, calendars and clocks were prominently displayed and frequently referred to, and much family discussion centered on the planning of future activities. The schedules of the surrounding community were brought into the home and used to organize family activities. A son was told to clean up his room because the family was going to a baseball game, and dinner was rushed to ensure they would be on time for a church activity. Missing the school bus, being late to church, or arriving at a tennis lesson after the group had assembled were perceived in this family as personal failures, and the children were reprimanded or punished for behavior which reflected a lack of attention to time. This family falls toward the monochronic end of Hall's continuum, emphasizing linearity and sequencing, closure, scheduling and planning, and promptness in meeting the temporal demands of their community.

The Andrewses' emphasis on linearity was evident in their patterns of TV viewing as well. Their children were encouraged, both explicitly and implicitly, not to engage in concurrent activities while viewing. The mother reported, for example, that "I really feel that when they watch TV

I want to see them watch TV rather than just have the TV on as a companion, you know?" In reference to her own behavior, the mother's attitudes were even more explicit.:

> If I'm going to watch television, I'm going to watch television. I'm not going to waste time and just sit there and—there might be a few programs on that you can just half watch, but I, if I'm going to let it take my time, I'm going to give it, give it all the senses I've got and try to get something out of it.

The father also reported that he believes that completing one activity before moving on to another, without overlap, is an "ideal way to do things." He worries about the differences between his own children and other children:

> I wonder if there's something wrong with my kids that they don't do something else while they watch television. You know, a lot of people, they'll read, or, now, do their homework.

The Bradys, on the other hand, evidenced more polychronic characteristics. Rather than a linear approach to the sequencing of activities, the Brady family engaged in multiple concurrent activities with an easy flow from one group to another. The emphasis was on interaction rather than closure. Instead of the frequent changing of activities, and the variety of types of activities that characterized the Andrews family, the Brady family tended to engage in large blocks of general activity within which there were numerous polychronically organized lesser activities. As reported by the mother, "I am always trying to get twelve things done at once, and I never get anything done." The wash would be ready to change to the dryer, dinner would be half cooked, the children would have the television set on but would be engaged in playing with friends who were visiting for the afternoon. Although lip service was often paid to the value of "getting things done," in fact the children often laid aside one task in the middle, particularly if an opportunity for social interaction arose. The ability to do several things at a time is not only encouraged but rewarded in this household, and the mother reported that "the confusion is frustrating at times, but that's the way we are." There was one clock in the public rooms of the home, and no calendar. Planning and scheduling were rarely discussed, and, when they were, the discussion included qualifiers and conditional statements.

It is important to emphasize that there is no value judgement implied in the use of the terms "polychronic" and "monochronic" (difference, not deficit), and that there is a coherent "sense" to the temporal organization of the Brady household, just as there is in the more linear Andrews household. One source of evidence for this coherence is that I was able to learn to function as an equally competent temporal member of both households. One source of difficulty, however, is that the Brady family's use of time is discontinuous of that of the community which surrounds them. Members of the Brady family are often late for school, work, and prearranged meetings.

This polychronic organization was also reflected in their use of television. TV often seemed to be a backdrop to ongoing family activities and interaction in this home, similar to the "constant television households" described by Medrich (17). The television was operated during dinner, during play, while the mail and newspaper were read, and even during the reading of a bedtime story in the same room. Rarely was television viewing an exclusive activity, receiving a family member's undivided attention.

Temporal organization, then, provided a clear example of the family's power to influence, at a very basic and to some extent unconscious level, the exposure of its members to television. The family's organization of television reflected their organization of the rest of their lives, thus supporting the notion of an active audience, organizing television rather than being organized by television. Attentional styles of individual children also appear to be related to their family's organization of time.

The third family in the ethnography, the Chapmans, combined both polychronic and monochronic features, thereby emphasizing the dangers inherent in any effort to typologize the complex behaviors of families. On the level of the family as a unit, they would fall closer to the monochronic end of the scale, in that the personal timetables of the members were synchronized and allowed for a rather linear pattern of activities, if taken as a whole. At the individual level, however, the members of the Chapman family were extremely polychronic, or "multi-channeled" (15, p. 242). Multi-channeled individuals can do several things at once, and do them effectively and comfortably. At the family level, however, these diverse individual temporal styles seemed in this family to fit together to create a linear and accountable movement from one activity to another, with joint efforts to be prompt. The Chapmans would be relaxing in the lounge room, for example, with both the radio and the television on, with mother reading a newspaper and talking on the phone, and the rest of the family conversing, crocheting, and playing with toys. Yet, when asked individually, they were able to report accurately what had been taking place on the television or radio, as well as what their mother had just said on the telephone. This family activity of "leisure time" was then superseded by a trip to the local community fair, where again each individual member engaged in a number of simultaneous activities while concurrently taking part in an organized and linear family activity.

Temporal organization provides a grounded example of the ways in which families mediate the experience of television by their members. It documents the power of everyday life, and belies suggestions that television dominates families. Rather, these families were seen to use television as one medium through which to establish social meetings and carry on the acculturation process. Television must be viewed to result in learning, and the family plays a major part in determining the amount and nature of that viewing.

The next step in the investigation of family time and television, in my view, was to explore the time use orientations of additional families. Each of the families studied in the ethnography had included an 8-year-old boy. Since evidence suggests that time orientations may change over the developmental life span of a family (6), I wanted to continue looking at families with young children. A related question raised by the ethnography, although one that will not be addressed at any length here, was the role of the family's temporal curriculum in the child's management of nonfamily contexts. Would children perform better in schools which matched the time orientation of their families, with M-time children being perceived by their teachers as more successful in M-time schools, and less successful in "open" classrooms organized more polychronically, and vice versa? A further study of nine families with preschool aged children was undertaken to address the above questions.

TEMPORAL ORGANIZATION IN FAMILIES OF PRESCHOOL CHILDREN

This further research effort began with the identification of a preschool program for 5-year-olds which was organized along monochronic principles. The schedule for each 3-hour session was planned and publicly posted a week in advance. The director of the program reported that teaching the children to anticipate and plan for activity changes was an explicit educational goal of the program, as was the child's learning to complete one activity before moving on to another.

The two program teachers were interviewed about the time-related behavior of each of the 24 children enrolled in the program, and asked to give a prognosis for the later educational success of each, relative to the other children in the class. The interviewers were an undergraduate student and an educational psychologist. Neither interviewer had any further contact with the project after the interviews, and the interview data were not available to other participants in the research process until all data had been collected. The parents of 18 of these children gave permission for their children to be videotaped in the preschool building. Each child was videotaped for two 10-minute periods. One period was taped during a unstructured play time, when the child was free to move from one activity to another. The second period was taped during a teacher-directed activity. In an effort to identify the child's temporal style, each tape was coded for the number of activity shifts, eye gaze shifts, and verbal activity within each 10-second span.

The mothers of the children were then contacted by mail and asked to participate in a lengthy, open-ended interview about the family's use of time, which would be conducted in the family home. Nine of the mothers volunteered to participate. Interviews were conducted by me and a research assistant, and were audiorecorded. The interview focused on the temporal organization of the family, and began by asking each woman to recount a day in the family's life, beginning with when the first member awoke and continuing until the last member went to bed. Additional interview topics included the family's scheduled activities, television viewing patterns, use of clocks and calendars, and their attitudes and feelings about time. Mothers were encouraged to talk freely about other aspects of their family which they felt were important for their child's development, as well as to recount specific time-related incidents, such as how the family went about organizing themselves to leave the house for a scheduled commitment in the community.

The triangular relationship between social values, time, and television was evident in the mothers' responses to the first request that they walk the researcher through a day in the family's life. No mention was made of television as a focus of the research prior to the specific television-related questions which were raised later in the interview, and yet, without exception, the recounting of the family's day resulted in lengthy statements about the mother's, or family's, attitudes toward television.

In each of the representative statements below the mother is referring to her 5-year-old child.

> After breakfast, um, he will watch TV if I'm trying to get something done. When he does watch TV I usually feel guilty that he's watching TV in the morning—that's when his energy level is highest and his mind is the most alert and I hate for him to watch TV during that time, whereas later in the day when he gets home from school at four, then if he wants to vegetate I don't think that's a real waste, you know?

> There isn't any regular TV, but sometimes maybe *Dr. Who* at 7 P.M. We're not TV watchers, see, and my husband's so against TV that the TV only registers the ETV stations well.

> I allow time for him to watch *Sesame Street* and *Electric Company* in the morning because that's his time, and he can do it without being interrupted.

These are only a few examples, but they reflect the fact that each of these mothers, when asked about time use in the family, reported not only the pattern of watching but placed that watching in a meaning context which always included family attitudes toward television and often included an emphasis on larger family values as well.

Each mother also clearly drew an association between television, time use, and her role as a parent. In a positive sense, mothers would report that they controlled television because of larger family values. An example would be the following:

> Just by taking a look at our schedules you can see that we maximize our time with the kids so they spend as little time with television or a babysitter as possible. That's like, at the core of our family, and that's the most important thing to us.

In a more negative sense, television was seen by some mothers to be a concrete example of their shortcomings in the parenting role:

> (In a family where the mother reports that the television is on "basically all the time the kids are home")
> TV is a conflict I haven't resolved yet – I'm just not strong enough. It's my responsibility. It's up to me to plan other activities, if I had the energy to do that. I let the TV take over.

Throughout the interviews, television is referred to in a frame similar to other kinds of activities (e.g., church, camping, walks), and each is presented as an operationalization of the family's values. Again, as in the earlier ethnography, television was reported by these mothers to provide the opportunity for the acculturation processes that pervade family life. These mothers explicitly presented their families as active audiences, establishing the meaning context for the television experiences of their members, often through the temporal placement of television in the family's life.

The interviews did not provide clear evidence of family temporal styles which were wholly polychronic or monochronic. Given the complexity of family life, it is intuitively sound that their behaviors do not fit clearly into any dichotomous typology. The concepts and the continuum they represent did, however, provide a useful tool for heuristic comparison. Mothers seem to have clear notions of their family's uses of time, and the kinds of attentional styles they are fostering in their children. One mother will report that promptness is secondary to having a good time, saying, "I want them (the children) to be on time when it's important to be on time. If they're having a good time here it's not important to be on time to school..." while another mother will say that learning the importance of promptness and completing activities is one of the most important things she tries to teach her children. There do seem to be clusters of values and behaviors, with less "time-conscious" families having more polychronic characteristics and being more likely to engage in unplanned, non-exclusive viewing, and the more "time-conscious" families reporting more planned and exclusive viewing. The importance of this clustering of temporal values and television attendance lies not so much in what it says about specific determinants of attention, as in what it reveals about the coherence of familial behaviors. It suggests that television is a part of a larger family construct, subject to the same rules and offering similar opportunities for acculturation as any number of other family activities.

The videotaped samples of children's behaviors in preschool, and the interviews with their teachers, support the intuitive notion that competence in educational settings has a large temporal component. Children whose behavior reflected more monochronic features (paying close attention to activities, completing one activity before moving to another, etc.) were evaluated by their teachers in a monochronic preschool program as being more likely to succeed and being better adjusted. The nature of the evidence prevents any generalizable conclusions about the extent to which the temporal styles of families are carried to school by their children, although comparisons between the family interviews and school data do show a consistency between the parents' expressed time-related values and behaviors and their children's activity and attentional patterns in preschool.

FAMILY TIME AND TELEVISION

What contribution can this inquiry into the family's uses of time and television make to our understanding of human social behavior and the media? Does it, in the end, add any new insights or perspectives, answer old questions or raise new ones?

The temporal dimension of family life does contribute to our understanding of the variable of exposure to the television medium. It supports previous research on the discontinuous nature of attention, and it adds complexity to the issues of content selection and choice. By documenting that exposure to television is part of a larger and coherent family organization, the micro-culture of the family is brought into the research equation of television's effects. Even the already refreshingly broad notion of an active audience is given added layers and breadth, because "active" must now encompass more than the shared meanings of immediate social action before the screen, and the history of viewing and interaction, to include the whole of a family's way of life.

Kantor and Lehr's (13) identification of time as a fundamental organizing dimension of family life is also supported here. The implications for media use include the fact that similar questions must also be asked relative to other such dimensions, such as the family's spatial organization and handling of power and affect. Research on technology and social behavior, it seems, must begin with a thorough analysis of the interactional system, and then look to see how technology is incorporated within this system.

Small scale social systems, with the family as a stellar example, must be considered as learning environments. What gets learned, the processes through which it gets learned, and the never-static process of building on and shifting that learning are the most basic questions to be addressed. Then, within such a framework, additions to that learning from external sources can be examined.

Family behavior is coherent and invested with a sensible (at least to its members) set of unwritten rules. These same rules apply equally to organizing family trips, family dinners, and the family's exposure to television. The meaning context created by the whole of these rules provide the basis for both exposure and interpretation of experience, including television.

Television viewing, then, is one possible label for a variety of family activities. In one family, watching the *Dukes of Hazzard* is a reification of the value of "doing things together," despite parental disapproval of its content. In another family, the same program is understood as a conflict, testing the mother's energy level and willingness to engage in conflict with her children. To study the complete web of meaning which surrounds each act of viewing, that is, to fully understand the determinants, experience, and consequences of an individual act, is beyond the abilities of current science. One beginning, however, is to study the processes through which this meaning is created and maintained, and how such acts come to occur. One entree to these processes is the place of television in the temporal organization of the family.

REFERENCES

1. Anderson, D.R., L.F. Alwitt, E.P. Lorch, and S.R. Levin. "Watching Children Watch Television." In G. Hale and M. Lewis (Eds.), *Attention and Cognitive Development*. New York: Plenum, 1979, pp. 331–361.
2. Anderson, D.R. and S.R. Levin. "Young Children's Attention to *Sesame Street*." *Child Development* 47, 1976, pp. 806–811.
3. Anderson, J.A. "Evaluative Principles for Naturalistic Inquiry Or: How Do I Know That You Know What You're Talking About." Paper presented at the International Communication Association convention, Minneapolis, May 1981.
4. Anderson, J.A. "Cultural Norming and the Active Audience." Paper presented at the Conference on Communication and Culture, Philadelphia, March 1983.
5. Bechtel, R.B., C. Achelpohl, and R. Akers. "Correlates Between Observed Behavior and Questionnaire Response on Television Viewing." In E.A. Rubinstein, G.A. Comstock, and J.P. Murray (Eds.), *Television and Social Behavior* (Vol. 4). Washington, DC: Government Printing Office, 1972, pp. 274–344.

6. Berk, R.A., and S.F. Berk. *Labor and Leisure at Home: Content and Organization of the Household Day*. Beverly Hills, CA: Sage, 1979.

7. Bronfenbrenner, U. and A.C. Crouter. "Work and Family Through Time and Space." In S.B. Kamerman and C.D. Hays (Eds.), *Families That Work: Children in a Changing World*. Washington, DC: National Academy Press, 1982, pp. 39–83.

8. Bryce, J. "Television and the Family: An Ethnographic Approach." Ed.D. dissertation. Teachers College, Columbia University, 1980.

9. Bryce, J., and H.J. Leichter. "The Family and Television: Forms of Mediation." *Journal of Family Issues* 4, 1983, pp. 309–328.

10. Comstock, G., S. Chaffee, N. Katzman, M. McCombs, and D. Roberts. *Television and Human Behavior*. New York: Columbia University Press, 1978.

11. Glaser, B.G., and A.L. Strauss. *The Discovery of Grounded Theory: Strategies for Qualitative Research*. Chicago: Aldine, 1967.

12. Hall, T. *Beyond Culture*. Garden City, NY: Anchor Press/Doubleday, 1976.

13. Kantor, D., and W. Lehr. *Inside the Family: Toward a Theory of Family Process*. New York: Harper and Row, 1975.

14. LaRossa, R., and M.M. LaRossa. *Transition to Parenthood: How Infants Change Families*. Beverly Hills, CA: Sage, 1981.

15. Leichter, H.J. "The Concept of Educative Style." *Teachers College Record* 75, 1973, pp. 239–250.

16. Leichter, H.J. "Some Perspectives on the Family as Educator." *Teachers College Record* 76, 1974, pp. 175–217.

17. Medrich, E.A. "Constant Television: A Background to Daily Life." *Journal of Communication* 29(3), 1979, pp. 171–176.

18. Robinson, J.P. *How Americans Use Time*. New York: Praeger, 1977.

19. Szalai, A. (Ed.). *The Use of Time: Daily Activities of Urban and Suburban Populations in Twelve Countries*. The Hague: Mouton and Co., 1972.

Chapter 7

Media-Logic-In-Use: The Family As Locus of Study

Paul J. Traudt

Dept. of Speech Communication
University of New Mexico

Cynthia M. Lont

Dept. of Communication
George Mason University

Husband: Maybe next year you'll [Researcher] come around and [there will] be a dish[Satellite Dish] in the back. . . .
Wife: Oh, I doubt it.
Husband: Screw cable!

This communication exchange was but one of many observations generated in a case study that explored the relationship between selected family members and the mass media. The exchange also demonstrates the rapport and acceptance that can develop between media ethnographers and family members. This chapter will provide a theoretical perspective, a discussion of methodology, and an exemplar for case study research examining the influence of the mass media, notably television, on family members and their social actions.

The interpretive sociologies of empirical phenomenology, symbolic interactionism and ethnomethodology have all, in due course, examined how it is that individuals, through the symbolic realm of communication, demonstrate competence as members of a social order. Only recently, however, have scholars turned their attention to the study of how mass media contribute to this social order—how audience members use the mass media in the practice of everyday life. Our purpose in this chapter is not to justify the perspectival approach, most of which is subsumed under the umbrella of phenomenology, but to demonstrate how television can become the mantlepiece for personally held meanings and interpersonal actions within a specified social realm. More specifically, our aim is to demonstrate how social reality is constructed by members of the family household, and how television contributes to the common stock-of-knowledge shared by family members within this process of social construction.

All social research, whether motivated by phenomenological or positivist directives, must be grounded in certain fundamental assumptions about the relationship between the communicator and social environments. We have chosen as our theoretical foundation the work of Altheide and Snow (1). Their ideas reside within the concepts of *media logic* and *media consciousness*. Our goal in adopting their perspectives is to provide empirical support for and demonstrate these concepts as they are practiced within the context of the family household.

The foundation for Altheide and Snow's work is embodied within the premise that audience members come to acquire a sophisticated series of expectations which they bring to their consumption of television, film, radio, and so on. These expectations are based upon the media user's previously acquired knowledge regarding the form and content unique to each of the mass media. The authors refer to these sets of expectations as *media logic*:31

> the thesis we propose is that social reality is constructed, recognized, and celebrated with media . . . Our claim is that in contemporary society the logic of media provides the form for shared "normalized" life. Our aim, then, is to view social life from a "media-centric" perspective, seeking first to discover as well as clarify how media logic operates, and then to describe what media culture follows (1, p. 2).

We share the authors' assertion that the mass media provide, in varied shape and form, and contingent upon individual differences, the fabric for a host of "realities" within day-to-day social settings. Intrinsic to our consequent arguments and claims, however, is the authors' description of how the form and structure of the various mass media come to provide a pervasive resource for the audience member's daily social regimen:

> The present-day dominance of media has been achieved through a process in which the general form and specific formats of media have become adopted throughout society so that cultural content is basically organized and defined in terms of media logic. It is not a case of media dictating terms to the rest of society, but an interaction between organized institutional behavior and media. In this interaction, the form of media logic has come to be accepted as the perspective through which various institutional problems are interpreted and solved (1, p. 15).

This proposition is based upon the recognition of a number of conditions in society. First is the generally recognized pervasiveness of the mass media, especially television and its many forms of transmission, delivery, and storage. Second, and fundamental to all consequent discussions in this chapter, is Altheide and Snow's notion of the interactive process that goes on between the audience members within a choice of social settings and exposure to various mass media institutions. Interaction presupposes process, particularly a process based on prior experience and expectations developed through ongoing social encounters. Finally, and most important to the current study, is the authors' notion that the media logic acquired by the audience member is seen to have direct bearing upon the individual's consequent use of such logic for interacting within a host of social settings. Taken further, media logic, for many audience members, comes to represent a legitimate model on which to base their communication strategies within a host of social settings. More recent work by Snow provides useful elaboration:

> people relate to media on the basis of personal identities and then use media as sources of information and situations to play out those identities. Media's influence is that it serves as a respository of information and situations for voluntary action by audience members. Therefore, media influence should be understood not as a cause beyond an individual's control but as something consciously used by people to varying degrees. The media world can become an environment for total immersion, a world tempered by critical evaluations, or an aspect of culture almost totally rejected by an individual (11, p. 219).

Ultimately, the adoption of the media logic perspective leads the social observer to conclude that most audience members bring to any social setting a consciousness formed, totally or in part, by the media logic provided by various media vehicles and their corresponding messages:

> we feel it is not too pretentious to claim that our approach to media analysis is relevant for the sociology of knowledge (analysis of the conditions and processes that yield knowledge). We feel that through adopting media logic people have, in effect, developed a consciousness that affects how they perceive, define and deal with their environment. What emerges as knowledge in contemporary society is, to a significant extent, the result of this media consciousness (1, p. 16).

We take this to mean that the individual nature of audience members, the social contexts in which media are consumed and consequently utilized as parts of social strategizing, and, in large part, the type of media under examination all contribute to the degree of media consciousness characterizing each of our own unique social realms. There are, however, certain milestones, recognizable to us all, which demonstrate the propensity toward a shared collectivity of media-based consciousness. Kreiling provides a useful scenario that suggests empirical application within a number of social realms:

> The media have become arenas in which people find imaginative worlds in which to live, appealing styles of life by which to live, and compelling images and visions through which to identify with the social dramas of those new-found worlds. Thus the population organizes itself into various media publics—The New York Times readership, the fans of Fellini films, the Johnny Carson audience, and so forth—which become worlds of social experience in which people find expressions of their sensibilities (5, p. 207).

A two-staged plan of investigation is suggested in the ideas by these authors. The source of media logic rests within the institutional ethics within each of the mass media industries, and the day-to-day representations of that logic directly observable in their products by means of various transmission devices. For the audience member, mass media logic-in-use becomes an ongoing, synthetic process, where the conventional forms for presenting mass media content are incorporated into behaviors appropriate for everyday social actions.

One may easily extend the scenario of various expressions to the social setting of the family. Surely we can all relate to those "compelling images" of family as provided by a host of television dramas both present and past—of those idealized models of motherhood and fatherhood provided by certain domestic dramas and comedies of the 1950s, 60s, and 70s, of the prototypic professional roles of lawyer and doctor, and of the ideal forms of parenting and child behavior evident in a host of exemplars from televison programming.

One may ask, at this point, whether television and other mass media, as proponents and creators of cultural form, create or simply reinforce these ideal forms that contribute to our social consciousness. The question begs the familiar chicken and egg metaphor. The best answer, we think, lies within a consideration of the relational dependency each audience member brings to the media event, and the individual's needs which motivate their pursuit of these idealized forms through mass media contents:

> In the use of media for both practical information and the establishment with media personalities, the audience member is selectively attentive to particular kinds of media and media content for the purpose of validating personal identifiers. Now the question may be asked, to what extent do personal identities and the perspectives that inform these identities originate

from the media itself? For some people, media may define what it means to be an adult, a female, an accountant, and so on. In addition, media may supply the identity achievement strategies and the sources for validation that are used by the audience member. When this occurs media have reached the zenith of influence, and we may speak of people as having developed a "media consciousness" within a media culture (11, p. 125).

Media consciousness, then, characterized by the audience member's utilization of various sources of media logic, becomes a matter of personal degree, based upon the individual's dependency upon the mass media for the point of origin and maintenance of personal self—achieved largely through social interaction. We can all, after introspection, recognize those examples where we utilize the form—the media logic—provided by mass media. This utilization, as Snow suggests, represents a complex process that runs the gamut, from our use of a story retold from the evening television news in order to converse at an informal gathering, to the adoption of an idealized persona represented in a favorite daytime soap opera for our own intimate social encounters.

The concepts developed by Altheide and Snow, and supported by Kreiling, suggest certain empirical avenues. To summarize, each audience member incorporates the presentation of media logic in one or more ways as the form for their own social construction of reality. The degree of this process of incorporation represents each individual's level of media consciousness. We see the degree of this incorporation in daily behaviors as the individual's demonstrated media-logic-in-use. Our goal in this study, then, is to examine this media-logic-in-use as it is demonstrated in the individual's social construction, born out of exposure to the mass media, specifically television. When the individual is a significant member of a social order, such as the family, then that individual's demonstrated media-logic-in-use may be evident in the way that individual relates to other family members, the way media-logic-in-use may provide validation for the family member's structured responsibilities within the family unit, and so on. It is to the systematic investigation of this media-logic-in-use that we now turn.

The notion of media-logic-in-use, as represented in an individual's media consciousness, has tremendous theoretical appeal. What remains is the systematic development of empirical research documenting the process of media-logic-in-use in everyday activities. The requirements of method become a process whereby procedures must allow for the first-hand observation of the audience member's patterns of exposure to media logic and, concurrently, the investigation of the process of social action influenced by media consciousness. These methodological demands place a high priority upon the tools of ethnography, generated with keen allegiance to mainstream philosophical phenomenology (4).

Contrary to the beliefs of many, qualitative field research is motivated by clear theoretical assumptions as to the nature of human social actions—the mass media audience member's practice of media-logic-in-use as demonstrated in daily life and communication. The open-ended and often inconsistent nature of the data-collection process represents one of the strengths of this perspective. As Willis stresses:

> It is indeed crucial that a qualitative methodology be confronted with the maximum flow of relevant data. Here resides the power of the evidence to surprise, to contradict, specifically developing themes. and here the only possible source for the "authenticity," the "qualitative feel," which is one of the method's major justifications . . . This is not to allow back an unbridled, intuitive "naturalism" on impoverished terms. Even with respect to what remains unspecified by the larger "confession," we must recognize the necessarily theoretical form of what we discover. Even the most "naturalistic" of accounts involves deconstruction of native logic and builds upon reconstruction of compressed, select, significant moments in the original field experienced (12, pp. 90–91).

Indeed, the complexity of observing and documenting an individual audience member's media consciousness and demonstrated media-logic-in-use requires a methodology open to inchoate information. As Willis further elaborates:

> We will find in any cultural form and related form of consciousness a submerged text of contradictions, inconsistencies and divergencies. If we are tuned into an illusory attempt to present a single valency account without interpretive or reductive work, we shall more usually miss (or, at best, simply reproduce) this sub-text. It is necessary to add to the received notion of the "quality" of the data an ability to watch for inconsistencies, contradictions and misunderstandings and to make theoretical interpretations of them. We must maintain the richness and atmosphere of the original while attempting to illuminate its inner connections (12, p. 91).

To predict that ethnographic observation would produce consistent accounts of behavior undermines the purpose of such methods. People, as social actors, are in themselves often inconsistent in their actions. The challenge offered by empirical phenomenology is one of making sense of the conscious ordering by individuals of their social world.

There is a growing corpus of study geared toward the ethnographic study of the audience member's perceptions and use of the mass media in natural settings. As expected, these studies vary considerably in focus and methodology, but they all share the phenomenological perspective that observing, talking and recording in the social world provide the keys to answering those questions regarding the role of the mass media in the strategic construction of social reality. The settings for this research vary. "Ride-along" ethnography by Pacanowsky and Anderson demonstrated how police officers use televised portrayals of law enforcement roles to describe to ethnographers:

> the irony and conflict [they] felt about themselves and their colleagues in relation to the larger social universe . . . [and] as a dramatic authentication of the value of police work . . . and as a negative referent . . . in the police officers' explanation of the "real" world of cops (8, p. 753).

We see from this one study how a subset of society uses the presentation logic of crime-dramas on television to perform a number of significant social strategies. Police officers, though they no doubt as a majority can discern the very real differences between action-packed crime dramas and the normally mundane nature of police work, also use televised portrayals to refer to themselves and other colleagues. Media-logic-in-use, for the police officer, then, demonstrates the relevance of examining the audience member's identification with televised portrayals as they may relate to occupational roles.

The practice of television viewing outside of the home was examined by Lemish (6) in her study of the unique social "rules" displayed by strangers in public televiewing locations. Observations and a range of interviewing techniques were incorporated for a number of settings, including bars, student lounges, airport lobbies, and department stores. The results indicated that televiewing in public places is characterized by an indentifiable set of communication rules, "in general, and specific public viewing rules in particular (which) are created, molded and practiced" (6, p. 779). This study clearly demonstrates how a collective media-logic-in-use contributes to a sophisticated set of codes governing public behavior.

The relationship between television and childrens' play has been documented by Reid and Frazer (9). Their 3-month observational study of children from 10 households revealed how children use both the content from television programming and the television set itself as the objects of play. Media-logic-in-use, then, can be seen as established at a very early age. Television provides both the substance and form for early social interactions.

The household, because of its traditional and extensive locus of sociological study from a number of philosophical viewpoints (10), has also been the object of ethnographic study on the relationship between household televiewing practices and family members' social worlds. Lull (7) examined the process by which family members select television programs and how family roles and communication patterns influence this selection process. His study showed a downward hierarchial structure from adult through older siblings, characterized in the communication process of program selection.

We may further suggest that, as children utilize televised portrayals to provide the substance of play, and for other social encounters, so too can the communication encounter of programming selection be seen to provide opportunities for the day-to-day practice of parenting. Choosing, monitoring, and regulating television programs represents part of the media-logic-in-use of being a parent. These behaviors constitute a good part of how parents practice and exhibit their beliefs about parenting. Wolf, Meyer, and White (13) demonstrated in their longitudinal study of one married couple how television provided a ritualized order to daily life and significant impetus and substance to routine conversations in the home between the couple and their neighborhood friends:

> The case of [names deleted] illuminates the various ways in which television, as a medium per se, and as a purveyor of viewer-selected content can be used to communicate values, feelings and thoughts which all contribute to how they make sense of the environment around them (13, p. 828).

The Wolf et al. study observed the communication behaviors of a married couple engaged in extensive and predictable televiewing and communication behaviors. As suggested earlier by Snow, this couple could be characterized as exhibiting a "zenith of influence" in terms of their media-logic-in-use.

The use of television content providing the substance of social life and discourse is also demonstrated in Hobson's (4) study of English housewives and the mass media. The women in her study were habitual viewers of "realistic" television programming (e.g., dramatizations, soap operas) which related to their own home-bound lives, and how the "everyday" problems encountered by favorite female portrayals "and the resolution or negotiation of their problems within the drama provides points of recognition and identification for the women viewers (4, p. 113).

We can generate a number of conclusions from these previous ethnographies as to how audience members, in various social settings, demonstrate media-logic-in-use. Servants of the public make reference to televised portrayals to refer to themselves and others in the work setting. Televiewing in public as a communication context strikes an awkward balance between personal behaviors for televiewing in private domains, and the rules for appropriate social behavior in public. Children pursue the entertainment forms of television, intent as well on acquiring models for social skills and knowledge about their surrounding world. The exercise of family roles is demonstrated through the selection, regulation, and consumption of television programs. Television provides the substance and impetus for conversations, and provides a source for coping with and learning about familial roles, norms, and expectations.

The corpus of previous research also speaks to the dreadfully slow and inconsistent production of longitudinally based ethnographic accounts of media consciousness. The trend is already clear, however, regarding how these individual accounts provide both rich and revealing insights into the relationship between individuals and television. They also speak, some more explicitly than others, to the conclusion that, no matter what the context for study, the social institution is revealed through the perceptions and observations of others in their practice of mass media and social interaction. Our attempt with this study is to provide further understanding of how it is that individuals, within the social institution of the family, use the mass media—its logic-in-use.

To order our analysis of the data, we set down certain questions for inquiry. We have organized these questions into two categories: basic research questions and theoretical questions. Our research questions guided the formulation of specific observation strategies and questions put to family members. They included:

1. How does each individual describe her or himself, other familial members, and members of relevant outside social settings?
2. How do individuals describe their actions and relationships with the mass media?
3. What forms of content and patterns of media consumption are practiced by each individual—with what system of delivery?
4. What is the chronology for the practice of content and pattern of use for each family member?
5. What are the physical settings for media use?

The data from these basic questions provided us with the substance for demonstrating:

1. a media-logic-in-use for individuals based on the form and content of individual mass media; and
2. the individual's construction of social reality based on the breadth and sophistication of their media consciousness.

The volunteer family for this ethnography met the basic profile deemed necessary for demonstrating Snow's notion of media consciousness as prominent resource for the social world. The family subscribed to both basic and pay-cable services, they taped and stored video by means of a VCR, they played home video games, and, upon questioning, they considered theirs a home characterized by "heavy" media consumption – notably television.

Upon initial contact, the purpose of the study was explained as exploratory and nonevaluative – that the goal was basic information about the family members' descriptions about their use of television in the home.

Others have discussed the many roles the researcher may adopt for gaining entry and developing relationships with subjects for qualitative study. These roles are seen to include ones of leader, supervisor, advisor, and friend. The role of friend was adopted for this study, "a role based on the combination of denial of specific authority, and the desire for positive social relations" (2, p. 171).

The field study was conducted for 3 months during a recent summer, consisting of 14 visits and over 15 contact-hours with family members. Most visits spanned 1 to 3 hours. A total of 7½ hours of interaction were audio tape recorded, and included both interview sessions for later transcription purposes and sessions with family members present within televiewing proxemics. Family members created records of televiewing patterns by maintaining two 1-week quarter-hour television logs. These logs, distributed during the initial week and near the end of the field study, provided structure to the course of fieldwork. Patterns and preferences of televiewing behavior evident from these logs could then be confirmed and further observed firsthand in consequent visits to the home. In time, periods became evident when family members could be interviewed with semi-structured and open-ended questions.

The family for this study consisted of five individuals. They lived in a modest home in the suburbs of a midwest university town. The family's one-story home consisted of three bedrooms, bathroom, livingroom, kitchen, and a single-car garage on the ground floor. Most family activity occurred in and around the televiewing "pit" in the basement. The entire basement was finished with wall paneling and contained the only televiewing area, a serving bar, another bathroom and a laundry. The basement floor was covered by wall-to-wall carpet. The "pit" was the central place for family activity in the home. These activities included studying for school, playing with toys, entertaining friends, and using various forms of video. The family owned two forms of transportation, a truck-van and a late model two-door sports coupe.

The actual televiewing area was approximately 12 by 20 feet, enclosed by a modular arrangement of comfortable sectional sofas. This sofa was constructed in a large "U" shape, positioned directly in front of the television set. The television set was a large-screened, color floor model contained in a hardwood cabinet with a self-contained speaker. A remote control unit was used by family members sitting on the floor or sofa to control television speaker volume. Two 35-channel cable converters were used to change stations. One was permanently situated on top of the television set, while the other was moved around to various locations in the televiewing area with the assistance of a long extension cord. The television set's location was permanent; the size of the unit prohibited mobility.

Other video equipment was neatly stacked on or near the television set. A standard VHS home video tape recorder and playback unit was situated on a small wheeled stand to the televiewer's left of the large monitor. A dozen or so cartridge tapes for this machine were arranged bookshelf-fashion on the top of the television set's hardwood cabinet. VHS capacity included standard playing speed, fast-forward, fast-reverse, freeze frame, and fast forward search. A "playlist" for VHS tape cartridges was kept close by for easy reference, though the father explained that both he and his wife knew each tape just about by heart, and no longer used this reference. Tape boxes were coded by assigned number and/or color of tape box. An ATARI-version home video game rested on top of the television monitor when not in use, complete with assorted cartridge games and player joysticks. Long extensions on game-player joysticks enabled the playing of video games from as far back as the remote regions of the "pit."

The father was 26 years old and worked as a daytime manager in the frozen foods section for a regional grocery-store chain. He had been working with the same firm prior to high school graduation. The father had resided in the same town since birth.

His regimen was occupied with work, and had included working on Saturdays for as long as he could remember. He normally had Sundays off and another weekday, usually Thursday. His working hours were from seven o'clock in the morning until four o'clock in the afternoon, freeing up considerable time for volunteer, late afternoon coaching of a little league baseball team.

The mother in this family was 27 years old, and attended a local community college on a full-time basis in pursuit of a nursing degree. She had been in school for over 3 years, and looked forward to graduating soon and beginning a recently secured job in surgical nursing at a local university hospital. Her anticipation was, in part, based on the fact that both parents looked forward to returning to the ranks of two-income families — an economic reality not realized by either individual since they had started their family. The mother was raised within one hundred miles of her current home.

The three children in this home were preschoolers. The oldest daughter was 4, the second daughter was 3, and the son was soon to celebrate his first birthday. Further discussion of the children will be limited to the two daughters, as both observations and corroborating evidence by parents led the researchers to conclude that the son's current media-related activities were extremely limited if not nonexistent.

A good portion of the children's summer weekdays was spent at the home of their maternal grandmother. Here they were cared for when both parents were at work or school. The children were usually brought home (by parent or grandmother) by five o'clock in the afternoon.

The family's practice of television was patterned, consistent, and predictable. Newspapers, radio, and magazines also followed a consistent pattern of usage, but never approached the frequency of use of the dominant medium of television.

The principal consumer of video fare was the husband. Typically, he read very little in the way of magazines or books and usually just skimmed a state-wide newspaper while on break at work. His use of radio was limited to the time spent driving to and from work, averaging no more than 1 hour per day, and typically tuned into the one album-oriented FM rock station in this small midwest market.

Comparisons between the two quarter-hour television logs provided a rough measure of the time spent with basic and pay cable channels, video-tapes and videogames. The father watched an average of 25 hours of cable television, 2 hours of video recordings, and played home-video games for 2 hours during each week that records for such activities were kept by family members. The father's general viewing pattern was considerable when compared to his other household activities. This tele-viewing pattern varied from 1 to 4 hours, and found him normally positioned directly in front of the video monitor—reclining in some area of the "pit." His programming tastes spanned most generally recognized forms and genres of televised fare—and included HBO and CINEMAX movies, syndicated reruns of newer and older situation comedies, and sports. Videotaped program preferences included *Star Wars, The Empire Strikes Back, Connections,* and varied forms of X-Rated adult movies. His video game playing was always limited to *Space Invaders,* an older yet popular version of the video arcade game.

The father's day periods for televiewing were relegated to the early to late evening weekday hours. He often fell asleep in front of the television set at midnight or one o'clock, only to wake up at two or three o'clock in the morning, when he would turn off the television set and head upstairs to bed. The father would occasionally watch television during mid-day periods as well, during his day off from work. Weekend viewing for this subject occurred typically during mid-morning, followed later in the day by weekday-evening viewing patterns.

The mother's media profile included some newspaper, radio, and relatively little time devoted to television fare. She regularly read the regional newspaper while interning at the nursing clinic. Her radio listening was relegated to time spent driving the car, and was normally limited to a local FM top-forty formatted station. Radio use in the car was supplemented, in part, by stereo eight-track recordings of favorite musical groups, including the Doobie Brothers and The Beatles.

The mother participated in a weekly average of 12 hours of cable television. Time spans devoted to programming or other video fare were consistently shorter than her husband's pattern. The mother's viewing patterns did occasionally involve more than 1 or 2 hours in front of the television set, but, typically, household activities requiring her attention interrupted a consistent pattern flow. Her programming preferences included HBO and CINEMAX movies, syndicated re-runs of older and more recent situation comedies, dramatic family series, and medical/ hospital based dramas. The mother did express a loyalty to a favorite soap opera, *General Hospital*, but rarely had the opportunity to view this program during the mid-day.

The mother's participation in videotaped materials was limited to occasional screenings of the movie *Grease* with other family members, or portions of X-Rated adult movies with her husband.

The two daughters did not yet read magazines, but liked to have stories read to them. They only listened to local radio broadcasts or tape recordings in the company of their parents while in transit around town. The 4-year-old daughter watched about 10 hours of television per week, and shared most of these televiewing sessions with her younger sister. Viewing periods over at the grandmother's house were typically mid-day and early afternoon periods. The two daughters were allowed to watch only 2 hours of television during these periods—a rule established by their grandmother. Typical fare at the grandmother's included public television's *Sesame St.* The daughters' home viewing preferences included Saturday morning cartoons, Nickelodeon in the late afternoons, syndicated situation comedies, and HBO and CINEMAX movies.

Periods devoted to televiewing on the part of these two youngsters varied, and were observed to range from as little as 2 to 3 minutes to 2 to 3 hours. These children also regularly screened the family's video tape of *Grease*. The oldest daughter was beginning to play *Space Invaders*.

These life profiles and televiewing patterns paint a picture of the varying degrees of television's media-logic-in-use for each family member. The father's dependency on television is clear, and characterized by consistent and heavy usage of the medium. The mother's relationship with television is less clear, and appears more limited both in terms of frequency of use and dependency upon the medium. A good deal of her time spent with television enables the fulfillment of concurrent social functions, time spent with other family members. The older children in this family were only beginning to use television in a consistent pattern. The theoretical discussion, therefore, will necessarily concentrate on the media-logic-in-use as demonstrated by the parents' televiewing behaviors and their perceptions of those behaviors.

Our initial probing into a media-logic-in-use captured only surface accounts of television's importance for the father:

Researcher: You keep saying "junk" and "garbage" when using language
             to refer to TV.
Father: Uh Huh. [Affirmative]
Researcher: Can you put a definition on that?
Father: Here's a perfect example. [Researcher, Husband, and Wife
             are in the "pit" watching *Halloween II* on HBO]
Researcher: But, it's great entertainment, right?
Father: Oh . . . just terrific. [Sarcastically] [Laughs] It's garbage.

Yet, when pushed for specifics regarding the influence of television's media logic on his children, the father's deeper understandings were revealed. For example, the increasing diversity of televised information forced the parent to consider what his children should and should not be exposed to within the dearth of availabilities. The practice of parenting, and the individual's perceptions of his role as parent, are beautifully displayed in the regulation of televison content:

Researcher: What do you think about television and your kids?
Father: Uh . . . it's . . . I dunno . . . it's a tool that you like to use, not
             so much to brainwash 'em, but to . . . uh "there's a world out
             there type of thing" . . . so we let 'em watch. Of course, they
             don't go near the dirty movies [on videotape]. I hope they
             don't know that those exist. As far as nudity goes . . . uh . . . I
             let it go, but no porn.

This father recognizes the importance of exposing his children, through televised portrayals, to worldly events portrayed in a televised context. He perceives television through a variety of frames; first as garbage and second as a useful tool for his children, if regulated properly. In the following excerpt, he discusses the importance of television to daily life, the institutional goals behind its creation, and its power to influence human behavior:

Father: No, but, without the, the, box of the world, uh, it would be
             very boring around here, because a lot of people think that's
             [reliance on television] awful, that you rely so much on TV,
             but you just, it's a window, it widens your perspective as long

	as you use it the right way, I guess. Often times I don't, but I do catch some news once in a while. . . .
Researcher:	What's the "right way?"
Father:	Well, as long as you don't let the media hype get things out of hand. I still don't know where to put my finger on the Beirut incident going on . . . it's uh, crazy, You're not sure which way to go with it, but it's obviously a media hype. Everything that Israel's doing is wrong, but yet they say it's O.K. . . . and the Falkland Islands was another prime example of a "good war." Yeah . . . I don't know. As long as you can separate truth from fiction . . . think you'll be alright watching T.V. But uh . . . often times what they want you to believe is truth isn't the same either.
Researcher:	Who's they?
Father:	The networks. As far as . . . as far as whether I believe that, that, uh, the kid uh, wasted . . . where was all that people in Florida?
Researcher:	The Zamora case?
Father:	Yeah.
Researcher:	Yeah.
Father:	[Chuckles] I don't buy it in a minute. I don't know. I've seen 'em hooked up to uh, different machines and I can see that they . . . watching one particular kind of show raises the brain waves and stuff like that as opposed to watching somebody skating on an ice rink or something like that. I can believe in it.
Researcher:	Uh huh.
Father:	But as far as pushing someone over the limit to going out and blowin' a couple of people away . . . uh . . . I think it's gotta be a different motive.

The historical patterns of exposure to television programming also emerged as a significant factor in the parents' demonstrated understanding of the media logic of television, and, more important to the current study, their utilization of these accumulated histories toward a media-logic-in-use. Both the father and, to a lesser extent, the mother expressed their awareness of television's effect on their own social roles within the family:

Researcher:	That's one thing I wanted to talk to both of you about. Let's take you [wife] first. Something that may be very important is that a lot of our habits and behaviors around TV are probably a large function of how we used TV as kids. We all grew up in the TV era, uh, did you have a TV as long as you can remember?
Mother:	Uh hmmm. [Affirmative]
Researcher:	Did you used to watch *Leave It To Beaver?* [Question drawn from TV diary data]

Mother: Uh hmmmm. *Beaver,* and *Hazel,* and *Father Knows Best,* and all those . . .

Father: [Interrupting] Yeah, where did all those guys work? Did you ever ask yourself that? Where did Ozzie work? What job was he in?

Researcher: That's right.

Father: Where did Beaver's dad work? I think, uh, *My Three Sons,* he was in aeronautics, wasn't he?

Researcher: Yeah. He was an engineer.

Mother: Yeah. All those shows were great . . . loved 'em.

Father: Where did he come from when he came home from work?

Researcher: Yeah.

Father: Ya know . . . little Beaver was gonna get his butt whacked when he came home from work, ya know?

Researcher: Did that bother you?

Father: No, we were talking about that a year ago. It bothers me now. Where did all those guys come from? Ya know? I know my dad worked at the place of business.

Mother: I think I'm missing the point. What's the point?

Father: All the moms stayed home . . .

Mother: Yeah?

Father: All the fathers went to work, but yet, now, the kids know where I work. I involve them in the store, they know all my buddies and all like that. Work is part of my life, so they should be associated with it. In those days the father went to work and he was gone, ya know, for 8, 10 hours of the day, while all the little kids pulled their little pranks . . . had their little fun. It's kind of weird perception that we grew up on. . . . When you [Researcher] bring that up.

Researcher: How about you? [Same question directed toward father]

Father: Our TV . . . we always had black and white, in fact, my parents to this day do not have a color TV. So the importance wasn't really on TV. In fact, I think the only reason they bought it was for my sister and I. And we did most of the viewing of it, and my sister's 5 years difference of age [older], so of course her watching techniques were a little different than mine. I wanted more garbage shows and she wanted more adult ones. So there was always a lot of bickering. There were few shows that she liked and I liked and vice versa. I can remember watching a lot of *The Smothers Brothers* on Sunday nights. That used to be the thing, I'd go up and get pop up at the corner store and come home and watch *The Smothers Brothers,* which was one of my favorites back then. *Laugh-In* was great, of course, all those kid type shows that we watch now and regret that you watch them [chuckles.]

Researcher: Now you said last Wednesday, or something, that you characterized yourself as kind of a redneck as a kid.

Father: Yeah.
Researcher: And a lot of those shows . . . things like *The Smothers Brothers*,
               Laugh-In had sometimes even anti-war connotations. Did
               you pick up on that?
Father: Yeah. But that's kind of what made it funny, I guess, to me. It
               was absurd to think that like . . . I can remember one of the
               quotes or one of the skits that they had was, uh, uh, two guys
               were in a foxhole and he says, "Now we're gonna go out and
               get those dirty reds," and he says, 'Yeah, and I can't vote."
               That was before the voting age was 18. And I can remember
               that now. It was a liberal type show. So was *Laugh-In*, I guess.
Researcher: Was it kind of like *All In The Family?* Archie Bunker? You
               know, different audiences could appreciate that show for
               what was said?
Father: I think so. I think so. I wasn't offended by anything that was
               said.
Researcher: Any rules in your family regulating TV?
Father: Ahhh. I don't think so. Like I say, my father barely watched
               it. The news was a rule, of course, and still is . . . six o'clock
               and everything's quiet. Uhh . . . outside of that there wasn't
               much, he really didn't care to watch it much, and, if mom was
               paying attention to it, she'd watch it, but that was primarily
               my sister's and my toy, I guess.
Researcher: Did you have any favorite shows?
Mother: I like *Leave it to Beaver*, like he [husband] said, but I don't . . .
               and I like used to love the movie that was the show *Eight is
               Enough*, until they took it off. I loved it. *Eight is Enough*.
Researcher: Why?
Mother: I thought that the family was really close and I thought that
               [closeness] was really needed. I like the . . . all the situations
               that the movie was made in.
Researcher: Did you ever watch the similar show, was it *Family?*
Mother: Yes. and I liked that too. I like *Eight is Enough* better, though.
Researcher: How about *The Waltons?*
Mother: Don't like *The Waltons*, maybe it was the time, the time the
               movie was portrayed in.

These transcriptions reveal the effect of the televiewer's history as it relates to the parents' understanding of television's use of formula, convention, and predictability—its media logic. The data also demonstrate the
audience member's corroboration and negation of televised portrayals to
actual lived experiences.

The mother in this family is clearly attracted to television's media logic,
as it serves to reinforce her own values regarding the importance of an ordered family life. Many of the family dramas and comedies she mentions
as both historical and current favorites portray idyllic, contemporary

home life. She appears to adopt these values of family as portrayed through television in their entirety, with complete suspension of disbelief in the contrast between televised portrayals of family as compared to her own setting. These programs serve to reinforce her own strong beliefs regarding a traditional and idealized family structure. The mother's utilization of media logic is also demonstrated in her attraction to the soap opera *General Hospital*. Though not evident from the data we've provided, the mother has always pursued television programming (*Marcus Welby, M.D.*, etc.) situated in a medical context. These programs provide an idealized model for her own interests and pursuits within the medical profession. Over the course of her lifetime, the mother has actively pursued television programming which has helped her structure her social world at home and at work.

The father, whose historical consumption of family-based drama roughly corresponds with that of his mate, recognizes the inconsistency between televised logic of family life and actual, day-to-day realities in the home environment. He questions the difference between adult male roles portrayed on television and his own experiences. For the father, the traditional family drama's portrayal of father represents a form of media logic inconsistent with his own belief system.

On a broader plane, the father's additional perceptions speak for the potential for multiple perceptions of the logic television provides in its portrayals. Television's media logic, particularly in comedic form, will be interpreted from the context the audience member brings to the televiewing event. What is one person's dose of liberal criticism of patriotic ideals represents another's ritualistic reaffirmation of those same ideals. What is one gender's idealization of family life as portrayed and reinforced in televised versions of family life may be the other gender's realization that things may not always be as they seem on the small screen.

Finally, media-logic-in-use as practiced in human communication can be demonstrated through some striking testimony by the father. The mother upon similar investigation, indicated that she never used television as a referent for engaging in communication with her family or the other members of her social milieu. However, the mother's active pursuance of domestic dramas and comedy, and her expressed interest in dramas situated in medical settings, clearly demonstrates how her media consciousness impinges on both her world at home and at work. The father, though, perhaps because of his unabated and expressive recognition of the role television plays in his life, captured the process of television as common social construct among fellow employees:

Researcher: There's some research evidence that suggests that children
               take a lot of what they learn . . . well, for example, the time

	you were telling me about [oldest daughter] and the end of *Grease,* how she reenacts that role. . . .
Father:	Yeah. Right.
Researcher:	Do you think adults do that?
Father:	Oh, yeah. Definitely. There's a show that was on several years ago, no several months ago, just when cable started up for [town of residency] area . . . *California Dreamin'* . . . uh . . . it was a real good show. Like I'd try to watch, what was it? *Movie Review* . . . on Thursdays when I ever get a chance to. . . .
Researcher:	On public television?
Father:	*Movie Review* is what it's called . . . yeah . . . the Chicago Sun Times and . . . these two guys get together . . . Gene Siskel and Roger Ebert? And, when they did this, when they did the review on that *California Dreamin'* they really liked it but it was one of those that just never, uh, made it at the box office for some reason. They couldn't figure it out because it was a good show. It just wasn't one of those blockbusters. But that was on, and when it came out the terminology on it . . . uh . . . cowabunga, narley, uh, different things like that. And we still do this, y'know, to this day we'll say "It's really narley out there," to refer to when it's a super bust [at work], or something like that. Or, we've got a couple of guys who are kind of goofy that work for ya, y'know . . . couple of part timers who are a little bit goofy and we call them kooks . . . stuff like that . . . [chuckles].
Researcher:	You and. . . .
Father:	The gang up at work . . . the little clique up at work. [chuckles]. And that, that happens with everything, you know. As far as a show that everybody kind of talks over. "Did you see this?" Ya'know? And you start talking the terminology in the show. So. . . .
Researcher:	Good.

Here, then, represents the "zenith of media consciousness' (via Snow) as demonstrated in the social environment of the workplace. Television-logic-in-use becomes the common referent for working colleagues to describe their mutual perceptions of developments within a common task of labor. Moreover, media-logic-in-use outlives the original novelty of the form of presentation and gets used as an agreed-upon term of shared meaning for other events that transpire in time. The father's testimony also shows how television content can become the object of such communication as well.

We would fail in our duties as ethnographers if we were to leave this scene without some mention of the role of more recent advances in video technology as they impinge on the family environment. The relative recency of cable in this midwestern market made relevant the investigation of certain pre- and post-televiewing pattern questions. Our observation of cable's influence in the home varied with each parent:

Researcher: Do you watch more now that you have cable?
Mother: No. I think I watched more before. But I wasn't in nursing school before, and didn't have kids before, either.

The mother's regimen as student and homemaker made few allowances for cable television's influence on her viewing regimen. However, cable television did afford her the opportunity to pursue, within her work schedule, favorite syndicated programming made more available through increased channel capacity.

As was expected, cable television has greatly affected the father's televiewing regimen:

Researcher: Since getting into cable, do you think you watch more?
Father: Oh, Jeez yeah! Sure, because right now I found myself flipping to the other network stations and there's just garbage on. And before, uh . . . well, like the wife was saying that she'd like to move out of town sometime so that I could be a store manager, you know . . . my first impression is, "Is that town gonna have cable?" Ya know? [chuckles] . . . cuz, uh, it's part of my life.

Cable television increases the father's duration of viewing periods. Cable television also affords the emergence of new episodic viewing patterns. The increase of channel selection afforded by cable technology serves to modify televiewing patterns characterized by more standard, over air broadcasting. The father watches more, but on fewer channels.

We have attempted to reconstruct the events surrounding one family's relationship with the mass media—with television as the primary focus. Readers of this brief ethnography might well question our role as gatekeepers in the process of selecting what we felt were the most illuminating aspects of our data in order to make certain claims. By way of initial departure, our selection of this specific family was motivated by our understanding of how media logic is defined and how media consciousness is practiced by subjects under observation. A family whose members included those who spent a considerable period of time engaging in mass-media behaviors would more likely exhibit patterns of social behaviors and express their views of the world in a way that was consistent with the theoretical notions provided by Altheide and Snow.

Our analysis of descriptive data, including that drawn from personal observations, audiotape recordings, and diaries maintained by the parents, came to represent a formidable task. This analysis would have been without direction given the absence of a theoretical foundation translated into pragmatic research goals. As Willis (12, p. 91) would have it, all subjective accounts provided by society's players require both the deconstruction of "native logic" and the reconstruction of personal accounts toward theoretical ends. As researchers, we felt most confident in those reconstructions supported from a number of methodological angles (i.e., direct observation, testimony provided by subjects during interviews, and televiewing logs). The reader has been provided with those excerpts from data we felt best exemplified, as evidentiary support, the family member's demonstrated media-logic-in-use. As the organization of our ethnography would suggest, a number of constructs emerged in our analysis of the data. These included: (a) the context for the conduct of family life, (b) the context for televiewing activities, (c) a day-to-day profile for each family member, (d) individual and group patterns of mass-media usage, (e) parental perceptions of the role television plays in family life, (f) historical patterns of television program consumption, and (g) the direct or indirect utilization of television programming for communicating in a number of social settings. These constructs were applied to our goal of empirically demonstrating a media-logic-in-use as practiced by family members. We feel these constructs represent a point of departure for other media ethnographers intent on demonstrating the same in other studies, though the range of possible familial settings would suggest that other constructs might also be relevant.

What has crystallized from this study is our understanding of how it is that family members, in varying degree and styles, exhibit through their actions and words an acute awareness of television's presentational logic—how programming content is perceived as both highly formulaic and predictable. We have also provided glimpses as to how television's presentational logic comes to represent a media consciousness on the part of family members, and how this logic comes to represent, not only possible sources for social behaviors, but, in certain cases, the preferred behavior for a host of social settings. Family members come to utilize both specific portrayals from television fare and an historical aggregate of these portrayals in order to construct their own identities appropriate to a number of social realms. Television provides a significant resource for the construction of experiences and knowledge regarding one's self, one's role as a family member, and one's role in life outside of the home.

REFERENCES

1. Altheide, D.L., and R.P. Snow. *Media Logic*. Beverly Hills, CA: Sage, 1979.
2. Fine, G.A., and B. Glassner. "Participant Observation With Children: Promise and Problems." *Urban Life* 8, 1979, pp. 153–174.

3. Grimshaw, R., D. Hobson, and P. Willis. "Introduction to ethnography at the Centre." In S. Hall, D. Hobson, A. Lowe, and P. Willis (Eds.), *Culture, Media, Language: Working Papers in Cultural Studies, 1972-1979.* London: Hutchinson, 1980, pp. 73-77.

4. Hobson, D. "Housewives and the mass media." In S. Hall, D. Hobson, A. Lowe, and P. Willis (Eds.) *Culture, Media, Language: Working Papers in Cultural Studies, 1972-1979.* London: Hutchinson, 1980, pp. 105-116.

5. Kreiling, A. "Television in American Ideological Hopes and Fears." *Qualitative Sociology* 5, 1982, pp. 199-233.

6. Lemish, D. "The Rules of Viewing Television in Public Places." *Journal of Broadcasting* 26, 1982, pp. 757-781.

7. Lull, J.T. "How Families Select Television Programs: A Mass Observational Study." *Journal of Broadcasting* 26, 1982, pp. 801-811.

8. Pacanowsky, M.E., and J.A. Anderson. "Cop Talk and Media Use." *Journal of Broadcasting* 26, 1982, pp. 741-755.

9. Reid, L.N., and C.F. Frazer. "Television at Play." *Journal of Communication* 30(4), 1980, pp. 66-73.

10. Scanzoni, J. *Shaping Tommorrow's Family: Theory and Policy for the 21st Century.* Beverly Hills, CA: Sage, 1983.

11. Snow, R.P. *Creating Media Culture.* Beverly Hills, CA: Sage, 1983.

12. Willis, P. "Notes on Method." in S. Hall, D. Hobson, A. Lowe, and P. Willis (Eds.), *Culture, Media, Language: Working Papers in Cultural Studies, 1972-1979.* London: Hutchinson, 1980, pp. 88-95.

13. Wolf, M.A., T.P. Meyer, and C. White. "A Rules-Based Study of Television's Role in the Construction of Social Reality." *Journal of Broadcasting* 26, 1982, pp. 813-829.

Chapter 8

Commentary on Qualitative Research and Mediated Communication in the Family[1]

James A. Anderson

Department of Communication
University of Utah

The notion of family is obvious, yet difficult (21, 24, 32). Most of us were born into one. Many of us have chosen to create another; a sizeable number of us will dissolve and create many. A family is an intimate, committed, and significant organization which typically begins when individuals choose to associate for reasons which include propriety, economics, affective support, sexual access, sodality, child rearing, and many others. The nuclear family of industrialized societies is intimate in that membership is restricted and the viability of the organization is dependent on the individuals involved. That is, particular families are formed by the assembled individuals and fail when those individuals withdraw, are expelled, or die. Even in this day of intentional couples, the family remains a committed association in its expected duration and involvement of membership. And it is significant because it has standing in the larger society. Udry (31, p. 16) comments:

> It is inaccurate to say that the nuclear family has become less functionally significant for the society and for the individual. In many ways, the nuclear family has become more important as a social unit, since it provided the major source of emotional security for adults and children during most of life. Marriage is the longest and most significant relationship in life. It is the major source of companionship for adults and provides the setting for the great preponderance of sexual activity in the society. The nuclear family is the basic consumption unit of the economy. It provides the only basis for initial

---

[1]Portions of this chapter appear in: "Cultural Norming and the Active Audience." In Satya P. Sharma (Ed.), *Culture and Ideas: The Interface of Anthropology and Communication.* New Delhi: New Concepts Press, (forthcoming).

status placement of individuals in the community. More than any other single institution, it determines what kind of life a child will grow into and what his chances will be to amount to something. It is hard to see why some social scientists have arrived at the conclusion that the family has few functions today. It simply has different functions, and it has become the only major focus of emotional life in society.

PERSPECTIVES ON THE FAMILY

Even a cursory examination of the literature on family studies reveals a substantial number of views that can be taken of the family. Nye and Berardo (28) list 11; Burr, Hill, Nye, and Reiss (7) give another five. When one collects those views, it appears that the concepts of structure, function, system, and dramaturgical interaction form a core around which variations appear (5, 6, 14, 15, 18, 23, 26, 27). In addition, these concepts can be approached using different levels of entrance into the family (12, 17, 19, 25). A comment or two on each follows:

Structure. The family is a formal organization defined by the culture in which it appears and, in part, archived in law (34). Its formal organization is governed by the twin principles of reciprocity and legitimacy, which organize social alliances and provide for the entry of new members in society (9). The family is also a natural organization as developed by the members. As such, it shows itself in many variants, some of which are sanctioned and some not. And it is a contingent organization—an adhocracy—which appears in response to the particular moment. College roommates or army buddies may serve as family when circumstances require (8, 30).

Function. The family is the setting for the accomplishment of a number of functions (4, 10). Among them are included: providing a place for the individual in society; carrying on transactions with the environment by managing economic and social utilities; being the primary setting for nuturance, socialization, sexual access, childrearing, emotional expression and other social processes; and organizing the methods of exchange and the management of conflict.

Systems. From one systems view, the family is an interactive unit within the ecosystem of its sociological environment (2). It is a component of society interdependent with other institutions, such as the school, church, and government. In a different focus, the family is also the ecosystem for its own members—a dynamic conditioning field which members both define and to which they are focused to respond (3, 11, 13).

Dramaturgical Interaction. In interactional theory, the family is seen as a set of roles governed by role expectations and evaluation of role performances (16). Drawn from a symbolic interaction heritage, this con-

ceptualization defines the family through a structure of roles, but analyzes it in terms of the meanings and expressions that develop within that
structure. As interaction moves closer to its dramaturgical metaphor, the
family is a scene in the theatre of life. In the dramaturgical metaphor,
members give performances in their various roles. The family is a collection of actors and audience with individuals trading places on the stage
and in the seats.

Level of Encounter. Family members can be encountered at different levels (29). There is, of course, the level of the family itself that contains the
concerns of membership, territory, access and the attributes of ethnicity,
class, status, power, and the like which result from membership. Within
the family, there are the interpersonal relationships between adults, siblings, parents, and children. And there is the individual per se who pas-
ses among family memberships and fills roles within them.

FAMILIES, MEDIA TECHNOLOGY, MEDIATED CONTENT, AND NATURALISTIC INQUIRY

In some way, we approach the structures, functions, systems, and
dramaturgical interaction of the family from the perspective of its external
transactions, internal organization, or individual members when we em-
bark on its study. When we approach that study from the particular focus
of mediated communication (mass media is no longer an appropriate
term), our intent is to explain the presence, functions, and influence on
the content and technology within the structures, functions, systems,
and interaction of the family. When the study is taken from the naturalistic perspective, we seek to document the social action of the situated
family for the purpose of understanding the socially constructed meanings of a family's structures, functions, systems, and interaction. Our research domain is the situated family, the data reside in the social action,
and our explanation illumines the socially constructed meanings of the
members.

Exemplar questions that a reader might expect such studies to address
would be: How does a particular family express the functions of nuturance, socialization, emotional support, and the like? How does mediated
communication appear in these functions, have some purpose, or influence that expression? What roles does a given family construct imply,
and what content or technology, if any, does it use to define role expectations or role performance? How are content and technology used in the
relationships defined by parent and child, brother and sister, husband
and wife?

Naturalistic inquiry has certain problems in approaching any specific
questions such as these. An exquisitely inductive method, it can address

only what is presented in the social action in which the researcher is a participant and which the researcher understands from a member's perspective. In the intimate membership of the family, some social action will never be presented in the presence of a nonmember (22). Other action may be redefined in response to the more public context of observation to be consonant with societal images. Further, most familial social action is well practiced and its meaning held deeply beneath its appearances. Consequently, the researcher faces a schedule of contacts of significant duration (perhaps a year or more) in order to report on whatever access was granted. The result is a characteristic pattern of a few well-defined explanations and several partial sketches. The reader has to realize that the well-defined explanations come from those parts of the household where the windows of social action were open. They do not represent the whole, nor necessarily the significant occasions, of media use. It is important for us to realize that our understanding of families to be gained from naturalistic inquiry is expansionistic. It develops as case after case adds to an ever expanding discourse.

EPISTEMOLOGICAL GAINS FROM NATURALISTIC INQUIRY

Naturalistic inquiry into families and the presence and use of mediated content within them has a short history, with only a handful of studies available (1). There is, however, a significant conclusion that can be drawn from those available. We can clearly see that media technology and content are not pipelines of meaning into the hearts and minds of family members. Rather, meaning is constructed from that content and for that technology by individuals within their systems of social reality. The ordinary viewing of television, or participation in any medium, is not an unstructured pastime. It is the normal case that every incidence of viewing has a coherence which connects the particular incident with what has happened in the immediate past and with what will happen in the immediate future. Media use happens within connected skeins of behavior, accomplished practices, if you will, which constitute and maintain our social realities. Family viewing, for example, is no more casual and spontaneous than the family dinner. It is accomplished by competent actors with great improvisational skill. In the Utah media research studies, every family we visit has a set of practices. Every individual shows a practiced accomplishment of media use — from the youngest to the oldest. It is in these practices that media content and its technology come to be interpreted.

   The following three examples drawn from research directed or conducted by this author demonstrate the notion of the methods and practices of reception. While they are unique to the given circumstances, they are not unusual, in that any set of observations could find equally compelling examples.

The first example is taken from an observational study by Weaver (33)investigating the concept of group viewing of television. Weaver was interested in the ordinary circumstances surrounding the gathering of college students to view specific programs. While college groups such as this one are commonly seen with "soap operas," Weaver's group gathered each weekday afternoon to view the syndicated program *Leave It To Beaver*. The viewing required effort and subterfuge. Television sets were frowned on in individual dorm rooms. Reception of the distant channel which carried the program was possible only by illegally tapping into the cable drop in the student lounge.

Each afternoon, Poz and Malcolm, two leaders of the group, would string the cable from the lounge to Poz's room. At about 3:20 in the afternoon, one of the group members would range up and down the hall calling out, "Beaver Time." The members would begin to assemble. Weaver writes of one episode:

The nine individuals seemed quite comfortable together in the close confines of the small, uncluttered room. Some were lying on the bunk-bed, others lounged on the floor, and still others stood leaning against the closet door. Everyone in the room was talking during the commercials between the cartoons and *Leave It To Beaver*. But as the familiar music of the television show echoed through the room, everyone abandoned their talk and turned to the television set. Two members began a new conversation:
"I liked the other beginning better."
"Why?"
"I don't know. . . . It was just better."
"No, this beginning is much better than the other one, I mean it shows the Cleavers as they really are, America's only two lawnmower family."
"What?"
Before anyone can respond, Poz turns with an angered stare and says, "Shuss!" Everyone remains quiet as the first segment of the day's *Leave It To Beaver* begins (pp. 7–8).

The next two examples come from family home situations. The first involves a play group which regularly gathered at the home of the author; the second, a family observed in the Utah studies. They are again presented as narrated episodes constructed from field notes.

Like many weekday afternoons, the doorbell rang at 5:00, followed immediately by an impatient knock. "That's got to be Eric; right on time," she said to herself as she got up to answer the door. "Come on in; Amy and Eden are already downstairs with Angela." Eric, the 4-year-old, next-door neighbor, was dressed, as always, with an apron around his shoulders for a cape, vinyl cowboy boots, and his gun belt wrapped twice around his shorts. He was dressed as his favorite superhero; it was time to watch the show. Eric joined the three children downstairs. After watching for a few minutes, they began to act out part of the scene they were watching, which quickly evolved into one of the regular fantasy games they played. The television became a back-drop for this play activity. When a particularly exciting scene was signaled by the audio, they would stop to watch and then go back to play. The television show was over long before the playing stopped.

Each workday, the mother left early in the morning before Ellen and John were off to school. She depended on Ellen to clean up the breakfast dishes and to see that she and John made it to elementary school on time. This morning the two children had gotten up late. In their rush to make it to school on time, Ellen had left a mess on the table.

Dinner was over about 7:00 each workday evening. The children would get up from the table and go into the living room to sit on the long couch and watch television. Their mother would join them after she had finished the dishes. They were a close family. The children would snuggle up on each side of their mother and watch until bedtime. They rarely spoke during this time together but seemed to enjoy the closeness of one another. Tonight, the mother came into the living room and said: "Ellen, I left those cereal bowls for you to finish. You go on in there now and get them done. I can't be doing those things for you." Ellen began to cry. "Go on, girl," her mother commanded. Ellen cleaned the two bowls in the kitchen but, still feeling the sting of rejection, spent the evening in her bedroom.

These three examples show the very different contexts in which content and technology get interpreted. It would be incredible to argue that the *Leave It To Beaver* gang, Eric, the playgroup hero, and Ellen our budding housewife would arrive at the same functional meaning while watching the same content in their different viewing conditions. It would be incredible because one would have to ignore the circumstances of reception and argue that the meaning properties of content are like a noninteractive object such as a stone, the properties of which presumably persist regardless of who observes it. But naturalistic studies demonstrate clearly that the meaning properties of content are quintessentially interactive. Meaning is constructed in the interaction between the characteristics of content and the character of the reception as interpreted by the individual.

Similarly, it would be incredible to argue that these contexts are not the result of the methods and practices of these particular individuals. To argue that any play group would provide the same context as Eric's is to ignore the fact that Eric, Amy, Eden, and Angela have expended great effort to negotiate just what their playgroup means.

The interpretive process of meaning construction does not end with the moment of reception. Meaning is both promiscuous and prolific. It is promiscuous because meaning is aroused in each of us as we interpret content. It is prolific because, each time we encounter that content, new meaning arises. Meaning construction, then, is an ongoing process which reaches well beyond the moment of reception. It is continued in the circumstances of each situation demanding interpreted content. It appears to me from my own practices and from the naturally occurring accounts that others give of their media practices, that we interpret media content retrospectively in the subsequent uses we have for it. Interpretation certainly begins in the practices of reception which form the enlarged context of understanding. But further interpretation awaits an occasion in which media content is seen to have some utility. There its meaning is established by what the individual wants to accomplish with the occasion. Meaning is prolific, arising in the situations that I and my fellow members create.

An interpretive system, then, begins with my everyday practices, which create the situations in which I find myself. When media content or technology is used in those situations, it comes to be interpreted according to the contingencies of each situation. That use, of course, reflexively maintains the initiating practices. and the spiral continues. Interpretation begins with what one actually sees, hears, reads, and the like, continues through the practices of media participation, and concludes in the hundreds of occasions in which content may be put to use. In this manner, media content and technology are accommodated in our everyday life.

A CONCORDANCE TO THE RESEARCH WORKS IN THIS SECTION

We can see this accommodation in the two pieces that precede this commentary chapter. In the sections that follow, I would like to underline the contributions that the authors of these works make in their research and to offer a cautionary note or two where I feel the perspective of naturalistic inquiry has come in for some rough treatment.

Bryce's Family Time and Television Use. Jennifer Bryce's analysis of the Andrews, Brady, and Chapman families demonstrates how these families have negotiated different concepts of time and how television viewing becomes incorporated within those time concepts. For the Andrews family, television viewing is a chosen activity deliberately selected from a matrix of competitive alternatives. It is a well-defined activity from which some outcome is presumed to result. Intensive viewing is encouraged. In the Brady family, in counter distinction, "watching TV was often a part of the contextual background of family life rather than an activity in and of itself" (p. 127). In both of these families (and in the Chapman family), television is a reality element which is managed within the constructions of the families themselves. The meaning of its content and technology emerges within those constructions. Television is a different force of life for the Andrews, Brady, and Chapman members.

Bryce's analysis clearly shows that the consequences of television viewing (or any media attendance) cannot be approached solely on the basis of content characteristics and exposure to them. The members of the different families invest different meanings in the content presented, and even exposure itself is a different act.

I do have a reservation to express in this examination of the Bryce article. When Bryce takes the concepts of monochronic and polychronic time out of their naturalistic setting and uses them as sense-making templates to overlay the interviews of nine mothers, the notions begin a rapid slide toward distortion. This reader gets the feeling of responses being cranked into these two categories with considerable force. The power of inductive constructs is that they are inspired by intimate contact with the particular instances they help to explain. The notions of monochronic and polychronic time help us understand the Andrews and the Brady families. Moving them to the status of objectified attributes of the institution of family is reasoning in warp-drive. The reader could be better guided through this perspective shift.

These comments are not to say that Bryce's view of family time is not a useful contribution. It is a particular insight. It is also one which should be more credited to her than to Kantor and Lehr (20), whom she cites. Their predominate metaphor is space which time helps define.

Traudt and Lont's Media-Logic-in-Use: The Family as Locus of Study. Traudt and Lont encounter their family on the level of the individual member as they explore "the relationship between selected family members and the mass media (p. 139). In fact, it is the father who comes alive to the reader. This level of encounter results in a quite different analysis from that of Bryce. Whereas, in Bryce, we see the family as a meaningful system, in Traudt and Lont we have the view of an individual finding his way through the maze of life contexts. In this article, the family is the place where the father engages television.

Traudt and Lont have restricted the naturalistic approach with two powerful, a priori, sense making concepts: media logic—the "use of formula, convention, and predictability," and media consciousness—implicitly stated as the correspondence between content attended and reality constructed. These two notions do not arise from the analysis, but rather are impressed upon it. This departure from the inductive character of naturalistic inquiry raises certain difficulties for the reader in assessing the evidence that Traudt and Lont present. The conclusions of media logic and media consciousness seem to be sprung too quickly, as if one found what one was looking for.

For example, the authors conclude that the introduction of cable television has significant effects on the father's use of that medium. I have a palpable desire to understand how this family with three children under 5 has provided the time and opportunity for some 30 hours a week of video contact by the husband. It is clear that this family is not a center of liberation. Further, the authors themselves seem caught up in the taken-for-granted chauvinism when they write: "His working hours were from seven o'clock in the morning until four o'clock in the afternoon, freeing up considerable time for volunteer, late-afternoon coaching of a little-league baseball team (p. 149). Presumably, grandmother is babysitting (the eldest child is a 4-year-old girl), and mother is doing her studies, the cooking, and the wash. It is possible that televiewing and coaching are justificatory activities which help construct a traditional male role? If such is the case, then the direction taken in describing the effects of video technology—technology impacting on the father—is deceptive. The technology is first used by the social system before it influences it.

I have a similar problem with the conclusion that the mother of this family uses her program choices of family and medical soaps "to provide an idealized model for her own interests." There are two other systems which would appear to be important but are given little comment. First, the mother operates within a successfully functioning extended family. Second, she is attending school for the health professions. In both of these systems, standards and models would be expected to be everyday content.

In many respects, the Traudt and Long article faults come from reaching too far, in attempting too broad an analysis from data which are extensive by any measure but limited in approaching the intimate relationships of family. It is particularly noteworthy that the authors use interviews as the primary evidence of their claims in the article. The tenets of naturalistic inquiry would hold that interviews are performances in their own right, rather than surrogates of another social action. That is, interviews *do not reflect on but start from* the social constructions in which the respondents operate. In interviews, one's actions are interpreted according to the ideology in place. Consequently, they inform us only obliquely—if at all—of what is taken-for-granted and known-to-be-true by the members.

Despite these concerns, there is much to be gained from the Traudt and Lont article. Foremost among these gains is the concept of maintenance as a function of the social influence of media. Traditional research approaches have been particularly concerned with *change* as the primary (and perhaps, only) function of social influence. Traudt and Lont demonstrate that the use of media content and technology to maintain social meaning structures is a more significant avenue of social influence because it affects such a broad base of social action. It is clear that the adults in this family assemble both technology and content to support the way that they live. They create an environment of information and values which promotes the meaning systems they construct. In creating this environment for themselves, they also create it for their children. By creating this environment, the media are moved into the process of the socialization of their children.

Both the Bryce and the Traudt and Lont articles reveal families to us and provide us with concepts for the understanding of other families. They accomplish their purposes in the best of traditions.

REFERENCES

1. Anderson, J.A. "Forms of Argument in Naturalistic Inquiry in Communication." Paper presented at the International Communication Association Convention, San Francisco, 1984.
2. Anderson, R.E., and I.E. Carter. *Human Behavior in the Social Environment* (first edition). Chicago: Aldine, 1974.
3. Andrews, M.P., M.P. Bubolz, and B. Paolucci. "An Ecological Approach to Study of the Family." *Marriage and Family Review* 3, 1980, pp. 29–49.
4. Belsky, J. "Early Human Experience: A Family Perspective." *Developmental Psychology* 17, 1981, pp. 3–23.
5. Berardo, F.M. "Decade Preview: Some Trends and Directions for Family Research and Theory in the 1980's." *Journal of Marriage and the Family* 42, 1980, pp. 723–728.
6. Berardo, F.M. "Family Research and Theory: Emergent Topics in the 1970s and the Prospects for the 1980s." *Journal of Marriage and the Family* 43, 1981, pp. 251–254.
7. Burr, W.R., R. Hill, F.I. Nye, and I.L. Reiss (Eds.). *Contemporary Theories About the Family* (Vol. 2) New York: Free Press, 1979.
8. Cogswell, B.E. "Variant Family Forms and Life Styles: Rejection of the Traditional Nuclear Family." *Family Coordinator* 24, 1975, pp. 391–406.
9. Coser, R.L. *The Family its Structures and Functions* (second edition). New York: St. Martin's Press, 1974.
10. Ericksen, J.A., W.L. Yancey, and E.P. Ericksen. "The Division of Family Roles." *Journal of Marriage and the Family* 41, 1979, pp. 301–313.
11. Feiring, C., and M. Lewis. "The Child as a Member of the Family System." *Behavioral Science* 23, 1978, pp. 225–233.
12. Galligan, R.J. "Innovative Techniques: Siren or Rose." *Journal of Marriage and the Family* 44, 1982, pp. 875–886.
13. Garbarino, J. *Children and Families in the Social Environment.* New York: Aldine, 1982.
14. Hill, R. "Whither Family Research in the 1980s: Continuities, Emergents, Constraints and New Horizons." *Journal of Marriage and the Family* 43, 1981, pp. 255–258.
15. Hareven, T.K. "Cycles, Courses and Cohorts: Reflections on Theoretical and Methodological Approaches to the Historical Study Of Family Development." *Journal of Social History* 21, 1978, pp. 97–109.
16. Heintz, P., T. Held, and R. Levy. "Family Structure and Society." *Journal of Marriage and the Family* 37, 1975, pp. 861–870.

17. Hodgson, J.W., and R.A. Lewis. "Pilgrim's Progress III: A Trend Analysis of Family Theory and Methodology." *Family Process* 18, pp. 163–173.
18. Holman, T.B., and W.R. Burr. "Beyond the Beyond: The Growth of Family Theories in the 1970s." *Journal of Marriage and the Family* 42, 1980, pp. 729–741.
19. Huston, T.L., and E. Robins. "Conceptual and Methodological Issues in Studying Close Relationships." *Journal of Marriage and the Family* 44, 1982, pp. 901–925.
20. Kantor, D., and W. Lehr. *Inside the Family: Toward a Theory of Family Processes.* New York: Harper and Row, 1975.
21. Knox, D. "Trends in Marriage and the Family—the 1980s." *Family Relations* 29, 1980, pp. 145–150.
22. Larossa, R., L.A. Bennett, and R.J. Gelles. "Ethical Dilemmas in Qualitative Family Research." *Journal of Marriage and the Family* 43, 1981, pp. 303–313.
23. Lee, G.R. Kinship in the Seventies: A Decade Review of Research and Theory." *Journal of Marriage and the Family* 42, 1980, pp. 923–934.
24. Macklin, E.D. "Nontraditional Family Forms: A Decade of Research." *Journal of Marriage and the Family* 42, 1980, pp. 905–922.
25. Miller, B.C., B.C. Rollins, and D.L. Thomas. "On Methods of Studying Marriages and Families." *Journal of Marriage and the Family* 44, 1982, pp. 851–873.
26. Nock, S.L. "The Family Life Cycle: Empirical or Conceptual Tool." *Journal of Marriage and the Family* 41, 1979, pp. 15–26.
27. Nye, F.I., and G.W. McDonald. "Family Policy Research: Emergent Models and Some Theoretical Issues." *Journal of Marriage and the Family* 41, 1979, pp. 473–485.
28. Nye, F.I., and F. Berardo (Eds.). *Emerging Frameworks in Family Analysis.* New York: Macmillan, 1966.
29. Reiss, D., and M.E. Oliveri. "The Family's Construction of Social Reality and its Ties to its Kin Network: An Exploration of Causal Direction." *Journal of Marriage and the Family* 45, 1983, pp. 81–90.
30. Sussman, M.B. "The Four F's of Variant Family Forms and Marriage Styles." *Family Coordinator*, 24, 1975, pp. 536–576.
31. Udry, J.R. *The Social Context of Marriage*, (second edition). Philadelphia: Lippincott, 1971.
32. Walters, L.H. "Are Families Different from Other Groups." *Journal of Marriage and the Family* 44, 1982, pp. 841–850.
33. Weaver, J. "Field Notes: 'Beaver Time.' " Unpublished manuscript, Indiana University, 1982.
34. Wieting, S.G. "Structuralism, Systems Theory, and Ethnomethodology in the Sociology of the Family." *Journal of Comparative Family Studies* 7, 1976, pp. 375–395.

PART III

SUBCULTURES
AND
INSTITUTIONS

Chapter 9

Ideology and Pragmatics of Media Access in Prison

Thomas R. Lindlof

Dept. of Telecommunications
University of Kentucky

A total institution is typified by the uniformity of treatment of its residents, the routinization of their activities, and the hierarchical execution of "a single rational plan" (8, p. 17). In the case of the prison, the logic of the rational plan is simple: *control* of the activities of the persons under its jurisdiction is both the means and ends of its operations. In such circumstances, where personal autonomy is continually constrained and normal relations with the world become tenuous, access to media may take on unusual importance.

Previous studies of television in institutions have concentrated on the program preferences and perceived gratifications of residents, and its utilization in therapy (16). This study relates media use opportunities to prison inmate behavior from an interactionist perspective. The interactionist study of subcultures seeks to identify the information exchanges that occur among culture members, as well as the artifacts and communicative means that facilitate those exchanges (5, 8, 10). Empirical research in this vein focuses on the lines of action developed by inmates in response to the exigencies of incarceration. Classical research of deviant subcultures (1, 14) investigated those people's conceptions of the legitimacy of their activities and the labelling processes carried out by agents of the mainstream culture. In the correctional institution, however, this type of "deviance" is not especially at issue. An inmate's previous criminal career and convictions are neither sources of stigma nor largely relevant to his career qua inmate. What is at stake in incarceration, instead, is the search for appropriate ways of behaving that are consistent with the inmate's constructured identity. Systemic investigation of media in institutions must consider, as well, how staff personnel construe their effects and formulate policy and procedures with those effects in mind. Beliefs that are expressive of a media policy may operate in contradistinction to the real terms of approbation that guide its implementation. This chapter reports some of the ways in which mass media resources in a particular prison are defined by both those who use them and those who make them available.

THE INMATE CAREER

The construct of inmate "career" refers to a sequential process of adaptation to a variety of problems that confront the inmate: legal, administrative, custodial, and peer-related. As correctional systems and inmates' biographies vary widely, a single model of that process oversimplifies the plurality of adaptive modes that inmates can and do adopt. Useful descriptions of convict social organization have been developed, though, that explicate subcultural codes and their associated behavior patterns.

The prison experience actually begins with a series of post-sentencing actions, including psychological, vocational, and intelligence assessments, classification, and transfer through state or federal correctional systems (2). Phenomenologically, these actions induce a *mortification* of self (8, pp. 23-44) in which the inmate's personal effects and designations are removed and replaced with a standard issue of inmate number, cell, clothing, and daily schedule. The institution is able to collect, manage, and selectively use various kinds of data about the inmate. That purview often extends to the monitoring of information going in and out of the institution as it relates to the inmate. The priority of security, the temporal structure of institutional life, and the open spatial arrangements of prison architecture leave the inmate with few zones of privacy (3, 18). Although newly-incarcerated persons often attempt to "prepare" for what awaits them, the shock of entering this system of extensive controls—in concert with separation from their familiar ties to family and friends—can be severe and long-lasting (19).

Long-term imprisonment also presents the inmate with great difficulties in using time and conceiving of future plans. Inmates fear the deterioration of their self concept (manifested in feelings of "retreatism" or "resignation") that may result from being unable to affect the course of near-term events (4, 6). Galtung (6, p. 113) explains the ongoing dialectic between the inmate's time perspective and his efforts at personal identity maintenance:

> The prisoner is precluded from changing his fate in an essential way through any act of his own. The minimum time to be served is perceived as

unchangeable, yet only those prisoners whose minimum sentence exceeds a probable lifetime [can] adapt themselves fully to the internal structure of the institution. . . . [Most prisoners] are painfully aware of the necessity of preserving an identity relevant for life outside when release comes, while at the same time playing a role in prison, however high or low its degree of relevance for life outside may be.

The inmate must deal with the problem of time perspective by choosing reference group commitments (10, 19). In effect, he develops a response to the question—How shall I do my time?—that allows pragmatic alignments to the simultaneous demands placed on him by the institutional ideology, staff members, fellow inmates, the physical environment, and the judicial facts and possibilities of his case. The inmate typically decides on the manner in which he will do his time shortly after admission, although that "decision" may change later. Irwin (10) identified three principal *prison-adaptive modes* that constitute models of behavioral style for fashioning a sustainable inmate career. Briefly, the *doing time* mode represents incarceration as a comparatively short-lived interruption in the inmate's outside way of life. The institution is evaluated for whatever nondemanding niches (e.g., favored prison jobs) and privileges (e.g., television ownership) can be obtained. Associations with other inmates tend to be casual and impermanent. In the *jailing* mode, inmates relinquish all orientation to either outside or administrative incentives, having habituated completely to a life in prison. Cliques are often formed with like-minded inmates in the economic and sexual trade operations in cell blocks. Exploitation of weaker inmates is common. The *gleaning* mode inmate accepts the institution's incentives for rehabilitation and actively seeks programs and relationships that can be expected to lead to educational, vocational, psychological, and/or spiritual improvements. Although both time-doers and gleaners are highly attuned to achieving early release, the latter conceive of their time in use-value rather than consumptive terms. A disavowal of the former subculture values often provides the pretext for gleaning, resembling a "conversion" process (8, p. 59).

The newly-admitted inmate enters into a situation where longstanding moral codes and interactional rules already exist. His adaptation consists in part in formulating a stance with respect to those codes and rules, with media use possibly augmenting that process in a variety of situations. The ways in which mass media are implicated will, of course, depend on the media access policies of the institution. Given an institution in which mass media are as freely available as security, budget, and other considerations allow, however, actual media practices should still operate as functions of the structural and social features of that institution.

RESEARCH PLAN

This study was undertaken in mid-1983 at a medium-security state correctional institution for male felons in the Northeast United States. The administration's concern about safety, security, and already strained staff resources precluded direct observation of the inmates' activities. Inmates' probable reactivity to the researcher's presence was also seen as an inhibiting factor.

Data were produced primarily through intensive interviews with 16 inmates and a number of administrative and line officers. The structure of the interviews was consistent for all inmates in terms of *sequence* and *areas of inquiry*: first, the circumstances of the inmate's incarceration; then, general adjustments to and impressions of prison life; finally, media-related matters. This structure allowed flexibility in formulating media-related questions, given individual backgrounds and dispositions toward incarceration.

Several criteria for selection of inmates for interviewing were developed. An earlier systematic-sample survey (13) provided both baseline quantitative data and the names and backgrounds of inmates willing to meet again for a personal interview.[1] The degrees to which an inmate aligns himself with the institution's preferred ideology (by joining in classes, formal groups, therapy, work programs, etc.) and maintains communication with the outside world (through letters, visits, and phone calls) were found to be salient indicators of inmates' orientations to both incarceration and media use. By forming a matrix of magnitudes of those variables with TV and radio use, theoretically relevant features of the inmate population were identified from which interview candidates could be selected (see 9, pp. 116–117).

Inmates were also considered on the basis of their articulateness and ability to perform well in an extended face-to-face interview. These were informally assessed by the earlier willingness of some inmates to engage in conversation with the researcher about the project as well as the length and quality of their written responses to some open-ended survey items. Not surprisingly, these criteria produced a somewhat more "intelligent" sample than the inmate population as a whole. Since there was little opportunity to get to know the inmates, the risks of an unusual sample as the cost of applying those criteria were considered to be acceptable.

Although all of the inmates understood the confidentiality protections, the level of their "confidence" in the researcher (and therefore the candidness of their remarks) was not easily ascertained. Yet the relative

---

[1] An incentive of $3.00 to participate in the interview was offered. On this basis, over 80% of the 93 inmates in the sample survey indicated a willingness to be interviewed; only one of the inmates contacted eventually declined to submit to an interview.

ease with which the inmates spoke of their own and others' (often con-flictive) activities and feelings about incarceration led the researcher to believe that the inviolability of the protections offered by his independent status was accepted. For the staff members, their separate domains of duties meant more individualized lines of inquiry. Thus, interviews with the administrative personnel centered around the ideology and overall functioning of the institution, while the interviews with the custodial officers provided mostly informant data on the effects of policies on inmates' lives (since they are line personnel in daily, quasi-informal contact with inmates). The primary source for administration views on media policy and correctional system goals was the Deputy Superintendent for Treatment, B. J., the second-ranking administrator at the Institution and the individual responsible for overseeing and providing access for the researcher's activities. Spread over several occasions, approximately 6 hours of conversation with him were recorded. The Director for Treatment (M. J.), who supervises the counsellors and psychologists, and the Administrative Assistant to the Deputy Superintendent (L. R.), who designs the block TV schedules, were also interviewed. Finally, two custodial officers were selected for interviews. The criteria selected for the guard interviews—several years' tenure, experience in many of the cell blocks, and a high level of articulateness—were well-satisfied in Officers K. R. and E. D.

Some documents were also available for analysis, including state corrections department policy directives, Institution brochures, block TV schedules, film screening schedules, inmates' open-ended written responses on television and their viewing, and drawings of cell location and contents made by inmates.

THE INSTITUTION

At the time of this study, the Institution had an inmate population of approximately 1250, with nearly equal numbers of black and white inmates. Due mostly to changes in state sentencing laws, the inmate population had been increasing faster than the ability to provide additional housing. Thus, the Institution, with a constructed capacity of 975, was forced to double up over one-third of its population in cells of 8-by-8' floor space dimensions. This double-celling practice had reportedly increased tensions in some cell blocks. The recent influx also resulted in the admission of some inmates with a higher security risk than had been the norm.

In addition to the four main cell blocks, dormitory, and administrative offices, the Institution maintains a dining hall and kitchen, chapel, educational building, visiting areas, cannery, maintenance shops, forestry camp, orchards, greenhouses, and a nursery on almost 7,000 acres in a rural setting. Work experience for the inmates is a central feature of this Institution's mission, and nearly all physically-able inmates are involved in work assignments. An array of educational programs (from elementary to college levels), vocational training, and therapeutic (including alcohol/drug treatment) programs offer services to several hundred inmates monthly. Direct contact with the inmate's outside community is especially encouraged through direct visits, letter writing, and telephone calls. Rules facilitating such contact are intended to ease the immediate pains of imprisonment as well as assist the inmate in his eventual reintegration.

Provision of media use opportunities is deemed vital to the inmates' well-being, although policies for individual media vary. Several state correctional system directives codify inmates' rights and privileges regarding mediated and other communications. Inmates may receive any publications through the mail, with the exception of materials concerning the manufacture of weapons and drugs, the overthrow of the government or its institutions, and "judicially defined obscenity." (The latter category is operationally defined in terms of violent or forced-sex portrayals.) The Institution has delegated the responsibility for monitoring all incoming publications for questionable content to a Publications Review Committee; the number of cases requiring the withholding of entire copies of newspapers or magazines or the excision of objectionable parts is reportedly minimal.

Certain broadcast media outlets are provided by the Institution. All cells are equipped with a cable and earplug through which four local radio stations can be tuned. Each cell block is equipped with a 25-inch color television with weeknight programming consisting of a block of composite programming from the local cable system; the schedule is expanded on weekends to accommodate sports events and movies. The Institution also books and screens first-run motion pictures for the entire prison population on Sunday nights.

Inmates may elect to purchase personal radio and television receivers. If two inmates occupy a cell, only one television may be used. The in-cell power supply of 45 watts limits not only the number of receivers, but also the type: most commercial color receivers exceed the power requirement. The cable franchise, which wired the facility several years ago, makes the basic 10-channel service available to inmates at one-third the normal rate, but the premium channels are not discounted. Partly because of broadcast signal interference caused by the heavy construction of the cell blocks, very few television-owning inmates do not subscribe to the basic service. At the time of this study, 687 inmates were cable subscribers, of whom 55 paid for at least one premium channel.

INSTITUTION IDEOLOGY

Deputy B.J.: I think the top reason for the existence of the correctional system is to protect society and to remove these individuals that society does not want in the community for a period of time. Now while they're here, the correctional system should provide a safe and humane environment for the individuals, should offer them a chance for rehabilitation if they desire to get involved. . . . And it also serves as a punishment.

Embodied within this statement is the suggestion of a tension between goals ("removal" and "rehabilitation") that, in practice, may act in either complementary or paradoxical ways. In the complementary sense, the "indirect coercion" used to persuade inmates to participate in Institution programs is rather directly tied to the methods available for reducing the length and degree of removal, such as parole or the home furlough program. And rehabilitation is construed broadly: "Even going to work every day. . . . If you can give an inmate a work ethic while he's in prison, you may have gone a long way in helping rehabilitate that inmate" (Deputy B. J.). The removal itself becomes a sort of interregnum in which the inmate can engage in self-enhancing activities sanctioned by the state. As Director M. J. commented, "Whether [the treatment programs] have any carry-over to the street, I really don't know. I wouldn't be awfully optimistic."

But providing a "humane environment" by allowing visits and phone calls, or by allowing the personal use of media, both softens removal and makes it more salient for inmates. As the administration views it, contact with their former community and access to media are different, albeit contributory means for inmates to reintegrate with life outside. Contact with families prevents total immersion in prison life. In addition to (or in the absence of) that contact, mediated communication attenuates some of the more debilitative effects of incarceration:

Deputy B.J.: You know, you have sensory deprivation that's occurring, and I think that sensory deprivation can occur in different levels. You know, I can talk to all the other inmates here, but if I don't have any contact with the community, there is a deprivation to something that's going on around me, and something very important to [a life] I'm going back to someday. So I think that's where media fit in, is being a crucial part of their eventual reintegration back into the community.

Staff members alluded to another reason for media access: that of an activity that simply keeps inmates active. The use of media policy as a potent tool for controlling inmate behavior was articulated by Deputy B. J.: "Regimentation and boredom can really be a problem, because if people start getting bored, if they don't have anything to do with their time, they're gonna get in trouble. . . . So [TV] is entertainment, it's an activity, and it keeps boredom from coming in, and consequently it aids in the overall good order and adjustment of the Institution." Making personal media available for inmates to efficiently dispose of large amounts of time relieves the strain on staff resources. Inmates are less likely to congregate outside their cells during their free time. Security demands are therefore relaxed. Although many inmates commented on the time-consuming character of televiewing, only one showed some reflexive awareness of the Institution's intentions in that regard: "So, TV's the best babysitter, about the best babysitter they could get" (S. T.).

To enhance their effectiveness for behavioral control, certain of the media are considered "privileges" that can be withheld from their inmate owners for infractions of a variety of rules. In rationalizing those actions, the administration distinguishes between *entertainment* media (television, radio, the film screenings), which are "privileges," and *information* media (all print media). The Loss of Privileges (L.O.P.) assessments are made on a case basis and can range widely in severity (to include loss of phone and yard-out privileges, as well as television, radio, and film attendance) and length of time (from 5 days to 3 months). As Deputy B. J. put it:

> We don't do it with the idea of taking away their contact with the media. We do it as taking away a privilege. Most of them don't watch television to watch the news, you know, they're watching programs for entertainment. And I think that's what's being taken away rather than a contact with the outside world. Which is why newspapers and magazines and mail is never stopped from inmates, except for some real serious reason.

The administration perspective is based on a particular conception of how inmates use their media: although information-seeking may be a secondary aspect of radio and TV use, a more self-indulgent entertainment use is claimed to be characteristic of the inmates' affiliation with those media. Accordingly, the administration believes it is not compromising the rehabilitative value of the inmates' overall media access by selectively imposing the L.O.P. The temporary impounding of media property is not regarded as confiscation, but instead is justified as the literal removal of the privilege of having those media in the cell.

One reading of the administration position is that the basic provision of electronic media *demands* the privilege condition of the terms of their access, so that the L.O.P. can be adjusted to meet the exigencies of individual misconducts. In effect, by providing the "privilege" of personal media access, the Institution buys valuable leverage for its overall "good order." Support for this proposition comes from perceptions of the degree of hardness of the L.O.P. Both Deputy B. J. and the guards cited L.O.P. as being very effective, to the extent that some inmates would prefer going to the Restricted Housing Unit over losing their media privileges; one inmate purportedly destroyed his TV set before an officer could arrive to take it away. Several inmates also confirmed the effectiveness of L.O.P., although two of them, having experienced it, did not entirely regret the loss, as in the following:

O.R.: So they give me 25 days of L.O.P. until I was out of the [drug treatment] program. . . . It wasn't really that bad. Because I noticed that I was, like, used to having the TV and the radio there, right? And I got so used to it that I didn't realize that, you know, how much company they keep. How much time they take up. But since I like to read, they could have given me 25 days more L.O.P. and it wouldn't matter, 'cause I just got more of a chance to catch up reading.

Despite the information status accorded them, print media are more likely to be controlled at the level of specific content, as described earlier. Certain magazines (e.g., *Soldier of Fortune*) or articles/pictures may be withheld until a formal evaluation is conducted; in this procedure, the inmate has rights of appeal that can hypothetically extend all the way to the state attorney general's office. Generally, the inmates seemed able to anticipate publication acceptability, although some spoke of inconsistent treatment of pornography and survivalist/weapons magazines.

In summary, removal and rehabilitation goals become paradoxically related in that tensions induced by the removal priority are mitigated somewhat by the provision of media, with their presence bracketed as "rehabilitative." The Institution's formulation of access privileges, however, is based on an idiosyncratic conception of how inmates use and understand those media. By tying inmates' access to "entertainment" media to their behavior in non-media-related areas, the Institution attempts to augment or even displace some of its security activities. Such actions become coherent if viewed as an overall strategy to use media access as a tool for behavioral control.

BLOCK TELEVISION

Scheduling programs for the block televisions has been the responsibility of Administrative Assistant L. R. since 1973, when cable was installed at the Institution. His program selection procedure involves weekly consultation of the publications *TV Guide* and *TV Key*. The only content barred from block television screenings is depictions of prison violence or revolt. Systematic surveys or preference polls have never been conducted, although inmates can submit Request Slips for particular programs. L. R., whose office is far removed from the inmates' cell blocks, reported that he receives little direct feedback from inmates; it had been 2 years since he received a program-dislike complaint from an inmate. Deputy B. J. claimed that, although the programming is determined by L. R.'s discretion alone, "inmates do write to him and do suggest that he try something different." When all the inmates were queried on this subject, however, their "theories" regarding how programs are selected for the blocks varied widely. Three inmates provided a fairly accurate description of the process, but most professed ignorance. One inmate believed that the chaplain's wife was responsible for the selections, while another attributed an alleged prevalence of "cop shows" and college football to the guards' own tastes.

L. R. mentioned that the end of a guard's shift (or the 2:00 PM block sergeant roll call) provides daily opportunities to solicit information about inmates' responses to recently scheduled "new garbage" (his term for new entertainment programs) or unusual selections. However, Officer E. D. remarked that guards are never asked about either inmates' responses or about their own program preferences.

Once the schedule has been assembled, it is typed, photocopied, and distributed for public posting in all cell blocks by Friday for the next week's programs. The schedule is forwarded to the Superintendent every week, although L. R. never receives any feedback or directives from him regarding block television. (A previous superintendent did take a greater interest in the matter, and prohibited airing of documentaries or movies featuring prison settings.) The custodial officers' prescribed role in the block TV system is simply to activate the televisions and select channels in accordance with the schedule. They never deviate from the schedule except when preemptions occur, in which case the officers will generally spin the channel selector and tally a quick vote. Officer noninterference was corroborated by the inmates.

The governing rule for program selection, reflecting the basic constraint of having to construct one composite schedule from as many as ten basic cable sources, is based on an orthodox assumption: "attempt to satisfy as wide a range of tastes as much of the time as possible" (L. R.). Analysis of schedules from 4 consecutive weeks during July and August tended to confirm his rule. During the 6:00-9:00 PM weekday block-out period, for example, national news programs were scheduled three nights each week between 6:00 and 7:00, rotating a satellite news channel with the network news shows. For the 7:00-8:00 PM access period,

S.W.A.T. (eight schedulings), *Vega$* (seven), and sports events (six) were aired most frequently, followed by scattered schedulings of mostly off-network syndicated comedies. Yet some highly-situational exceptions were compelled by peculiarities of either the block viewing audience or the Institutional routine. For example:

1. Certain unique, less popular programs will be scheduled if L. R. perceives an intense minority interest in them. Religious programs are scheduled for Sunday mornings primarily because some inmates, for a variety of reasons, prefer not to attend services at the Institution chapel.
2. At one time, there was evident consternation on the part of white inmates that L. R. was programming for the black inmates. Since then, he has given increased attention to predicting audience preference with that factor in mind. Therefore, for one Saturday afternoon time slot, *Hee Haw* and *Soul Train* will alternate on successive weeks. Similarly, some sports seem to draw audiences along racial lines (boxing and basketball for black inmates; auto racing for whites), necessitating evenhanded scheduling of those events.

L. R. admitted that he would sometimes have a "gut response" to schedule a program that had a slightly negative record of inmate response (e.g., the PBS *Cosmos* series); his justification for such a move is to add variety to "the mix."

Although viewing behavior was not observed, descriptions of the block television audience (estimated by L. R. at between 50 and 150 inmates nightly) were quite consistent across both inmate and staff interviews. A nearly constant backdrop to the block television periods is high volume noise, due mainly to the receivers' locations at the guard stations where the inmates pass on their way to and from the yard. Often an escalating cycle of noise occurs, in which the volume of inmate talk combines with the TV audio, resulting in more requests for turning up the television. L. R. and the two officers maintained that the regular block TV viewers are "lower class" inmates with few outside resources, mentally "slower," and either disproportionately older inmates or young blacks from the most disruptive subgroup. The officers also claimed that a core group of the block TV audience "will watch anything," an observation that was corroborated by inmates in terms of an extremely passive viewing style.

Some personal-TV inmates expressed sympathy for those who are dependent on institutional television, noting the occasions when the schedule requires a channel change in the midst of an ongoing program. Television owning may in fact constitute a material status distinction in the prison system, where severe limits are placed on the types of goods that can be imported. Officer K. R. claimed that a personal television signals that its owner possesses real resources on the street ("Cadillacs, women, and expensive goods") whereas nonowners have no substantive backing for their claims. Most inmates did not explicitly refer to this, although one nonowner recalled an inmate whose conversations revolved almost exclusively around television and his street resources. It was apparent, however, that most personal-TV inmates held block viewing in low regard, as it exemplified institutional dependency in stark form, and its open, group aspect offered no protection against noise, surveillance, or undesired interactions.

PERSONAL MEDIA

In everyday associations, a person has considerable discretion in selecting "audiences" that will legitimate a sought-after idealized role identity (15). Gaining such role support becomes highly problematic, however, when identity glosses are applied and continually reinforced by institutional agents and by other residents. Thus, the simple act of acquiring media for personal use in a total institution covers a diversity of role-impelled motivations. Despite the influences that an institution may work on its residents' media use by the organization of physical space and staff-resident interactions (17), such acquisition often lends confirmation by self and others of preferred modes of doing time. This section explicates the themes of inmate adaptation to prison involving personal media that emerged from the interviews.

Ratification of the continuity of self. Many inmates have a need to remind themselves of the primacy of their original, pre-institutional personal selves. This is, in a sense, a ratification of self that usually remains concealed in an environment of extraordinary distrust of others. This may be especially important during the early stages of incarceration, as new inmates decide their social personas: "Penitentiaries, since I've been in two of them now, they all seem to be run that way. You either be a macho or you be a fag. Everybody's not that way, so eventually you knock somebody in the head that's trying to produce that or get that into you" (U. J.). A few inmates, usually those who intend to glean, will lay claim to the personal self at any cost: "I knew what I had to do. My thing was to impress these people that I'm not the common, ordinary stereotype of convict or inmate or whatever they want to call us. . . . I never knew nothing about this before, and I'm coming here in the blind and, 'See me, I'm different.' I *want* to be different" (J. M.).

For most inmates, personal media represent a natural dimension of their lives. The media qua artifacts, with their familiarity and locus of control, become highlighted in the prison context:

J.M.:   I always had TV at home, you know what I mean? . . . And I fig-
        ured if it was something I was allowed to have, I'd have it. I'd pro-
        vide myself of something they said I could have which might be a
        little bit of a comfort to me, a little bit nicer.
W.D.:   You know, you wake up in the morning and you can hear Marvin
        Gaye or somebody belting it out. Shoot, that brings you back, that's
        home. Anything you can identify with the streets, you take advan-
        tage of it.
M.R.:   [The TV] takes up a lot more time and space, even if just psycholog-
        ically, particularly the space. It just makes the room look so much
        better with it in there. It looks more lived-in, I guess.

Styles of personal media use emerge as a product of both the inmates'
normative viewing patterns in the outside world and the prison-adaptive
modes they have since adopted. Thus, the simultaneous use of personal
media was most common among inmates committed to a gleaning adaptation, since the operation of several media at once was more effective in
screening out the noises and movements of the other inmates. Time-
doing inmates, on the other hand, reported containing their attention to
one medium at a time; for them, media are occasions for "removal activities" (8) that cognitively distract the inmate from immediate circumstances.

Inmates' orientation to television content seemed greatly determined
by those aspects of their selves requiring nurture. Programs that prominently feature women (e.g., morning exercise and music/dance programs) elicited much interest. The absence of heterosexual relations,
however, may prompt occasional withdrawal from such content: "Sometimes I use to turn my TV off when I had 2, 3 years—and knew I had 7 or 8
go. . . . I didn't want to look at the R-rated flicks and know I can't touch no
woman" (J. M.). Solitary viewing is valued as a qualitatively different experience than block viewing. Because rules prohibit more than one inmate from being in a cell (except for double celling), moments of privacy
are particularly reinforced by fantasy-provoking programs. The mere
presence of others can intrude on the positive affect of the experience:

U.P.:   With guards on both sides it was like being in a theater. Sometimes,
        you see a little program, you know, and guards think maybe be-
        cause we're in jail we don't have any emotions, but you have feel-
        ings, you know. Some things might touch you at times, bring back
        memories or something . . . and you can talk to your roomie about
        this secret world, you know, and it's a little bit more private in your
        cell.
U.J.:   And, uh, I find myself every Saturday, right, 7:30, when [*Solid Gold*]
        comes on, I find myself trying to get a TV by myself so I can watch it.
        And if everybody's watching it, I'll stand in for a little while, but I
        won't stay.

The desire for control of program selection, evident in most owners' testimony of reasons for TV acquisition, was typically related to needs of the personal self that are inimical to negotiation with others or ongoing scrutiny.

Elements of identification with TV characters also surfaced in inmates' discussions of their personal media. The identification operated at either the level of association with aspects of their own personal history, or as a projection of desired characteristics. For one inmate, identification with the Hawkeye character from *M*A*S*H* and careful attention to the character's comedic style led to modifications in his own interactional methods:

> F.D.:   If somebody says something to me, the first thing I think of is something comical, in my head, even though I don't reply it. . . . Take a situation, and *hit them with it,* and they don't realize that I'm joking until after it's over with. Then it catches them, and they realize that I was actually just fooling around with them. It sounds like a serious statement until you think about it. That way, I'm not *ignored.* You know, they have to *think* of what I say.

This type of disclosure was rare. Without in-situ documentation, it is impossible to describe the prevalence and forms of media-derived public presentations of self. The interviews made clear, however, that media-derived *private* constructions probably vary in the degree to which they intersect with the inmate's social personas, from very low (e.g., one timid inmate's strong attraction to the TV characters played by Lee Majors) to very high (e.g., a reasonably self-confident black inmate's estimation of his likeness to the qualities of the Neil Washington character in *Hill Street Blues*).

Textualizing reality. In dealings with staff members and their fellows, inmates often find themselves repeatedly confronting the details of their past, their sense of personal responsibility, and the legitimacy of incarceration itself. Even though some inmates want to "rehabilitate," they may not desire to do so on the Institution's terms. Use of personal media helps inmates to give form to notions, sometimes inchoate, of the way the world is and the way it should be. Media content is transformed into a text, or grounds for argument, for negotiating their morally-ambiguous circumstances. Those interpretations may form the basis of solidarity with their fellows. Media texts can also force debates on the values of the Institution's *and* the convict subculture's codes of conduct.

The interest in media depictions of crime and criminal figures, for example, was complex. Inmates were highly sensitive to news reports about criminal justice and such reports were brought to the researcher's attention and directly critiqued. Their remarks implied that the news media had been co-opted by corrections officials into displaying a false picture of prison life. Two inmates cited a recent television report on a reunion of custodial officers held at the Institution; M. R. remarked:

> You know, they came with their families, man, it's a hell of a place to go for a reunion, come to this stinking-ass prison . . . they showed the trailers over here [new modular housing] and said it was an expansion for the overcrowded conditions. . . . They never mentioned it was a drug and alcoholic treatment community.

Inmates also expressed cynicism about televised representations of the motives and success of law enforcement as well as the nature of the crimes: "Criminal activities are depicted as more glorified on TV. I don't know about other activities, but as far as burglary goes, it's really haphazard. [T. L.: It's haphazard on TV?] No, it seems haphazard on the street" (M. R.). On the other hand, portrayals of powerful gangland figures, particularly in classic movies, were often admired. Some inmates, particularly first offenders, were struck by the ironic congruities between the movies' settings and their own. For most, the appeal seemed to lie in the movies' idealization of stoic brutality. How inmates interpret such programs is indicated by this episode:

U.J.:   They just had *The Godfather* on, everybody's televisions were on.

T.L.:   Why were they interested in *The Godfather*?

U.J.:   Oh, they were killing each other. They were showing *toughness*. It was masters of death. . . . Showing them that no one can do anything to me, but showing at the same time what could happen to you, too. You know, I found it interesting after, they had Michael— this was the guy that became the Godfather—you know how he had turned from a real nice party guy into a real nice gangster (laughs). The move was *graceful*, you know, it was different from what it really is. TV made it seem like he was a good guy or that, you know, he was having to do what he did, and he was still a good guy. And I asked them—we had a group sometime that evening—it was all out of place, but I wanted to hear what the crowd said. And I asked them, everybody watched that movie, what did you get from it? And everybody said, I loved it, I liked it, did you see what he did when he took that ice pick and stuck it in the—

T.L.:   What else did they like about it?

U.J.:   The killing, the guns, how they treated each other, what this world is coming to. Gangsters run everything. This is what everyone had to say. There was nothing about—I mean, here we are sitting up in jail, and they're talking about gangsters.

Media texts also provide continuing and detailed evidence of disparities between the stasis of prison life and the societal changes that surround but do not touch them. Certain information was regularly sampled (e.g., viewing *The Price is Right* to keep up on the current prices of merchandise; reading hometown newspapers), while inmates with short time or in their pre-release phase were particularly assiduous about monitoring the state of the economy and employment patterns. Several black inmates noted approvingly the progress made by blacks in television entertainment and news, but the same content was textually framed by some white inmates as examples of "race-mixing." One inmate who had recently gotten a cell to himself in order to do his time quietly commented:

L.D.:   Usually, if a black is on television, I just won't watch the show. Of course, boxing is all black, but the entertainment shows—I won't watch *The Jeffersons*. That's a minstrel show to me. They stereotype themselves. In here, I stay away from it. On commercials, I'll just turn away and do something else. I can't stand it. And they pander to the blacks, they cater to them. . . . It's not so much their color, it's their culture. And they perpetuate this same culture. They're in here, they talk in that street-corner black English.

T.L.:   With the black presence here at the Institution, it must be kind of difficult for you.

L.D.:   Aw, it's tough.

T.L.:   You must be switching the television a lot.

L.D.:   Well, you really don't see that much on. It's easy to change channels.

The Institution's recent exclusion of movies with racial conflict themes from public screening was invoked in clear recognition of the potential for actual disruption in the group viewing situation. Interestingly, many of the same movies appeared first on inmates' pay TV channels, where they can be viewed in private.

Organizing affiliations and disengagements. Personal media operate as malleable instruments for establishing settings of inmate conviviality—or for disengaging from prison routine. Within certain bounds, uses of media allow the inmate some authority over the occurrence and timing of interactions with inmates and staff. The content also provides common grounds for talk. Specific manifestations of social media use tend to conform to the modes of adaptation discussed earlier.

Among older inmates, recidivists who have tired of the usual recreations, and those in an extreme time-doing mode—"when they want to lay back and do a stretch"—televiewing consumes large blocks of time in the least complicated way. Personal media, especially television, often provide closure on an inmate career as the release date approaches. Officer K. R. observed that aggressive inmates will try to "pull 'em off their square." To avoid misconducts, therefore, which could result in parole postponements, yard-outs will often be avoided in favor of televiewing in the cell. O. R., who was entering the final year of his 6-year minimum sentence, exemplified this posture of disengagement via media:

> The bit I'm at now, I spend a lot of time in my cell. . . . It's simply because I've been *down* so long, and I've been into everything they have, I'm burnt out on it, and I'm more into, like, just kicking back now and letting this last year cruise by. . . . Most of my time I spend in my cell just reading and watching TV. Yeah, I'm just counting down. Just trying to stay out of the way.

During the middle passage of their sentences as well, times of either great stress or ennui will lead some to withdraw from their habitual inmate associations and "go into hibernation." Despite what is consensually regarded as a tightly-governed institution, the hegemony imposed on certain zones of cell blocks by cliques such as Muslims or young jailing-mode "jitterbug types" induces some inmates, particularly the more passive ones, to remain in their cells where personal media offer respite. For some, even that minimal level of routine isn't enough. Desiring separation for primarily self-protection reasons, they will intentionally get "written up" (i.e., receive misconducts) in order to get confined to the Restricted Housing Unit, a solitary detention unit where inmates are permitted no contacts, including media. The tactic is referred to as "going to the Bahamas for a month."

Those inmates using their personal media as a means for total disengagement from prison routine constitute a minority. More often, disengagement operates in a periodic fashion, as well-defined stretches of privacy backgrounded by the activation of media. Just as the towel or sheet draped midway across the front of the cell represents a make-shift barrier against visual surveillance, the use of ear plugs for radio and TV listening insures some auditory separation from the rest of the unit. Some of the commonest forms of media use for temporary disengagement, such as leaving the television set volume up low at night (instead of using ear plugs), entail some degree of rule violation. Such violations are either not enforced by guards or are subject to mild reprimands.

Disengaging by means of media can also lead to dilemmas it was meant to resolve. The Institution stipulates that all TV receivers be situated on a metal cabinet against the back cell wall, *facing* the cell door. This arrangement has a two-edged effect in terms of inmates' privacy concerns: although inmates typically view the set from their bunks with their backs to the door, ignoring activity in the cell block, inmates passing by the door are often attracted by it and may stop and watch for awhile. The fact that televisions often attract other inmates at unwanted times was cited by many owners as a chronic problem. And for inmates who have chosen to glean, the medium's "holding power" in the small confines of the cell often distracts from their study regimens.

For most of the inmates, however, personal media play in tightly with the interpersonal bonds and socio-economic alignments already functioning in the prison system. At one level, some media resources move into circulation along well-defined but unwritten lines. Magazines in particular will go from the subscriber to a "waiting line" of other inmates in the cell block, usually on a trade-off basis. Although an inmate may keep a personally valued magazine out of the rotation, the logic of a small network maximizing access to all of the members' subscriptions sustains the operation very well. The circulation of premium cable channel filter devices proceeds on a more deliberate and furtive basis, owing to the illegality of the operation. The inmate interviewees spoke freely about the underground economy in "cheat boxes." All reported that the devices, mostly stolen from the prison's electronics shop, work effectively, although reports varied regarding their normal cost (between three and ten packs of cigarettes).[2] Possession of the illegal devices is a Class One Misconduct, but the severity of the L.O.P. is usually contingent on the particular officer and how he perceives the behavior and reputation of the offending inmate. The fear of many inmates is that a routine cell shakedown will turn up a cheat box or other contraband. Thus, the inmates usually heed the Institution's rules regarding the amount of magazines and/or books permitted in cells, in order to avert the justification for a search.

Inmates are also prone to share their media on regular or ad hoc occasions, sometimes testing Institution rules in the process. Cellmates will normally "time-share" their access to the television, with the one who is in the cell when the other cellmate enters being allowed to finish viewing

---

[2]Although barter is common, the medium of exchange in this institution (and most others) is cigarettes. The actual exchange rate will vary, but inmate A. U. gives a succinct explanation of its operation: "T. L.: Can you tell me what a pack of cigarettes buys? A. U.: Oh, let's say, laundry, okay? I got three pair of good brown pants and three good shirts, and to get those washed, pressed, and brought back to me, which is illegal, but to get it done like that will cost me about three packs. Okay, a joint of marijuana will cost you three packs. . . . And then, if you run short or something, you go to the guy that runs the store in the block, it's two for one, you get one pack of cigarettes and you have to replace it with two. And sometimes, if you know the guy, he'll give you two for three. . . . So I guess the value of a pack of cigarettes is about a dollar."

his program; when a program-choice question arises, the owner's rights are usually invoked. The officers believed that introducing television into double-celled situations in itself entails no increases in conflict, because inmates are assigned in like pairings (either by race—e.g., black–black pairings; or by perceived dominance—e.g., a strong inmate is not paired with a weak one). In one case, however, an inmate thought a television would help him in achieving a manageable relationship with a cellmate, despite the fact that he had a history of discordant relationships with cellmates and desired to have his own cell. The inmate reported that, over time, relations with his cellmate deteriorated, mainly over issues of program selection. At the time of the interview, they were not speaking and the inmate was considering putting his television into storage for the remainder of his time in double-celling. Yet it was clear in the interviews that, more often than not, specific rules regarding the sequencing of in-cell media use are consensually arrived at that effectively allow double-celled inmates to pursue independent activities. In some cases, media availability may even facilitate the formation of a productive relationship, as evidenced in one inmate's report that he formerly watched a Spanish-lesson program every afternoon to help him in speaking to his Puerto Rican cellmate.

Sharing media access in double-celled situations is, of course, a legitimate activity. But entry by persons who are *not* cellmates to share tele-viewing, while not officially allowed, apparently does occur. Television-less inmates are often admitted into TV owners' cells. Friends will gather for a special program on a premium channel, or—in the case of inmate L. D., who happened to own a color set with low power requirements—simply stop in at random intervals to view. Precautions against discovery by officers are taken:

E.T.:   It's common to go in, especially way upstairs. The guard has to walk up five flights. You can't find two people at the bottom to walk with there [laughs]. They carry a walkie-talkie, too. You hear that and you stay outside the bars.

R.C.:   Uh, most of the guys stay *outside* the cell and look through the bars. And if you did go in somebody's cell, they'd have to give you a chair and you'd push it out, so you're outside the cell.

Another inmate reported that it was not uncommon for an officer who is approaching such a gathering to be purposely distracted by a sudden high-volume blast from a radio on another tier of the cell block. Although inmate–officer relationships could be generally characterized as correct, but not familiar, such tactics were regarded by nearly all the inmates as wholly acceptable in order to circumvent rules that were perceived as unnecessary.

Talk absorbs much of the inmates' energy, focusing it on such matters as recollections of the street, family, post-release plans, and the personalities and latest activities of staff members and fellow inmates. Due to the diversity of the individuals incarcerated in the Institution (and their relative equivalence in terms of lack of knowledge about each other's personal history), many of the judgments inmates make of their fellows are necessarily based on warrants found in talk. Talk often elaborates the essential insignificance of much of what the inmates do with their time:

> W.D.: You have a bunch of guys, 51 guys, telling a bunch of lies to each other. "This is what I did today," you know, and it wasn't that way. What you did is what I did, we took shit and put it in a spreader. You know what I mean? . . . But you sit and listen to them because it keeps you from being by yourself.

Inevitably, content from their personal media exposures are assimilated into the ongoing discourse. As much of the talk centers on sports, it has seasonal as well as cultural significance for the inmates; units of incarcerated time are differentiated and accented by their correlation with sports events just concluded and those that are anticipated. It was reported that for some types of programs, particularly soap operas and *M*A*S*H*, small cliques of inmates had formed in which some members kept others (who were absent due to work or other obligations) informed of the programs' happenings. Aspects of media content are also abstracted for their instrumental use in defining relationships within groups, as mentioned by some inmates with reference to the use of television characters' names. Instances of nicknames that eventually "stuck" were primarily comic characters applied to real persons with clownish characteristics: "Gilligan" given to an inmate who "acted dumb sometimes"; "Sergeant Schultz" (from the *Hogan's Heroes* program) given to a guard who would pull blankets off cell bars; "Benny Hill" given to an inmate resembling Benny Hill; and "Smurfs" given to two black inmates who were always together. In a similar manner, but without the intent to make personality classifications, a black inmate claimed to watch *Sanford and Son* reruns in order to use those "little racial remarks" with officers and inmates alike that are funny and serious simultaneously. The researcher himself was the subject of a blue jean commercial jingle sung by two inmates as he was walking across the yard—a comment, perhaps, on the pretensions of the visiting professional who chooses to dress casually. It may be that the use of media content in inmates' talk often deflects seriousness from what are, in fact, serious observations.

CONCLUSIONS

Few social settings offer more compelling evidence of the pragmatics of media exposure than the total institution. Prisons present a set of unusual and explicit incentives for behavioral conformance, some of which may be more salient than others at various stages of an inmate's sentence. The demands of inmate peer groups impose further bounds on self expression. Divorced from many of the normal resources for nurturing and presenting self, the inmate attempts to use both personal and institutionally-provided media to particular ends that are compatible with his chosen way of doing time. Media can be shaped to satisfy a number of situational needs in incarceration: diversion from predictability, control over environmental stimuli, artifactual continuity with the former life, materiel for learning and enacting functional roles, control over degree and type of social affiliation. The problem with such typologies, however, consists precisely in the great range of determinants of those adaptive behaviors. The interviews made clear that most inmates are in fact restless in their desire to wrest many dimensions of significance from their use of media. Two of those dimensions deserve comment. First, personal and institutional media (and perhaps these interviews as well) act to weaken inmates' reluctances to share their perceptions of the realities of the world and the institution itself. As indicated by the undercurrents of racial awareness and conflict in this prison, mediated communication may make manifest certain nascent themes of everyday life, and focus their precise usage later in other settings. Even in the absence of letters, phone calls, and/or visits with their outside community, the familiar settings and scenarios they view on television, or experience in other media, seem to provide a metric by which they can formulate conceptions of the worlds they live in simultaneously, the institutional world and the one outside. The validation they find in other inmates with similar media experiences contributes to those conceptions. Second, personal media empower inmates to control their information flows. Although the institution clearly mandates their ultimate access to media, it is equally clear that inmates are adept at finding ways to adjust their engagement with the prison system.

At the outset of the study, the fact that the Institution allowed personal media at all suggested a question: To what aspects of the Institution's mission are media presumed to contribute? To some extent, the Institution intends to create a type of "institutional sanctity" (18, pp. 80–1): viz., that its customary procedures, no matter how illogical, intrusive, or unpleasant, will become accepted as natural to inmates after a period of time. Interrogation of its officials and inmates led to the conclusion that security concerns were at the base of its media policy, rhetoric about rehabilitation notwithstanding. The operation of media at the Institution appears to exemplify a "loosely coupled system," as Weick (20) describes it. With media policy only temporally connected to the social systems in which media actually function, the intended effects unfold intermittently, if at all. The constant that mediates between the policy and the inmates' uses of media is the immediate social context of fellow inmates and line officers. In the loosely-coupled institution, *socialization* requires relearning subcultural rules for the actual situations of media use. The codified policy, and its intended effects for inmates, have little significance for inmates, except perhaps as a way of understanding the Institution's orientation to incarceration in general.

Uses and limits of informant data. With the option of direct observation closed, the possibility for detailed description of media-related interactions was also closed. Yet intensive interviewing is itself a form of participant observation in that a mutually-defining encounter between researcher and culture members takes place (9). The gulf of status between researcher and inmates, and the uncertain development of trust, are as problematic in face-to-face interviewing as in traditional participant observation (7, 11, 12).

Among the more efficient means of gaining access to institutionalized norms and status is the use of informants as an "observer's observer," especially when (a) critical parts of the social structure cannot be penetrated, or (b) information about incidents and histories is needed (21). Informant data can be misleading, however, when homogeneous pockets of complex systems are sampled (21, pp. 572-3). This has special relevance to the present study, since "[prisons] are social systems not bound together by basic consensus but rather organized around a cleavage in values and interests, knit together at certain places by patterns of accommodation and collusion, and frequently marked by conflict" (12, p. 126). Special care was taken to interview inmates from different cell blocks and with different communicational behaviors. Differences in perceptions or knowledge that were found in this study were often due to marked disjunctions in status (i.e., inmates vs. staff). Consistency could usually be found among those who had engaged in similar experiential trials. Private domains of media use—the meanings that content suggested for inmates, for example—were much more susceptible to variability in recall and motivations. The value of this type of account consists mostly in understanding the range of *possible symptoms* of media use rather than in developing a valid analytic framework.

REFERENCES

1. Becker, H.S. *Outsiders: Studies in the Sociology of Deviance.* New York: Free Press, 1973.
2. Bowker, L.H. *Corrections: The Science and the Art.* New York: Macmillan, 1982.

3. Burgoon, J. "Privacy and Communication." In M. Burgoon (Ed.), *Communication Yearbook 6*. Beverly Hills, CA: Sage, 1982, pp. 206–249.

4. Cohen, S., and L. Taylor. *Psychological Survival: The Experience of Long-Term Imprisonment*. New York: Vintage, 1974.

5. Fine, G.A., and S. Kleinman. "Rethinking Subculture: An Interactionist Analysis." *American Journal of Sociology* 85, 1979, pp. 1–20.

6. Galtung, J. "Prison: The Organization of Dilemma." In D.R. Cressey (Ed.) *The Prison: Studies in Institutional Organization and Change*. New York: Holt, Rinehart and Winston, 1961, pp. 108–145.

7. Giallombardo, R. "Interviewing in the Prison Community." *Journal of Criminal Law, Criminology, and Police Science* 57, 1966, pp. 318–324.

8. Goffman, E. "On the Characteristics of Total Institutions: The Inmate World." In D.R. Cressey (Ed.), *The Prison: Studies in Institutional Organization and Change*. New York: Holt, Rinehart and Winston, 1961, pp. 15–67.

9. Hammersley, M., and P. Atkinson. *Ethnography: Principles in Practice*. London: Tavistock, 1983.

10. Irwin, J. *The Felon*. Englewood Cliffs, NJ: Prentice-Hall, 1970.

11. Jacobs, J.B. "Participant Observation in Prison." *Urban Life and Culture* 3, 1974, pp. 221–240.

12. Kassebaum, G. "Strategies for the Sociological Study of Criminal Correctional Systems." In R.W. Habenstein (Ed.), *Pathways to Data: Field Methods for Studying Ongoing Social Organizations*. Chicago: Aldine, 1970, pp. 122–138.

13. Lindlof, T.R. "Social and Structural Constraints on Media Use in Incarceration." Paper presented at the International Communication Association convention, Honolulu, Hawaii, 1985.

14. Lofland, J. *Deviance and Identity*. Englewood Cliffs, NJ: Prentice-Hall, 1969.

15. McCall, G.J., and J.L. Simmons. *Identities and Interactions*. New York: Free Press, 1978.

16. Rubinstein, E., and J.N. Sprafkin. "Television and Persons in Institutions." In D. Pearl, L. Bouthilet, and J. Lazar (Eds.), *Television and Behavior: Ten Years of Scientific Progress and Implications for the Eighties, Vol. II*. Washington, DC: National Institute of Mental Health, 1982, pp. 322–330.

17. Sigman, S. "Why Ethnographers of Communication Do Ethnography: Issues in Observational Methodology." Paper presented at the Speech Communication Association convention, Louisville, Kentucky, 1982.

18. Sommer, R. *Personal Space: The Behavioral Basis of Design*. Englewood Cliffs, NJ: Prentice-Hall, 1969.

19. Toch, H. *Living in Prison: The Ecology of Survival*. New York: Free Press, 1977.

20. Weick, K.E. "Loosely Coupled Systems." Paper presented at the American Educational Research Association convention, Boston, 1980.

21. Zelditch, M. "Some Methodological Problems of Field Studies." *American Journal of Sociology* 67, 1962, pp. 566–576.

Chapter 10

Amateur Photography: The Organizational Maintenance of an Aesthetic Code

Dona B. Schwartz
Michael Griffin
School of Journalism and Mass Communication
University of Minnesota

Studies of visual media have primarily been object-centered, analyzing the form and content of pictures, whether films, video, photographs, or paintings. The research discussed here begins to elucidate the social meaning of a particular arena of visual production: camera club photography. The objects produced, the photographs, are viewed as a component part of ongoing social process, as visual artifacts emerging from communication activity. Thus, an analysis of camera club photographs, as objects, becomes primarily important for what it tells us about the social and economic relations which shape their creation. Birdwhistell (2) has argued the importance of studying the social contexts of communication in order to make statements about the meanings of communicational events:

> As our studies approach the point where we must deal with social meaning, we need clear statements regarding the occurrences. It is difficult, if not impossible, to answer the question: What does this symbol or that gesture mean? Meaning is not immanent in particular symbols, words, sentences, or acts of whatever duration but in the behavior elicited by the *presence* or *absence* of *such behavior* in particular contexts. The derivation and comprehension of social meaning thus rests equally upon comprehension of the code and of the context which selects from the possibilities provided by the code structure (p. 96).

In Worth's and Ruby's research proposal, "The American Community's Socialization to Pictures: An Ethnography of Visual Communication," they argue that the appropriate unit of analysis is not the product but "the *context—the community and the community members'* interaction with visual symbolic events" (32, p. 202, emphasis in original).

Object-centered analysis leads the researcher to interpret "texts" and make judgments as to the relative sophistication of form, structure, and/or the creator's skill. Given the primacy of the object, scholars often work through it to study the creator, attempting to identify qualities or characteristics of an individual personality as they are revealed within the content and style of the object. Rarely are the social networks within which a picture maker works, or the audiences to which a picture maker addresses him/herself, included as part of visual communication analysis. Viewing images as components of *communication process* forces the analyst to give equal weight to object, creator, viewer, and to the community which shares the symbolic conventions used. The specific forms and contents of symbolic communication result from tacit social agreement among community members as to conventional usage and meaning. The focus of investigation, then, may be usefully defined as the production system (composed of the interrelated activities of creators, viewers, and others necessary to the realization of visual symbolic events), and the social-historical context in which production takes place.

Proceeding from this perspective, and influenced by our own prior involvement in photography, we began to examine varied spheres of photographic activity. Because of the prevalence and accessibility of the medium, photographic production occurs in a broad array of settings, serving a wide range of functions. Simultaneous "worlds" of photography (1) operate in relative isolation from one another. Social scientists studying photography have related distinctive spheres of activity in which work routines, photographic styles, and evaluative standards differ sharply (4, 5, 6, 20, 24, 25). We had both completed research on children's development of visual symbolic skills, investigating media socialization and training as they relate to the nature of continued participation in visual production (11, 12, 26). Similarly, we became interested in studying the continuing involvement and recruitment of adults into visual production activities. Since photography is a medium which does not necessarily require years of technical training, and entry into photographic activity (particularly noncommercial production) occurs at a wide range of ages, organized amateur photography drew our attention. Camera club photography is an arena of symbolic activity with a stable organizational structure. Isolated from other worlds of photographic production (such as fine art photography, photojournalism, professional portraiture, wedding photography, advertising photography), camera club members simultaneously occupy the roles of creator, viewer, and critic. The aesthetic code of camera club photography has enjoyed historical longevity, providing predictable, stable standards of evaluation. As our research progressed, we found camera club photography to be particularly well-suited to an examination of the relationship between social process and pictorial aesthetic.

Camera clubs have received very little attention in the historical literature on photography, nor are they currently viewed with much interest. The history of photography has been written in elitist terms, with thorough texts devoted to "fine art" photography (e.g., 10, 16, 21). Insofar as documentary and early photo-reportage have been included in the construction of an art history of the medium, these idioms have received attention as well. "Home-mode" or snapshot photogaphy (4, 14, 20), family pictures made by anonymous multitudes, have recently been studied by historians and communications scholars. Camera club photography, artistic picture-making produced by unrecognized middle-class men and women, has been discussed only in terms of its relative mediocrity when compared to fine art or professional commercial work. The predominant evaluative, object-centered approach to studying photography has led scholars to ignore a major sphere of photographic activity. Thus, our research on amateur camera club photography also takes a step towards broadening discussions of the medium.

A variety of research methods were employed: participant observation, interviews (both formal and informal), and document analysis. Data-gathering began in early Spring 1979 and continued until August 1982. The authors joined the Miniature Camera Club of Philadelphia (MCC) in March 1979 as "family members." Family memberships (husband and wife) account for over half of the photographers who belong to the club. As a pair, we were accepted as a sociable unit, interested in friendships as well as pursuing photography. As stated in yearly programs, the purpose of MCC is

> to promote the art and science of photography. . . . We, at Miniature, offer the prospective member an opportunity to join with others of similar interests, to pursue a fascinating hobby and find stimulation with friendly and competent amateurs.

This blend of avocation with sociability characterizes more than a century of nationwide amateur club activity.

At our initial visit to the club we introduced ourselves, explaining that we were conducting a research project studying amateur photography, an interest stemming from our own avid interest in the medium. We were viewed with some suspicion at first. The ages of club members range from about 40 to 80 years; few were aged less than 40, while many were over 60. Many MCC members are retirees. Thus, we may have appeared as young infiltrators into a mature sanctum. Well into our second year as members, we were occasionally questioned about our "paper," although by that time most club members seemed to accept us as co-amateurs with somewhat esoteric academic interests.

During the course of our membership we attended club meetings, special events (exhibitions, photo-outings, dinners), and participated in club photography competitions. In addition, we volunteered jointly to fill the position of "club historian" (others showed little interest in taking on this particular task). We organized historical materials that had been collected by members during their tenure, and produced a short written history for distribution to the group. Thus, we were given the opportunity to study valuable records of club activities dating back to MCC's inception in 1933. As members, we attempted to limit participation in club affairs to a level at which we would be considered active, but not overly conspicuous or outstanding. While entering photo-competitions, we did not aim at winning prize ribbons. Instead, we each assumed the role of neophyte (easy as a result of our relative youth) so that advice could be readily sought and offered.

ACTIVITIES OF THE MINIATURE CAMERA CLUB

The Miniature Camera Club of Philadelphia holds meetings on the first three Thursdays of each month, from September through May. In January 1982, the club listed 97 members: 58 men and 39 women. Meetings are held in the rooms of the Engineer's Club (a professional's social club), commencing at 8 p.m. A small group meets earlier for drinks at the Engineer's Club bar, followed by dinner in the Club's dining rooms.

Program topics vary at MCC meetings. Often, an invited guest speaker presents a slide show which takes one of two formats: an instructional show detailing a specific photographic technique (at which the presenter her/himself excels); or a travelogue, an edited sequence of slides culled from the careful pictorial record of a vacation trip, accompanied by a spoken or tape-recorded narration. Occasionally, a manufacturer's slide-tape show on equipment and techniques is presented. The focal club events are photo competitions. Any member may enter his or her work in the appropriate exhibition categories. Competitions are judged by well-respected photographers from other local camera clubs or by representatives from the Photographic Society of America, the national umbrella organization of amateur photography headquartered in Philadelphia. Following each meeting, refreshments are served by one of the turn-taking women members.

During the season, MCC sponsors outings to camera-worthy sites in the Philadelphia area. Following the day's picture-taking, members head for a restaurant, chosen by the outing committee, to round out the event.[1] MCC holds two banquets yearly. The Christmas Dinner is held to celebrate the holiday season, and a member is asked to show a travelogue for the group's entertainment. The annual President's Dinner concludes the season with the presentation of club awards and an exhibition of the best photographic work entered in competitions during the year.

MCC is one of 28 camera clubs in the Philadelphia area which constitute the Delaware Valley Council of Camera Clubs (DVCCC). The Council organizes local inter-club activities, including an annual competition and photography workshops. The DVCCC also presents awards for service to the organization, and many MCC members have earned these honors. Area councils like the DVCCC provide regional links in the national network of camera clubs organized by the Photographic Society of America.

HISTORICAL CONTRIBUTIONS TO CURRENT ACTIVITIES

To understand current configurations of social behavior, historical data must be examined. A particular investigatory moment needs to be situated within its temporal context. Hence, in studying present MCC activities and the pictorial aesthetic of amateur photography, it becomes necessary to examine the historical evolution of a hierarchy of photographic activities.

When photographer-inventor Louis Daguerre published his daguerreotype process in 1839, he set in motion what would become the popular pursuit of photography. During the middle 1800s, the amateur photography world was composed mostly of science teachers and their students (29), but, as photographic technology advanced (i.e., became increasingly simplified), amateur activity swelled, admitting nonscientists into the ranks. During the 1880s, the number of photographic clubs or "societies" in the U.S. and Europe grew. Among the members were both amateurs and "professionals" (portrait photographers and commercial producers of travel pictures), a convenient arrangement for the latter, who were often paid to teach the beginning enthusiasts (29, p. 204). These organizations contributed to the advancement of photography by providing members with an arena for sharing expertise. Their joint efforts often resulted in new technological developments or applications. Societies held "salons" which were modelled after exhibitions of paintings, and the dialogue generated by these events helped to shape an emerging photographic aesthetic.

---

[1]Camera outings are a tradition among amateur groups. See (29) for descriptions of nineteenth century excursions.

In the midst of this burgeoning amateur activity, some photographers were concerned with promoting photography as a fine art. Contrasting their work with commercial and scientific uses of the medium, and with the unpracticed picture making of neophyte photographers, a small group of amateurs developed a photographic style which came to be known as "pictorialism." Pictorialists utilized printing processes which would yield soft focus effects, producing photographs that emulated the look of paintings. The surfaces of these pictures resemble the manual brushwork on the painter's canvas. Subject matter and composition were drawn from nineteenth century portrait, genre, and landscape painting (Figure 1). By virtue of these visual similarities, this group of amateurs argued that photography could be used to make art. They considered the pictorialist style to be the sole *artistic* form in photography.

Artist-photographers, a term which first appeared around the turn of the century (16, p. 88), sponsored exhibitions of pictorialist work. An American leader in this movement was Alfred Stieglitz, a prominent member of the New York Camera Club. He promoted *juried* salons of the "best" photography, a practice which was foreign to camera club members. Equal opportunity to participate and exhibit had been the hallmark of amateur clubs, and Stieglitz' screening process was viewed as an elitist infringement upon club members' rights. The majority of camera club photographers, unhappy with the "art movement's" stylistic and participatory exclusiveness, did not embrace pictorialism immediately. Long dedicated to experimenting with photographic technology, most amateurs did not view pictorialism as the only appropriate style.

In 1902 Stieglitz founded an organized group of artist-photographers called the "Photo-Secession." These amateurs promoted a "secession" from "commonplace" photographic activity, especially from commercial and technically-oriented amateur work. Stieglitz and his followers attempted to link their work with the modern movement in painting, both in the United States and Europe. As Stieglitz wrote:

> In Europe, in Germany and Austria, there have been splits in the art circles and the moderns call themselves Secessionists, so Photo-Secession really hitches up with the art world (21, pp. 105–6).

Stieglitz went on to establish institutions that would evolve into an elaborated "art world" of photography: a gallery devoted to showcasing art photography and avant-garde painting, and a critical journal which reviewed and reproduced the latest contributions to fine art. In addition he contributed to the formation of a network of art photographers, providing critical interaction and support.

The paths Stieglitz travelled led him away from organized amateur photography. Stieglitz bifurcated the amateur world, charging that activ-

Figure 1. Edward Steichen. The Flatiron—Evening. 1904. Courtesy the Minneapolis Institute of Arts.

ity which allowed equal participation by anyone choosing to take part would necessarily yield mediocre work. Instead, he publicized and elevated the work of an elite, leading to a hierarchical arrangement of noncommercial photographic activity. The rift between Stieglitz and camera club amateurs was concretized when members of the New York Camera Club ousted him from the club in 1908.

As photographic activity expanded around the turn of the century, the distinction between art photographers and the growing mass of amateur practitioners grew increasingly pronounced. George Eastman's revolutionary "Kodak," introduced in 1888, represented the first attempt to create a mass market of casual snapshooters. Prompted by his failure to successfully introduce the use of new roll films into professional studio or serious amateur work, Eastman went out to persuade the public that it too could make photographs. Operation of the Kodak required no technical expertise, and Eastman's famous ad campaign, "you press the button and we do the rest," enticed millions of untrained novice photographers (17, pp. 111–116). The development of factory-prepared gelatin dry plates in the 1880s had begun to increase the ranks of serious amateurs, since knowledge of the chemical production of photosensitive emulsions and the technical application of these emulsions to plates before exposure was no longer a prerequisite for photographic participation. With the advent of the Kodak, the complicated operations involved in processing and making prints could be bypassed as well. Anyone with $50 to spend for the initial purchase, and $10 more to pay for the processing and replacement of each roll of 100 exposures, could indeed simply press the button and let Eastman Company do the rest. By the early 1900s, introduction of packaged roll film which could be easily loaded and unloaded by novice photographers themselves, and the invention of the even simpler and less expensive Brownie camera (over 100,000 of which were sold in the first year), made snapshot photography a commonplace American leisure pursuit. For the first time, photography was easily accessible to anyone who could afford to own and operate a camera.

The fine art movement away from camera club photography was, in large part, a movement away from mass participation. Similarly, camera club photographers, serious amateurs themselves, saw a need to distinguish their own work from snapshooting. Influenced by Stieglitz and the attention given to pictorialism, camera club photographers eventually moved towards a pictorialist aesthetic as well (Figures 2 and 3). Just as the Photo-Secessionists had sought to distinguish themselves from other amateurs, camera club photographers increasingly adopted the tenets of pictorialism to separate their work from mass market snapshots. After 1910, the major distinctions between camera club and Photo-Secession activities revolved around issues of relative access to exhibition space and the opportunity for full participation by members of the group. Photo-Secessionists' desire to "hitch up" with the art world, and their interest in modern painting and sculpture, led artist photographers to establish an exclusive realm of discourse and interaction in which camera club photographers did not participate. Pictorialism declined as the marker distinguishing artists from camera club photographers, and by the 1920s the

Figure 2. Alfred Steiglitz. The Hand of Man. 1902. Courtesy the Minneapolis Institute of Arts.

Figure 3. Erno Vadas. Bahnhof. From the Third International Salon of Photographic Art, Milwaukee, 1936. Reprinted in *The Camera* Vol. LII, No. 2, August 1936.

Figure 4. Edward Murphy. Reprinted in *The Joy of Photography*, by the Editors of the Eastman Kodak Company, 1979.

Figure 5. Photograph by Jim Single, member Miniature Camera Club of Philadelphia.

pictorialist code was firmly entrenched as the normative standard of camera club photography. Coincident with the rise of camera club pictorialism, so-called artist photographers began to repudiate the pictorialist aesthetic. Once again, artists sought to distinguish their own work from amateur products; they viewed camer club pictorialism as overly sentimental and banal. "Straight Photography," sharp-focus picture-making once scorned by Secessionists, was to be the new fine art aesthetic code.[2] Despite the evolution of various fine art movements, camera club photography continued to maintain the pictorialist aesthetic of the early 1900s. The organization of the amateur photography world, and the role of the photographic industry in that world, combined to insure such aesthetic continuity.

THE MINIATURE CAMERA CLUB AND THE PHOTOGRAPHIC SOCIETY OF AMERICA

Thirty-five millimeter photography was introduced in 1924 with the first Leica camera. This new format provided an important advance: new lenses with larger apertures allowed photographers to work unaided by flash in "existing light," while using faster shutter speeds to freeze motion. The smaller, more lightweight camera also allowed the photographer greater mobility. This new "miniature camera" technology prompted yet another wave of amateur expansion. Even larger numbers of photographers swelled the ranks of camera clubs and, during the 1930s, many new amateur associations were founded. In March 1933, the Miniature Camera Club of Philadlelphia held its first meeting, and during the 1930s and 1940s the club's membership more than quadrupled. (As early as 1936, attendance was rising so steadily that the club decided it would have to enforce an admittance-by-membership-card-only policy.) At the end of 1933, the Photographic Society of America, or PSA, was founded (building upon the smaller American Federation of Camera Clubs) and made its headquarters in Philadelphia.

PSA was formed to coordinate amateur photographic activities and to serve as an organizational guide for hundreds of new clubs. During its first year, 51 clubs had joined PSA. By 1938, its member clubs numbered 373. Still the dominant nationwide umbrella organization for camera club and amateur photographic activity, PSA counted 1,265 affiliated camera clubs in 1978. The current president of PSA, Frank Pallo, estimates that 366,000 amateurs are associated with the Society individually or through club memberships, and an estimated 74,784 amateurs regularly receive

---

[2]See (27) for discussion of distinctions created and maintained which separate camera clubs and fine art photography.

the *Journal*, a monthly magazine published by PSA. Many leadership positions in PSA were filled by amateurs whose involvement in photography pre-dated the miniature camera explosion. They carried with them the pictorialist tradition, and, through the influence of PSA, newly formed clubs adopted the pictorialist aesthetic. Through their numbers, camera clubs institutionalized pictorialism as the accepted aesthetic code of amateur photography.

In addition to regular intra-club photo-competitions and shows, inter-club salons endorsed by PSA became an important exhibition circuit for many amateurs. Pictorialism provided the set of criteria by which photographic work was evaluated. Active and skillful PSA members could amass prize ribbons and medals. Salon "acceptance" stickers applied to the backs of travelling exhibition prints provided a conspicuous display of a photographer's success. International salons also attracted participation from ardent amateurs. Eventually a formalized point system evolved, allowing photographers to achieve "star" rankings, enhancing their reputations among PSA exhibitors and at their home clubs. PSA photographers can now earn the rank of one-star through five-star exhibitor. Beyond the five-star level, an additional "galaxy" ranking system operates. Success at salons and service to the Society lead to special honors. Titles like "Associate" or "Fellow" of PSA are bestowed upon worthy photographers. PSA salons continue to provide an important arena for amateur exhibition and competition. Through these activities, evaluative standards are assimilated. The pictorialistic aesthetic adhered to in PSA salons, and the exhibition categories used to organize these events, shape the ongoing activities of member camera clubs.

PSA AND THE PHOTOGRAPHIC INDUSTRY

Early in the history of organized amateur photography, the photographic industry took an interest in camera club activities. In the 1880s, amateur photography journals were the primary vehicle for industry advertising. Through these journals the photographic industry attempted to reach the burgeoning amateur market, delivering sales pitches for new detective cameras, gelatin dry plates, and other photographic paraphernalia. As the amateur pictorialist aesthetic evolved, photographic manufacturers presented their own advertising in such a way as to support and further the camera club visual style. Camera clubs and amateur journals became important vehicles for the diffusion of information on new technological developments introduced by the industry. As Manley Miles advised in his 1894 article "Hints for Amateurs,"

> Camera clubs and photographic periodicals must be looked upon as indispensable agencies for the increase and diffusion of knowledge relating

to the principles and practice of photography, and amateurs who wish to keep abreast of the progress of the times should not fail to avail themselves of these incentives and guides to improvement in the practical details of the art (19, p. 60).

Photographic industry executives and entrepreneurs were often involved in amateur photography themselves and not infrequently played active roles in the same clubs they solicited. Minutes of camera club meetings from the 1920s, 1930s, and 1940s are filled with accounts of visits and presentations by industry representatives. Recorded in the minutes of The Miniature Camera Club of Philadelphia for December 7, 1933 is the following account of one such visit:

the President called the meeting to order and introduced Mr. Pierce of the Weston Electrical Instrument Corporation who had come to Philadelphia at great inconvenience to himself, having recently suffered a severe automobile accident, to talk to the members upon the use of the photoelectric cell in exposure meters for photographic work. MR. PIERCE gave a history of the development of the photo electric cells and the use to which they had been put during the past ten years. He then showed to the members certain instruments manufactured by his Company, one of which was of particular interest as it gave a direct reading of light as affecting the human eye. . . . He then touched upon the application of the photo electric cell to photographic exposure meters. He illustrated his talk not only by means of meters but also by drawings and a large pasteboard model of the calculator. He called the members' attention particularly to the fact that with that type of meter it was possible to secure an exposure in any position upon the straight line of the H. and D. curve. To illustrate this point, he passed among the members negatives mounted upon cardboard with a tissue backing, so that by holding them to the light it was possible to see the different exposures obtainable. Some of these negatives showed under exposure, as well as over-exposure represented on the H. and D. curve by the toe and the shoulder.

MR. PIERCE answered numerous questions of the members and upon the conclusion of his talk, a rising vote of thanks was tendered to him by the club.

After another such presentation, MCC members were rewarded with free equipment. This entry in the MCC minutes appeared on January 18, 1934:

The meeting being called to order, Mr. Woods (the MCC President) stated that Mr. J. H. Kurlander, of the Westinghouse Lamp Co. had consented to talk upon the Use of Photoflood and Photoflash Lamps in Photography. That much to his surprise and appreciation five men of the Technical and Sales staff of the company were present to tell the members something about lighting problems in photography. That Mr. Gjon Mili Test Engineering Department of the Company would cover the subject in detail[3] and later Mr. Kurlander would talk upon synchronization of shutter and lamp.

Mr. Mili being introduced introduced his subject by by (sic) describing the process made in the manufacture of effectient (sic) and long life lamps. He illustrated this with different types of lamps. He then discussed the photoflood and later the photoflash lamps. The light giving power of each was explained and the life and efficiency of each together with construction details were discussed. His clear interpretations of the problems and their solution, illustrated by slides and charts or graphs, proved of great interest to the members.

Mr. Kurlander spoke upon synchronizing the photoflash lamp with the camera shutter. He pointed out that after much research it was finally accomplished but the apparatus required was too cumbersome and expensive for general use. No simple method has yet been devised to tie up the focal-plane shutter and the flash lamp. It may be done with a between-the-lens shutter. Mr. Kurlander's talk rounded out the subject and the members secured much valuable information upon lights and reflectors.

Mr. Kurlander presented to Mr. Woods a number of lamps of each type and the President graciously donated them to the members. Those submitting prints were given the first opportunity to select lamps.

Visits from industry representatives were commonplace through the 1940s, and programs sponsored by Leitz, Zeiss (leading German camera and lens manufacturers), Eastman Kodak, Ansco, General Electric, Westinghouse, Bausch and Lomb, and others, are recorded in the club's minutes.

Today, many high ranking officers of PSA also hold executive positions with corporations marketing photographic supplies and equipment. Frank Pallo, President of PSA, is also a vice-president at the Eastman-Kodak Company and holds the offices of Executive Secretary and Treasurer of the Photographic Industry Council, just as Eastman-Kodak and other companies are industrial members of PSA. Kodak "Here's How" books, which instruct amateur photographers how to reproduce the pictorialist aesthetic, are often written by expert amateurs who hold the honorific titles "Fellow" or "Associate" of PSA. Many of these authors also work full-time for Kodak. This Kodak literature is well read by amateur photographers, and MCC members report that Kodak pamphlets and books are among the most valuable informational resources available. Kodak's literature distribution center in Rochester, New York handles such a massive volume of mail that it has been assigned its own zip code number.

---

[3]Gjon Mili has become known in the literature on art photography because of his experimental manipulations of artificial light.

One Kodak publication is called "How to Run a Live Camera Club," a manual instructing readers how to found and organize a camera club. The manual covers drafting a club constitution and bylaws, strategies for raising money, and guidelines for running meetings and judging print and slide competitions. Of particular interest are sections which recommend appropriate club programs. In addition to suggesting the use of Kodak informational films and slide-tape shows, the booklet urges the prospective programmer to invite guest speakers frequently. Photo industry specialists are recommended, and an address is given at which Kodak representatives may be contacted. The booklet also recommends PSA officials as both lecturers and competition judges. When scheduling industry speakers, readers are advised, meetings should be publicized and opened to nonmembers in order to assure the largest possible audience. Questions concerning both programming and criteria for judging are referred to PSA headquarters in Philadelphia, or to Eastman Kodak.

From the beginning, the photographic industry established a close relationship with organized amateur associations, because camera club photographers constituted an important market for products. To better serve that market, the industry itself promoted the pictorialist aesthetic, providing neophyte amateurs with technical information as well as guidelines concerning appropriate subject matter, compositional rules, the creation of appropriate backgrounds, "more effective" manipulation of lighting, focus and exposure, and the most advantageous use of new equipment and products. As the photographic industry and PSA have grown, both have come to exert great influence on camera club photography, shaping the nature of club activities, competitions and salons, and the aesthetic code maintained by those activities (Figures 4 and 5). PSA and the industry's significant overlap in personnel is paralleled by certain shared mutual interests. Both promote the dissemination of photographic information and technical data. Kodak's literature (and the literature of other photographic manufacturers) has continually supported the camera club aesthetic, while PSA has provided a stable organizational framework for camera club activities which reproduce that aesthetic. The confluence of the industry and PSA, and the continuity of this close relationship over time, has helped to crystallize and maintain amateur aesthetic codes.

Recent interviews with industry executives and retail marketers have made it clear that the emergence of a mass SLR market of 35mm camera users has greatly diminished the economic importance of organized amateurs. Still, the apparent symbiotic relationship between the industry and amateur groups remains resistant to change. The industry continues to court "opinion leadership" groups like PSA. Kodak weekend seminars, day-long events which address technical and aesthetic issues raised in the practice of amateur photography, continue to be organized through regional camera club networks like the Delaware Valley Council of Camera Clubs in Philadelphia. Although held in public auditoriums and opened to the general public, our own observations indicate that these seminars are most often attended by the members of local camera clubs.

In cooperation with Eastman Kodak and the Photographic Industry Council, PSA also continues to maintain a Uniform Practices Committee (now called the Technical Standards Committee). This committee is primarily responsible for setting standards of picture exhibition and judging. The level of light in which photographs would be viewed, the type of screen slides should be projected on, the size and format prints should take, the distance from which a competition judge should examine entries, all aspects of proper picture display and photographic judging, come under the purview of PSA.

Current amateur/industry interconnections such as these represent long-standing historical relationships. Our observations and interviews, combined with historical research, suggest that present patterns of industry–camera club interaction result more from inter-organizational continuities than from an industry response to current market opportunities. The historical continuity at the level of organizational interaction is paralleled by the entrenchment of relatively invariant pictorialist codes in camera club photography.

THE CAMERA CLUB AESTHETIC

In recent years, art historians have turned their attention increasingly to the tradition of pictorialism and the re-emergence of pictorialist style in the work of art photographers dubbed "neo-pictorialists." While very little of this attention has included camera club work, an exhibition of photography from the Minneapolis Salon was hung in 1983 at the Minneapolis Institute of Art. In the exhibition catalogue, curator Christian Peterson describes pictorialism in this way:

> The pictorial style of photography emphasizes pure visual appeal, often bordering on the picturesque, in contrast to the documentary, straight and journalistic style . . . pictorial photography in all its phases was dominated by a constant preoccupation with beautiful imagery. This self-conscious attitude toward securing strong visual appeal perhaps reached its logical conclusion in the 1930s and 1940s. The expression of a concrete idea was not necessarily absent from work done over these decades but serious meaning was generally subordinated to pure pulchritude. (22, p. 9)

The requirement that a good photograph be beautiful persists among camera club members today. To be beautiful, a picture should show a beautiful subject: a pretty woman or child, a cute pet, a bucolic landscape, birds, flowers, or a nature scene. When less conventional subjects are chosen, beauty is attributed to the pictorialist style of depiction and the technical mastery exhibited. There are limits, however. A picture of someone suffering due to an automobile accident, or a picture of famine victims, is unlikely to be considered beautiful regardless of its rendering. Such pictures are generally considered inappropriate to camera club competition and are categorized as "photojournalism" or "documentary photography." A photograph of junk cars half buried in a streambed near Zion National Park was eliminated from one Miniature Camera Club competition on the first round, although members agreed that it was a "good environmental shot."

Camera club photography is nonconfrontational and unambiguous. Camera club members say that pictures should be "pleasing to the eye," "something you would want to hang on your living room wall." The pictorialist style has evolved and changed in a few respects since the early 1900s, yet the work of present-day amateurs maintains the same emphases on traditional painterly compositions, manipulation of a single subject to achieve immediate visual impact, nonobtrusive, controlled backgrounds, and "beautiful" subjects. Current pictorialists have rejected the hand-worked, soft focus impressionism of their predecessors, choosing sharp-focus "realism" instead. This shift reflects the introduction of new photographic technologies (faster lenses and filmstocks allowing photographers to produce sharper pictures in a variety of lighting situations) and the growing influence of professional and commercial photography (evidenced by the use of star filters and other devices used by professionals to produce special effects). Since commercial photography is similarly preoccupied with the manufacture of eye catching, "beautiful" imagery, amateurs have come to emulate much commercial work. PSA members are avid travellers, and many of their photographs resemble travel pictures seen in *National Geographic*, in travel magazines, in nature and wildlife magazines, and in Sierra club calendars. Portraiture is popular among camera club photographers and the influence of commercial studio work is clearly evidenced in their pictures.

PSA photographers can exhibit in several different picture categories, but Miniature Camera Club competitions we observed focused on two: "nature" and "pictorial." The best nature photographs are indistinguishable from the professional work reproduced in naturalist magazines and wildlife books. The best pictorial photographs resemble studio portraits, picture postcards, travel photography, and even publicity images. Industry literature regularly uses examples drawn from commercial photography, presenting commercial forms and techniques as models for their amateur readers. Much of our research indicates that industry, commercial, and amateur interrelations constitute what Stebbins (28) has called a "professional amateur public system," a system of amateurs and professionals tied together by common standards and goals, similar patterns of production and audience appreciation. The homogenization of photoaesthetic codes outside the art world supports the utility of such a concept for description of present-day photographic activity.[4]

Camera club photographers say that good pictures must have a "strong center of interest." When diverse, apparently unrelated elements appear in the pictorial frame, photographs are criticized as "distracting," a "hodge podge," or "confusing." Camera club pictures are designed to be easily and quickly understood, to have an immediate impact. Camera club work is without ambiguity.[5] A set of visual devices is used to augment their clarity. When pictures have a single subject, like a woman or a wildflower, the subject should not have to compete with anything else in the frame for the viewer's attention. Therefore, when backgrounds look "busy," photographers throw them out of focus, eliminating any distractions. To minimize tension between backgrounds and foregrounds, close-ups are often used, eliminating extraneous elements. One of the most frequent criticisms expressed by competition judges is "the photographer should have moved in closer" (Figure 6). For landscapes, where the subject of the photograph is the whole terrain, deep focus is required (Figure 7) and competition judges reject landscapes utilizing shallow depth-of-field.

Compositional arrangements lead the viewer's eye to the picture's "center of interest." "Leading lines," strong diagonals or S-curves appear regularly, and in Kodak's literature on composition these devices are rec-

---

[4]Comments made by authorities judging professionals' photography contests echo the aesthetic criteria we heard articulated repeatedly in amateur competitions and salons. The jury for the 1984 "Pictures of the Year" contest (sponsored by the National Press Photographers Association and Canon, a company manufacturing photographic equipment) consisted of photo ediotrs and photographers from *Geo* and *National Geographic*, as well as a Pulitzer Prize-winning photojournalist and a representative of the National Press Photographers' Association. According to a report on the contest published in the November 1984 issue of *Lens: On Campus*, "all of the judges agreed that content and technical quality were of prime importance in picking the winners" (18:32). One judge emphasized that "A picture either came across instantly or it was a non-picture" (18:32). In such contests, notions of appropriate subject matter often differ considerably from those held by camera club members, but standards of presentation, form, and technical execution seem nearly identical.

[5]Fine art photographers in opposition, value "mystery" and ambiguity. Art photography takes "ideas" as its subject (usually formalist "ideas"), and the complexity of a picture is a measure of the photographer's sophistication. For further discussion, see Schwartz (27).

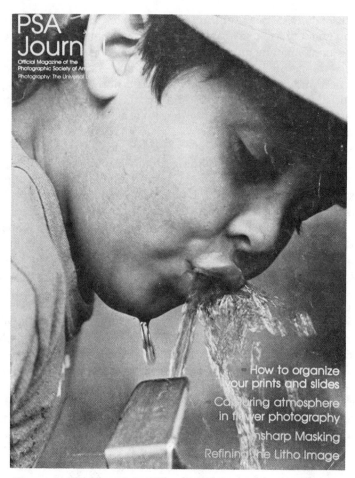

Figure 6. Photograph by Max Perchick, member Miniature Camera Club of Philadelphia, appearing on the cover of the *PSA Journal*, July 1981.

ommended. (Figure 6 utilizes the stream of water issuing from a fountain as a line leading to the boy's mouth and face, while in Figure 7 the brook, a luminous gold in the color original, makes an S-curve leading the viewer's eye through the frame). Repeatedly found in Kodak instructional books and pamphlets is the "rule-of-thirds," a compositional format used by club members to make pictures appear more "dynamic." Rather than centering the subject in the frame, producing what is considered to be a "static" composition, the "center of interest" is placed at one of the four points of intersection on a grid like the one which appears here:

Figure 7. Photograph by Harriet Richards, member Miniature Camera Club of Philadelphia, appearing on the cover of the PSA Journal, November 1980.

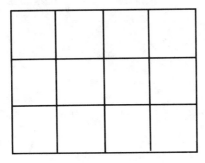

Figure 8. William A. Goden. Waiting. From the First Annual Exhibition of the Pictorial Forum of New York City, 1936. Reprinted in *The Camera*, Vol. LII, No. 5, May 1936.

Figure 9. William E. Mackintosh. Water Flower. From the International Club Print Competition held by PSA in 1981. Reprinted in the PSA Journal, Vol. 47, No. 10, October 1981.

In Figures 8, 9, and 10, camera club photographers have chosen moored boats as their subjects. Regardless of the specifics of location, the layout of docks (or lack of docks), or the type of boats, each photographer produces an image which follows the rule-of-thirds.

During interview sessions, camera club photographers were asked to critique a series of photographs. All agreed that Figure 11 exemplified the best in amateur work. All of the stylistic elements of camera club pictorialism are in evidence. The subject, children running down a winding lane, a barn on the horizon, is nostalgic and sentimental. Interviewees respond that it was "lovely," a "classic picture," a "delight." Following the rule-of-thirds, the children appear in the lower right-hand corner of the frame, and the barn and tree are both placed off-center. An S-curve is used to lead the eye through the frame. The compositional arrangement is echoed in Figure 12, a photograph which appears in Kodak's pamphlet "How to Run a Live Camera Club."

Figure 10. Photography by Charles Bowerman, illustrating his article "PSA Camera Tour: From Pagodas to Junks," appearing in the PSA Journal, Vol. 44, No. 6, June 1978.

Figure 11. Photograph from the PSA Journal.

Because camera club photographers adhere to a clearly defined aesthetic code, their pictures exhibit a high degree of conformity. Unlike fine art photography, which emphasizes innovation and rule-breaking as markers of creativity, in camera club photography expertise and creativity are communicated through conspicuous technical skill and mastery of the pictorialist code. Camera club photography exemplifies the "communication of competence," a concept discussed by Gross (13) in relation to artistic activity. Displaying photographic competence through control of exposure, focus, depth of field, framing, and composition is a primary goal for club amateurs. The evolution of the camera club aesthetic, and the organization of activity maintaining it, has provided stability and continuity in amateur picture making. Photographs praised in 1936 (Figure 8)

Figure 12. Robert E. Abernethy. Reprinted in a pamphlet titled *How to Run a Live Camera Club*, published by Eastman Kodak Company, 1979.

reappear over time (Figures 9 and 10) and continue to receive praises (see also Figures 2 through 5). The persistence of pictorialist tenets throughout the history of organized amateur activity is remarkable.

AMATEUR PHOTOGRAPHY AND COMMUNICATION RESEARCH

The research presented here emanates from a tradition of qualitative study focusing on contexts of symbolic production. Commercial mass media have been examined by social scientists (3, 7, 9, 15, 23, 25, 30), as has fine art production (1, 5, 6, 8, 13, 25, 27). Symbolic production operating outside of formally organized commercial production and distribution systems has received less attention. In his discussion of ethnographic semiotics, Worth (31) argues the importance of research which investigates symbolic communication process manifested in everyday life, and the links between varied production contexts.

Our research on camera club photography begins to delineate the nature of an amateur production system, charting interrelations among amateur, commercial, and fine art photography. Treatment of camera club work by photography scholars and historians has been sadly lacking. Since a concern with asserting photography's status as a fine art medium has predominated, organized amateur photography has been considered an unimportant subject for scholarly attention. Amateur pictorialism has been called sentimental, banal (21), even "indefensible" (33). We have taken issue with these viewpoints. As Stebbins (28) argues, within the "professional amateur public system" amateurs play an important supporting role for professionals, serving as sophisticated audience members, often graduating new professional personnel from the amateur ranks. Similarly, Gross (13) aruges that artistic communication is predicated on audience members' sharing symbolic codes with creators. Complex responses to symbolic production results from audience members' own media competence. Hence, amateurs, active and sophisticated producers themselves, influence professional production, providing a link between producers and their audiences. And, we would argue, amateur production is itself valuable activity. Camera club photographers learning to be competent manipulators of a visual symbol system become more competent interpreters of the visual messages they receive, and thus gain greater control over their own responses. Furthermore, camera club photographs merit aesthetic appreciation, as skillfully constructed, meaningful pictorial artifacts. As with art photographs, camera club pictures are valued within the social context of their production and use.

In our research we have examined the relationship between social organization and cultural production. The historical interconnections among amateur camera clubs, the developing fine art world of photography, and the photographic industry have shaped an emergent aesthetic code, maintained by the ongoing organization of amateur activity. The degree to which we were able to elucidate the nature of symbolic communications within this production context depended equally upon ethnographic data collection and historical research. Current communication activity is best understood when viewed simultaneously as part of a historical trajectory and as a part of ongoing social process. Our research suggests that more complex relationships, networks of influences, and mutual interdependencies fostering the diffusion of aesthetic codes await further investigation.

REFERENCES

1. Becker, H.S. *Art Worlds*. Berkeley: University of California Press, 1982.
2. Birdwhistell, R.L. *Kinesics and Context*. Philadelphia: University of Pennsylvania Press, 1970.
3. Cantor, M.G. *The Hollywood TV Producer*. New York: Basic Books, 1971.
4. Chalfen, R. "Tourist Photography." *Afterimage*, Summer 1980, pp. 26–29.
5. Christopherson, R.W. "Making Art With Machines: Photography's Institutional Inadequacies." *Urban Life and Culture* 3, April 1974, pp. 3–14.
6. Christopherson, R.W. "From Fold Art to Fine Art: A Transformation in the Meaning of Photographic Work." *Urban Life and Culture* 3, July 1974, pp. 123–157.
7. Denisoff, S. *Solid Gold*. New Brunswick, NJ: Transaction, 1975.
8. DiMaggio, P., and P.M. Hirsch. "Production Organizations in the Arts." *American Behavioral Scientist* 19, 1976, pp. 735–752.
9. Gans, H.J. *Deciding What's News*. New York: Vintage Books, 1979.
10. Gernsheim, H., and A. Gernsheim. *The History of Photography*. London: Oxford University Press, 1955.
11. Griffin, M. "What Young Filmmakers Learn from Television: A Study of Structure in Films Made by Children." *Journal of Broadcasting and Electronic Media* 29 (1), Winter 1985, pp. 79–92.
12. Griffin, M., B. Sutton-Smith, and F. Eadie. "Filmmaking by 'Young Filmmakers.' " *Studies in Visual Communication* 9 (4), Fall 1983, pp. 65–75.
13. Gross, L. "Art as the Communication of Competence." *Social Science Information* 12 (5), 1973, pp. 115–141.
14. Hirsch, J. *Family Photographs: Content, Meaning and Effect*. New York: Oxford University Press, 1981.
15. Hirsch, P.M. *The Structure of the Popular Music Industry*. Ann Arbor: University of Michigan Institute for Social Research, 1960.
16. Jeffrey, I. *Photography: A Concise History*. New York: Oxford University Press, 1981.
17. Jenkins, R.V. *Images and Enterprise: Technology and the American Photographic Industry 1839 to 1925*. Baltimore, MD: The Johns Hopkins University Press, 1975.
18. "At Last: Looking Ahead." *Lens' on Campus* 6 (6), Nov. 1984. Hearst Business Communications, Inc.
19. Miles, M. "Hints for Amateurs." *International Annual of Anthony's Photographic Bulletin*, Vol. 6 for 1894.
20. Musello, C. "Studying the Home Mode: An Exploration of Family Photography and Visual Communication." *Studies in Visual Communication* 6 (1), Spring 1980, pp. 23–42.
21. Newhall, B. *The History of Photography: From 1839 to the Present Day*. New York: The Museum of Modern Art, 1964. (Revised Edition, 1982).
22. Peterson, C.A. *Pictorialism in America: The Minneapolis Salon of Photography*. Minneapolis, MN: Minneapolis Institute of Arts, 1983.
23. Peterson, R.A. "Cycles in Symbol Production: The Case of Popular Music." *American Sociological Review* 40, April 1975, pp. 158–173.
24. Phillips, C. "The Judgment Seat of Photography." *October* 22, Fall 1982, pp. 27–63.
25. Rosenblum, B. *Photographers at Work: A Sociology of Photographic Styles*. New York: Holmes & Meier Publishers, 1978.

26. Schwartz, D.B. "Toward a Developmental Sociology of Art." Unpublished Master's Thesis. Annenberg School of Communications, University of Pennsylvania, 1979.
27. Schwartz, D.B. "Camera Clubs and Fine Art Photography: Distinguishing Between Art and Amateur Activity." Unpublished Doctoral Dissertation, Annenberg School of Communications, University of Pennsylvania, 1983.
28. Stebbins, R.A. *Amateurs: On the Margin Between Work and Leisure.* Beverly Hills, CA: Sage, 1979.
29. Taft, R. *Photography and the American Scene: A Social History, 1839-1889.* New York: Dover, 1979.
30. Tuchman, G. *Making News: A Study in the Construction of Reality.* New York: Free Press, 1978.
31. Worth, S. "Toward an Ethnographic Semiotic." Paper delivered to introduce a conference on "Utilisation de L'ethnologie par le Cinema/Utilisation du Cinema par L'Ethnologie," Paris, UNESCO, February, 1977.
32. Worth, S., and J. Ruby."The American Community's Socialization to Pictures: An Ethnography of Visual Communication (A Preproposal)." In S. Worth, *Studying Visual Communication.* Philadelphia: University of Pennsylvania, pp. 200-203.
33. Yochelson, B. "Clarence H. White Reconsidered: An Alternative to the Modernist Aesthetic of Straight Photography." *Studies in Visual Communication* 9 (4), Fall 1983, pp. 24-44.

Chapter 11

Thrashing in the Pit: An Ethnography of San Francisco Punk Subculture[1]

James Lull

Department of Theatre Arts
San Jose State University

Young people came to San Francisco with flowers in their hair in the 1960s. Now it's a place to go with a dog collar around your neck. This special city is a magnet for the unique and disenfranchised, a promise of hope for those who seek a new and better way — immigrants from Mexico, El Salvador, Nicaragua, and the rest of Central America, Asians from the entire Pacific Basin, young Europeans, American intellectuals and poets, Midwesterners, gays, young runaways, and others looking for a fresh start in an exciting and aesthetically unsurpassed urban setting.

Unconventional lifestyles are not merely tolerated in San Francisco, they are expected. It was strange, then, that when the punk uprising began in England, Europe, and the Eastern United States in the middle and late 1970s, San Francisco was not one of the cities in which the "scene" developed quickly. Perhaps it was because the apparent ideology and lifestyles of punks was inconsistent with the peace and love, flower-children image that had been cultivated so tenderly in this city during the previous two decades. Things have changed now. The punk movement has become more prominent in "the city" in recent years, and this deviant community is one among few visible entities to offer some form of resist-

[1]The author wishes to express thanks to Philip Wander and Michael Marx for critical readings of previous drafts of the text. Special thanks is given to Michelle Wolf for her extremely valuable help in collecting data during the early stages of the investigation and for her insightful comments on the punk phenomenon in San Francisco. Several numbers of the punk community, especially my chief informant "Christy," were instrumental in helping me understand the subculture. Limitations on the length of the manuscript preclude a lengthy discussion of the methodological aspects of the study. A summary of the method employed in this research is available from the author.

ance to the status quo, suggesting, not just alternative personal appearance, but ways of thinking that are far more complicated than they appear to be.

In this essay I will try to explain what the punk subculture of San Francisco represents. This article is one product of many years of study of the punk subculture in England, Europe, and the United States and, particularly, of a 2-month ethnographic investigation of the punk situation in San Francisco, where I live. The data result from hundreds of hours of participant observation and interviewing in the locations where punks congregate—the places they live, eat, hang out, and attend music shows. One emphasis of this writing is on the communication of the punk subculture—including both the domains of symbolic interaction, where so many of their images are nurtured, and the social processes that constitute their modes for living. Punk communication is reported and interpreted in the natural contexts of its occurrence, giving rise to the discussion of philosophical and practical exigencies that bear upon or help define the subculture.

DEFINING PUNK

The term "punk" had connotations in the United States long before the movement developed. It has always meant something negative: "He's just a punk kid." Or, "I'm feeling kind of punk today." The traditional primary reference for "punk" has been in terms of a feeling or attitude, rather than an appearance. That distinction still has merit. One member of the subculture said that punk is "a state of mind . . . it's the way you think." How can one punk tell if someone else belongs to the subculture? One girl said it is possible "by the vibes you pick up." In San Francisco, at least, the subculture is a kind of community, and many members know each other. Besides providing an ideological resting place for alternative-thinking people and an agent of expression to the uncovered, punk is a friendship space, a network of people, most of them very young, who develop relationships with others based on shared sentiments and community activity. Defining the subculture, therefore, is an exercise in pragmatism for those who engage. Authorities from the straight world and certain street inhabitants may view the subculture as deviant, disrespectful, sick, or weird. Persons having some connection with the music industry may see the subculture as a resource for new material or as a subgroup of potential consumers. People who define themselves as punk may see each other as members of a special minority of correct thinkers who offer the warmth of friendship and the possibility for creative and interesting social interactions.

Without question, the punk community is diverse and, naturally enough, the label is insufficient. Nonetheless, shared characteristics of all those who are considered here to be punks are at least: anger, expressionism, unconventional appearance, and a preference for what can be loosely-termed "nontraditional" rock and roll music. Another feature that sometimes characterizes punk is a focused resistance to the politics and economics of the dominant culture, but, as will be discussed in detail later, there are significant distinctions to be made here between punks and "skinheads," a group that is generally considered to be part of the larger movement. Differences between members of the subculture are sometimes extreme. One punk said, "We might look the same to outsiders, but there are big differences between us."

Level of ideological commitment does not define a punk. While San Francisco punk bands like the Dead Kennedys and The Dicks proselytize from the stage about political issues, punks on the street may define the subculture other ways. One 19-year-old told me: "Punk is getting fucked up and having fun. That's what it is. That's all it is." Another Mohawked young man said that members of the subculture can be identified, not by their commitment to any set of ideas, but by their willingness to dance in the punk style. Others claim that it is a "way of living" and has nothing to do with appearance or dance style.

Although it may not be posssible to determine exactly who is part of the subculture (a problem not peculiar to this group, of course), authenticity is valued. Two types of people that may appear to the outsider to be punks are strongly disliked by members of the subculture. The first of these is "new wavers," also sometimes called "punkers." These are people who try to look like punks, and often buy expensive "punk chic" clothing in fancy stores. They may also be high school boys and girls who use their allowances to buy punk outfits and to attend punk concerts, but are entirely dependent on and responsible to their parents. The second group not recognized as punks are rock and roll artists or bands that have become commercially successful, turning their backs on their punk origins. The prime example is Billy Idol, a solo artist now who previously helped form the British band Generation X (also known as "Gen X"). His case is particularly troublesome to the punks since the ideology expressed in his early work is completely contradicted by his metamorphosis, a commodification of the punk ethic. One of the first songs recorded by Gen X is "Promises," with lyrics such as:

Our hair was short, we said what we thought
We'd never be scared, never be bored.
Never sell out like they did, they did.

Since the creation of this song, Billy Idol has become a major recording artist, having made a fortune with songs such as "Dancing with Myself," "Rebel Yell," and "Flesh for Fantasy." He is a major figure on MTV Music Television with his videos of these and other songs. Commercial success is unacceptable within the punk community. Even the local Dead Kennedys are faulted by some of the punks for their financial earnings, though the band has actually made very little money.

Authentic punks are extremely aware of the new hard-edged music, and various subdivisions within the subculture are demarcated by preferences for particular groups. The concept of a "band" is crucial to punk, focusing on a community of singers and players rather than a solo artist. Unlike other genres, there are no real punk "stars," although lead singers have become well-known from the very first punk bands (Johhny Rotten of the Sex Pistols: Joe Strummer of the Clash) and this popularization continues in the United States today (e.g., Jello Biafra of the Dead Kennedys; Lee Ving of Fear; Henry Rollins of Black Flag). Still, as will be discussed later, punk groups are the essential unit.

Fine discriminations can be made among the punk groups and their followers. Punk types are defined by particular bands. The young history of punk still lives, and a profound reverence is expressed for "Original Punk" or "77 Punk," a reference to the first well-known punk bands from England, especially the Sex Pistols and the Clash. Many punks continue to listen to this "old" music. The first albums made by these bands have become classics within the community and, to a certain degree, American punk bands have all been influenced by them. The Clash and members of the Sex Pistols continue to make music in the mid-1980s, but these modern groups do not have the same respect that the original bands commanded. In fact, wearing a new Clash t-shirt would probably signal lack of commitment to punk among the more dedicated current members of the subculture.

A more contemporary offshoot of the founding British punk bands is "oi" or "British hardcore" bands often associated with the Skinhead movement there and here. Bands in this category include Cockney Rejects, Screwdriver, Business, and the Foreskins. In the United States, "thrash" bands such as D.R.I. or "American hardcore" groups such as M.D.C., Minor Threat, and Straight Edge create the fastest, most aggressive-sounding music within the genre.

In San Francisco, the "peace punk" bands such as Crass (a British group), Crucifix, and the Dicks have become a distinct component of the punk scene. There is a "psychedelic punk" movement represented by one of the most talented bands, the Butthole Surfers. And there is "Rasta Punk," owing to the Jamaican Rastafarian subculture; "funk punk," claiming a rhythm and blues base; and "punk funk," music created by black artisits such as Rick James owing primarily to the influence of white punk music. The subtleties of these music subdivisions represent real ideological layers within the punk subculture. Considerations having to do with varying orientations toward ideological issues will be raised in the following sections of this paper. The punk subculture is a complicated and heterogenous sociocultural phenomenon that cannot be understood easily.

THE PUNK LIFESTYLE

In the following paragraphs, descriptions of aspects of typical punk life will be made. Of course, there are punks who do not participate in all the activities mentioned below or hold attitudes exactly consistent with what is described here. Nonetheless, the behavior outlined in this section is representative of a great many San Francisco punks, particularly those that are the more authentic members of the subculture.

Appearance. There are no uniform requirements. Some of the more stereotypical appearances hold true: short hair, often shaved on the sides to approximate a Mohawk look, shaved altogether, or very short with a shock of hair at the front only, a common cut for girls. A moustache or beard is normally out of place, as is extremely long hair or sideburns. Coloring the hair is common, so long as it doesn't look like it was contrived in a beauty salon. There are the more extreme styles, where locks of hair stand straight up from the top of the head.

Clothing. Generally, clothes are not colorful or fancy in any normal sense of fashion. Authentic punk clothing is shabby and often torn. It is practical. There is a strong military and leather influence. Colors, then, are often green, black, grey, and other subdued shades. Like young people everywhere, lots of punks wear Levi's and other denim clothing. Shoes are inexpensive tennis shoes or boots, sometimes military boots, worn especially by the Skinheads.

Although the basic clothing is simple, the appearance given off is disturbing to some people outside the subculture. The extreme punk appearance is typically created by unusual hairstyles together with the jewelry and other acoutrements that are often worn. Common forms of jewelry are metal and leather items placed everywhere on the body. Dog chains and collars are worn around the neck and wrists. Metal belts are draped around the stomach or buttocks.

Punks often write slogans representing their political positions, cultural attitudes, or music preferences on their skin and clothing. Tattoos are common, among the Skinheads especially. Often the tattoos are placed in visible places, such as the hands, neck, or face.

Punks write things on their clothing. During the course of my observations, it was clear that most of the phrases written on shirts, jackets, and pants were political messages, sometimes original, at other times quoting the lyrics of punk songs that have political connotations. The most common phrase, for example, is "Fight War, Not Wars," an expression that can be found written on the clothing of dozens, if not hundreds, of San Francisco punks. Other common inscriptions are: "Amnesty International," "Support Nicaragua," "Part-time Christians," "Drunk and Disorderly," "Grim Coexistence," "No Future," "What Are We Going to Do?" and "Reagan for Shah." Often, the logos of favorite bands appear, or lyrics from punk songs such as "No War, No KKK, No Fascist USA."

The writing on the clothing is self-made. Punks generally don't wear buttons or badges; they are more likely to inscribe sentiments directly onto the surface of clothing with a marking pen. The overall effect of this is a "busy" appearance.

The most common insignias worn are Christian crosses and Nazi crosses and swastikas. Crosses are often worn as earrings, especially by men. The more shocking or original, the better. While punks downplay traditional concern for stylized appearances, there is a value placed on looking a certain way. Nonetheless, the overall look is unsexy and frumpy. One common style is to wear a jacket or shirt tied around the waist in the front, with the body of the shirt covering the buttocks. As part of the parody that punks engage in, eye makeup is often worn at night by men when they attend music shows.

Living quarters. Members of the subculture may share an apartment, live at home, or "squat" in abandoned buildings. Squatting is part of the authentic punk commitment—living with minimal constraints. It has also become a controversial issue in the city as police attempt to remove squatters from their homes, creating considerable media coverage.

The concept of squatting and "squatters' rights" is ideologically attuned to the punk movement. The punk music community has supported squatters by playing benefit shows to raise money in the city's "rock against rent" campaign. Members of many of the punk bands are squatters themselves. To live in a squat is one respected measure of true commitment to the punk lifestyles.

The San Francisco punks are organized in their effort to find buildings in which to live for free. The political activists within the movement typically locate buildings that can be used. This is done by driving around in a car looking for apparently abandoned buildings, or checking out leads that someone has given them. A list is made of candidates. The best places are then checked again by walking the neighborhood, noting access routes to the building, and determining the likelihood of trouble with the neighbors.

Various members of the subculture have special talents that are useful for making the squats livable. Screwdrivers, bolt cutters, and crowbars are passed among the various informal groups that are trying to break into a building. Electricity, gas, and water can be turned on with the tools in many cases. Punks and other street people who occupy the squats move their few belongings into the building and set up their living spaces.

An effort is made to match the potential squatter with the squat. At one squatters' meeting, a spokesperson reported the availability of a new squat and suggested that "Albert is the best person for that squat. No offense, but a punk (reference to appearance only) can't go there. Albert is mellow, low key. He goes to school a lot. He's a very respectable person."

When new buildings are located, a small number of squatters will move in, followed during next days and weeks by others who hear of the availability of a building. Punks are extremely willing to admit new people into the squat, so long as they are "cool" and don't create scenes that will get the entire group evicted or arrested. There have been numerous busts during the past year in San Francisco by the police, uprooting the living quarters of many punks.

Punks are not the only ones who live in squats. At one squatters' meeting, a 50-year-old man looked around at the group and said, "Beatniks, hippies, and punks. We're all here." The common bond among squatters is their homeless state. Also, there are separate squats for women and men in some cases, and other distinctions that may keep Skinheads or others out who disrupt things.

Food. Again, some punks may live in situations where food is provided, like their parents' home or school dormitories. For the street punk without a job, of course, finding food is a major task for survival. There are at least seven places in San Francisco that serve free and nutritious food for homeless people. Punks eat at these places regularly. A *Diner's Guide to Free Food in San Francisco* has been published, and is often consulted. This publication lists the primary places where people can eat for free in the city, including the addresses and menus of the most popular spots. Often these kitchens are located in churches or temples (e.g., St. Anthony's, Krishna Temple, One Mind Temple). The diner's guide notes when a mandatory sermon is served along with the food. Some places are recommended for lunch; others for dinner. Some places are good on weekends; others during the week. In one case, showers can be had in the same building where food is served, and this place will also do a small amount of daily laundry for anyone.

Punks become experts on food disposal. They don't always eat at the free food places, and often just pick up some day-old bread or bagels at small stores. Many punks know where and when the best food is thrown out.

Work. Meaningful employment among punks is rare. Many of them cannot find work, or can only find work that they sometimes term "exploitation jobs," where they are paid minimum wages or some small amount of money to work as "slaves" in a restaurant or some other demanding environment. There is little or no motivation to work in these conditions. Of course, the punk appearance is often discriminated against by employers, further limiting job possibilities.

School. Traditional forms of schooling are part of the dominant culture that this subculture resists. Nonetheless, many punks are young and may still attend high school. Some are enrolled in junior college or the local state college. The requirements placed on students, however, are not particularly agreeable to the punk lifestyle. The vast majority of street punks are not enrolled in school, and many of them are high school dropouts.

Religion. There is very little affiliation with traditional religion within the punk community, though a moral code that is based on the Judeo-Christian heritage is often observed. Some punks regard religion as a structural obstacle to personal and social fulfillment. One punk said, "Religion? No way. It's time to get off our knees!" Punk names and paraphenalia often incorporate religious artifacts. Two popular bands, for instance, are Bad Religion and Crucifix. As mentioned previously, the Christian cross is an icon that is often used for jewelry.

Money. There isn't much of it in the punk community. Money has negative ideological implications, but of course it is necessary for certain things, including bus rides and admission to many punk music shows (though not all, many punk shows are free). For punks who are politically oriented, money signifies what they are fundamentally opposed to—materialism. Punks generally have few possessions. One overheard conversation provides insight: "You know Debby and John have been making me a little sick lately. Did you see all that shit that they bought? I don't care where they got the money, I just care that, to begin with, that they even had the money. And then, what they spent it on. . . . Donna asked them for some money and they said they were flat broke. They're lying, and that's not good either."

Making money off the punk scene is always questionable, except for the bands, who are not faulted for this unless their profits become large (e.g. Billy Idol). Of course, the "punk look" has been picked up by department stores everywhere and marketed to other sectors of the public. An 18-year-old punk girl with a shaved head except for a long shock of hair falling in her face said, "If any fucker was making money off the way I look, I'd punch him in the mouth."

Drugs. All drugs, even the hardest ones, are generally acceptable. Alcohol is commonly consumed, especially by the Skinheads. Heroin, cocaine, barbituates, marijuana, and alcohol are all used by various members of the punk subculture, and it would be out of character for anyone to "come down" on someone else for their use of drugs. There is also a movement within the punk commmunity known as "straight edge," where the avoidance of drugs is advocated. Some San Francisco bands have taken this position.

Marijuana is an interesting case. This drug gained great popularity in the United States during the 1960s as part of what can be loosely termed the "hippie movement." It was often used by members of that generation to escape, or "get mellow." This orientation conflicts with the predisposition of most punks. A 19-year-old punk, Bill, explained that the problem does not reside with the drug itself: "Everybody smokes marijuana. It's the way they (the hippies) did it that's wrong. We don't believe in sitting in some field somewhere smoking a joint. You got to fight violence with violence." This man had attended a "marijuana march" during the previous summer in San Francisco where he and others openly smoked marijuana in defiance of the laws against it.

Marijuana has a tendency to make some of its users passive and accepting, a personal condition that runs counter to the general orientation of most punks. Jello Biafra, lead singer of the Dead Kennedys, has written a song titled "Drug Me" where he chastizes people who want to get "stoned out and just want to sit around and space out."

Gender relations. Like most subcultures based in part on rock music, punk is in many ways a male-dominated scene. The tough look of many punks and the strenuous dancefloor activity lacks a traditional female character. For that very reason, of course, some girls and young women are attracted to punk as an alternative to the sex-role behaviors they are expected to perform in American society. Nonetheless, the very essence of punk, its music, is extremely masculine. There are, for example, almost no female punk bands.

Females generally expect the males to be nonsexist. Sexism is an issue for most members of the punk community. Most punk girls do not dress in a way to be sexy. Bare legs are rarely shown. When skin is exposed, it usually is done in some mocking fashion. Females who enter into the punk scene expect to adopt nontraditional orientations toward their bodies. Lee Ving, the lead singer of the Los Angeles-based band Fear, announced a song this way at a show: "This next song is a love song. Ladies' choice. But first you have to make the choice to be a lady." Customary orientations toward gender are disrupted ideologically by punk.

Nonetheless, punk sex is almost exclusively heterosexual. Loving relationships form within the subculture, and sexual activity between members of the punk community is not much different than that between men and women of the same age who are not part of the subculture. The rough appearance of punks sometimes misleads observers into thinking that they are all engaged in some kind of bizarre sexual behavior. While some of them are, the numbers probably do not outweigh those who have similar orientations but are not punks. Normal sexual contact takes place within the punk community far more than do deviant forms. Although many men wear facial cosmetics and interact primarily with each other at shows, they are almost entirely heterosexual. Gays are barely noticeable on the scene. Skinheads are extremely opposed to gays, referring to them as "fags" in a very negative way.

Enemies of punks. There are categories of people that for one reason or another cause problems for the punks. These groups also occupy the streets, where they come in contact with the punks. In many cases, they are other oppressed minorities. Generally, the conflict that takes place between punks and others is a function of multiple occupancy of the street.

The most powerful and feared opponent is the San Francisco Police. Punks say that uniformed police often harrass them for their appearance or behavior, particularly loitering. Proprietors of shops and boutiques also sometimes telephone the police if they believe a congregation of punks near their place of business is hurting relations with potential customers. Police are also looking for runaways and they sometimes question punks about the whereabouts of young people reported to be in San Francisco. There have been numerous police busts of punk squats. Further, police and punks sometimes clash at the site of demonstrations. David, a 24-year-old punk, told the *San Francisco Chronicle* that a friend was beaten during a peaceful anti-war demonstration because the jacket he was wearing said "One Million Dead Cops," the name of a San Francisco punk band. Another Mohawked punk said he is routinely bothered by the police on the street because of his appearance. "I told the fucking police, okay, if you want to be macho, go ahead and beat me up."

Undercover police are spotted by the punks observing them whenever they try to organize something. Several punks said police watch from across the street at the Anarchist Book Store, one of the favorite hangouts, especially among the more politically active members of the subculture. The undercover police were not present one night when several of us met at the bookstore. One punk said: "No cops tonight. We must not be a problem. How do we know that we're not still a problem? Because we're still here. They waste people who are really causing them problems."

Punk girls in particular feel a lot of tension between themselves and young black males they encounter on the streets. The blacks often make derogatory comments about their appearance, referring to them as "dykes" or "boys." According to the girls, the young blacks cannot understand why they underplay their "feminimity." Several girls said that they think the blacks feel threatened by their lack of conformity to a sex-object stereotype.

Skinheads have been carrying on street warfare in San Francisco with the "Cholos," Mexican street gang members who are also sometimes violent. Other punks suffer from this conflict too, since the Cholos tend to categorize Skinheads together with other punk types.

Some people cause problems for punks at the music shows. In particular, "jocks" are cited by punks as causing problems since they confuse the hyperactive dance style of punk ("thrashing") with random violence. This gives the jocks a chance to "show off their muscles." Interestingly, it is difficult to tell punks from jocks sometimes, since they both typically wear short hair styles. Jocks have no commitment to the music or the ideology of the punk movement, and only participate during the shows. "Bikers" have also caused problems at the shows with displays of violence.

In general, the enemies of punks are males who are encountered in living environments. In no case was a group of females mentioned by the punks as their opponent, with the possible exception of the "imitators," who are just as likely to be female as male. The more abstract ideological competitors, businessmen and women, for instance, are not generally mentioned by the punks as their enemies. Their conflicts are generally related to the reality of the streets and to those who share or monitor the passageways of the urban environment.

PUNK MUSIC

This is the primary aspect of the subculture. Punk records, tapes, and especially the live shows are central to the movement, serving the same basic purposes that music has performed for countless cultural groups in the past. Punk music reinforces the ideological tenets and the aesthetic characteristics of the subculture to its own members. At the same time, the music is an agent of expression to the outside world. Special attention will be paid in this section to the functions of music for members of the punk subculture, with special emphasis on the role of the live show and the form of physical expression that punks engage in while listening to live music in public—thrashing.

Punk music was from the outset a reaction against mainstream forms of rock and roll music in England and the United States (1, 2, 3). The idea behind punk is that anybody can make music, and they should. A punk performer is not a rock star, a concept that will be discussed in considerable detail later. Punk bands are composed of members of the subculture who happen to play instruments or sing.

Nonetheless, the bands that get the most attention within the punk community are the ones that achieve critical success with good songs, tight arrangements, vocal harmonizing, solos, and some other features that original punk avoided. There are anthem songs that have been created by the original British punk bands, but also by American groups such as the Dead Kennedys (considered by many to be this country's most important punk band), Fear, the Circle Jerks, and Black Flag, among others. Punk music sounds like fast, unmelodic shouting to many outsiders, but punks immediately recognize their favorite songs and have often committed all the lyrics to memory, not unlike a teenager who learns all the words to Michael Jackson's music. It must be made clear that punk is simply a slightly different genre of music, a subset of rock and roll, that should not be judged negatively because of its sound. Most important, the driving energy of punk music reflects the activist orientation of the subculture.

In that sense, punk music strongly reinforces the lifestyle decisions that punks have made. It legitimizes the subculture for its adherents, providing an ideological base for members. At a more mundane level, it gives punks something to do that they identify with and enjoy. One punk said that the music "gives me an opportunity to meet the right people." When punk shows are presented in the city, especially the large, outdoor events, people who are attracted to the punk scene can meet each other. In this sense, punk music serves the same social purpose as classical music concerts, or art galleries, or libraries, for people with other lifestyle orientations.

The uses of music within the microsocial realities of punks is not much different from uses made by occupants of other social situations, except that it may be used more frequently. People who are attracted to the punk scene have often been introduced to it through music. Punks, therefore, are often more involved with music in various ways in their lives than are others who are less oriented toward music generally.

The uses of music by youth have been documented elsewhere (4). They include: background noise, dancing, lessening inhibitions, distraction, asserting personality and image, getting attention and approval, alienating parents and other authority figures, escape from reality, diversion, establishing and changing moods, enhancing or intensifying a variety of activities including sexual behavior and private moments of introspection, covering up other sounds in the environment, reality exploration, stimulating fantasies, passing time, companionship, relaxing, general entertainment, peer group acceptance and reinforcement, conversational topics, the physiological buzz of loud sound, and reminiscing. All of these uses apply to punks as well as to others. Certain uses of music are central to the punk lifestyle.

The angry sound of much punk reflects and stimulates the subculture's critical orientation. Themes of punk songs typically concern social or political problems rather than personal relationships. Punks say that they learn a lot from their music. The lyrics, easily overlooked by those outside the movement because of the harsh textures of the songs, are important to many members of the subculture. Punks claim that lyrics "teach me a lot" or "make me more politically aware." One punk said "We know Reagan sucks but we need to find out why. The songs teach reasons why." A 23-year-old female said that "you don't just go buy an album, you buy information."

What would happen to the punk movement if there was no music? "There would be a major breakdown. I wouldn't meet people. I'd be bored," according to a 17-year-old. Another claimed that music gives him a chance to meet people "who aren't mindless." Another said that "music is an important thing to share. That's what we believe in, sharing . . . sharing even with people who are not punks . . . when I talk about this it seems trivial. It is *not* trivial. It's who we all are, music."

The agitated beat of punk music stimulates many young men and women to get out their hostilities or aggressions by listening to it or by thrashing at the shows. This is regarded by many of them as a kind of cathartic experience where violent reactions to the world around them can be expressed, but no one gets hurt by it.

Nearly everyone has immediate access to music. In the living environments, particularly the squats, access takes the form of tape recorders and tapes that have been duplicated at little cost from albums. Punk musicians often practice in the squats. There is a rather constant presence of music in the living situations, creating a problem for those who want to sleep. A resident of a squat said, "The only real decision that I have to make is whether or not to play this or that. Like, some people I live with just don't want to hear hardcore in the early morning."

The shows. Punk music shows are given in a variety of venues in the Bay Area. Many of them are simple warehouses that are rented or otherwise expropriated for the occasion. Larger gatherings take place outdoors. Often the shows are given in conjunction with some political demonstration. Shows are basic to the punk subculture.

The most popular site for the presentation of punk music, however, is Broadway Street in San Francisco's famous North Beach area. One of the first clubs to put on punk shows there, On Broadway, has since changed to a gay bar. Now, the place to go is Mabuhay Gardens, a Filipino-owned and managed establishment that serves Asian cuisine in the early evening, then changes into a punk rock club for music in the late hours every night. Across the street and one block down is The Stone, a fancier location that books various shows, including punk.

Broadway Street is a spectacle. Punks, tourists, fashion elites in fancy cars, beggars, and every other type of person can be found on this street. Mabuhay (pronounced Ma-boo-high) Gardens is in the midst of it. Neon signs, hookers, drug dealers, and fancy restaurants all impinge on the senses here. A live sex show featuring "Hot Spanking and Nightmare Bondage" and "San Francisco's Hottest Male Strip Show" are presented in clubs nearby. Across the street is the Chi-Chi Club, that advertises itself as the city's "most elegant night club." Two doors away is a hole-in-the-wall Mexican restaurant. A video arcade and amusement center is next door to Mabuhay on one side, and a valet parking lot is situated on the other side. Punks by the dozens, sometimes by the hundreds, mill around outside the club every night, with the largest gatherings on the weekends. An alley separates the nightclub from the amusement arcade, and this area is used for private conversations, sexual fondling, fighting, and urination, in addition to its original purpose, the loading and unloading of supplies and materials for the club, including band equipment.

In front of the club, the manager walks around, quietly picking up bottles and gently encouraging the punks not to loiter so that the police won't close the club down. The sidewalk in front of Mabuhay Gardens is a regular meeting place for San Francisco's punks. Many of them cannot afford to attend the shows priced at six or seven dollars on weekends. Many try to enter the club without paying, either by claiming to know somebody in one of the bands, or by rushing past the ticket taker. The cost of entry promotes a form of violence at the door that continues throughout the night. While most punks appreciate the venue as an outlet for their music, someone has written "same old shit" under the sign that announces "Tonight's Bill:". It is not unusual to see some fighting and lots of mock fighting in front of the club. Punks sometimes pass out there too, usually reacting to too much alcohol or drug consumption.

The Stone is a different scene. This club has no commitment to punk rock, and puts on concerts that its owners believe will make money regardless of the kind of music. During the observation period, bands or artists ranging from the Dead Kennedys to Jerry Garcia (singer and guitarist of the Grateful Dead, the king of hippie music) and the Plimsouls (innocuous Los Angeles pop artists) all appeared at The Stone. Unlike the stark and dirty interior of Mabuhay Gardens, The Stone has fancier tables and decorations and very straight-appearing cocktail waitresses. Bouncers regulate the line in front of the club so that people don't stand in front of neighboring stores. In this way, punks are arranged by the club's management into neat groups as they await entrance to the club, a curious posture for this disorderly subculture. At the door is a sign that announces: "No cameras, no tape recorders, no spikes, no skateboards." None of those items is prohibited at "the Mab." Punks under 21 are admitted to this club, but they must purchase a mandatory soft drink at $1.50 above the admission price of $7.00 for most shows. These requirements are extremely irritating to the punks, who yell and gesture disapprovingly outside.

Punk shows are unique. People who attend them for the first time sometimes are alarmed by the intensity of the performances and the forms of physical expression that accompany the music. The two most common distinguishing characteristics are thrashing and stage diving. When punk bands play, many audience members assemble in the middle of the floor (the pit) and take part in a group activity ("slamming" or, more generally, "thrashing") that may or may not be considered a dance. Everyone who takes part begins to move around in a circle, much like they would at a skating rink. When the music goes very fast, the group moves rapidly, with some participants occasionally falling to the floor.

Punk shows are a masculine scene. Very few females brave the activity near the stage or in the pit. This is a major difference between punk and other forms of rock and roll, where girls typically get as close to the stage as possible to admire the boys in the band. Audiences for the Beatles or contemporary likenesses such as Duran Duran are comprised of completely different kinds of people who behave in a much different way.

There are no special effects at punk shows. It's absolutely unthinkable, for instance, that the lighting would constantly change or cast multiple colors on the bandmembers, or that a solo spotlight would illuminate one of the players. Rock conventions such as smoke bombs or macho-strutting are not present.

At a good show, there is an extreme sense of chaos on stage and in the pit. Band members and audience members throw themselves off the stage into the crowd, while others churn around the pit in an aggressive motion that often terrifies those seeing it for the first time. Others stand around the periphery of the pit, or further back where they can listen and view. Punk shows are a spectacle of sound and sight. There is a normal amount of socializing that goes on away from the pit. The shows bring together lots of members of the punk community in a kind of communal celebration of the subculture, but punks mingle with nonpunks here too. On the weekends, there are always a large number of new wavers who show up. Modern-day hippies and other street people are also attracted to punk shows, as are various curious onlookers, some of whom become disgusted by the scene and leave.

There is a great deal of mockery within the subculture, and some forms of it become apparent at the shows. Punks push and shove each other a lot, on the streat and in the pit, but they almost always mean no harm by it, and to perceive this activity as a fight is incorrect. Most of it is a mocking of machismo. Similarly, a punk guitar player might play his instrument with his teeth for a moment as a way to mock the self-indulgent stage displays that some guitarists from nonpunk rock bands create.

Performer–Audience Relationship. One of the fundamental philosophical tenets of punk life can be noted by observing the relationship between punk bands and their audiences during performances. Despite the importance of live performance, the formalities and expectations of the rock "concert" are not in evidence at punk "shows." Normal rock concerts are one-way affairs. Audience members buy a ticket that entitles them to an assigned seat in a large hall. In other cases, the "festival seating" arrangement, ticketholders stand on the floor and face the stage, perhaps moving around a bit in place but not dancing or interacting in any way with other spectators. At punk shows, the distance between creator and consumer of the music is lessened greatly. Band members are expected not to act as if they are somehow better than their audiences.

There are several indications of this unique relationship. To begin with, audience members do not applaud when the band comes on stage. Even the most popular punk bands do not elicit an ovation. There is no pretense of stardom. When the Dead Kennedys were late arriving on stage, for instance, one of the stage hands grabbed the microphone and explained that one of the band members "was taking a shit," and could everybody hold on for a second?

There is very little applause given by the audience after each song, or even after the show is over. Punk bands rarely are asked or are willing to perform an encore. When the crowd applauded the Butthole Surfers, the guitarist yelled loudly, "Shut up!" When the applause continued, he yelled, "Shut up!" again. One audience member yelled, "Buttholes . . . buttholes" at the band after each song. In days past, bands and audiences spat at each other during shows.

After performing, members of the "opening" bands walk around the hall, mixing with the audience members, many of whom are their friends. There are no "rock star" pretenses. As soon as the band Detox finished its set at the Mabuhay, the bass player unplugged his instrument and put it in a case. This is unlike most rock bands, where the players leave the stage after putting their instruments down while some hired hand comes out to remove them and put them away.

Set-up time on stage for each band is very short. In rock concert situations, the amount of time taken to get the instruments on stage and to perform a sound check is long, serving in part to create an air of expectation among the spectators. This formality is not part of punk, caused partly by the simple set-up required by punk bands, but also by the subcultural rule that does not permit the creation of unnecessary distance between the performer and the audience member.

One signature characteristic of punk shows is the interaction of the band and the audience on stage. In overt defiance of the norm for rock concerts, audience members are permitted to jump on the stage and dance around, even touch the band members harmlessly, and then dive back into the audience. Similarly, band members sometimes jump into the crowd during songs. In this way the distinction between artist and audience member is broken during the subculture's definitive moment—the live performance, suggesting an ideological orientation toward human equality that is not so strongly felt in other concert situations. This behavior is called "stage diving."

Stage diving is one of the more shocking aspects of the live show. From the back of the room, it appears that people who throw themselves off the stage will be badly hurt when they land on the floor. Some stage divers take swan dives or do backflips off the stage into the crowd. But the divers are rarely hurt. They are caught by fellow audience members and either gently released to the floor or hurled back onto the stage where the act is repeated sometimes several times over.

Stage hands or security police do not show anger toward the divers except in very unusual circumstances. When one bouncer at The Stone needlessly applied a lot of force to remove one of the stage dancers, he was immediately reprimanded by a senior employee. The rules for stage dancing and diving are understood by the participants—band members, audience members, security guards.

During the Dead Kennedys show, a young blonde punk dove from the stage and fell to the floor, hitting his head and knocking himself unconscious. Jello Biafra stopped the show after completing a song, and asked for someone to attend to the boy. He then told the crowd, "When somebody jumps off the stage, fucking catch them! This isn't the seventies, you know. This isn't a fucking fern bar. We've got to help each other." This example illustrates one of the defining characteristics of the San Francisco punk subculture, the importance of cooperation and unity in the face of whatever struggles are encountered. Imagine the trust that exists in the minds of stage divers as they hurl themselves backwards into the crowd.

The overall feeling that is created at the shows is a collective expression of subcultural values through the production of live music. Punk shows are highly communal. An 18-year-old punk girl said that "the bands don't play *for* you, or anyone. They are right there *with* you. It's your show. You know, it's a very communal experience, like our living situation and general views of life." Perceptions of the meaning of the shows differ greatly for members of the subculture, in comparison to views likely to be held by an outside observer.

Thrashing. Punks don't usually say that they want to go dancing. They want to "thrash" or "slam," a physical activity that bears some resemblances to traditional forms of dancing, but has some distinct characteristics that separate it from most conceptions of dance.

Participation in thrashing is one measure of belonging to the subculture. The thrashing ritual accompanies virtually every punk music show. Thrashing is an extremely physical activity that many punks say helps them get out their aggresson—a means for channeling their anger. A 23-year-old punk male from the Noe Valley area said, "it's been a rough week. I think on Friday I'll go to the Mab to let go. I really should go sooner, someplace. I need to thrash."

Like stage diving, thrashing has a violent appearance to it, but in reality very little physical damage is experienced by thrashers. There are no steps to learn. Recalling the previous discussion, people who participate congregate in the middle of the floor ("pit") and begin to move around in a counter-clockwise circle to the beat of the music. It's a group experience. No one dances *with* anyone else, although a common style is for one person to climb onto the back of another and join in "piggyback." The normal rules for social dancing are broken. Everyone moves around in the circle on their own terms, usually with arms held at chest level for protection. The overall feeling is of a churning union of everyone in the pit. Thrashers have the right of way on the floor. No one else should expect to stand in the vicinity of the pit unless they are willing to be run over by the group.

Thrashers usually just walk in a kind of possessed way around the circle, sometimes ramming into people in front of them, often falling to the floor. A thrasher does not become angry if contact causes him or her to fall to the ground. The person who causes another to fall has an obligation, however, to assist the fallen individual to his or her feet. Similarly, if a thrasher collides with an onlooker on the periphery of the pit, it is acceptable for the bystander to shove the thrasher back into the churning flow of bodies. If the thrasher falls because of the shove, the bystander must then rush to the floor and pick the person up. That way it is clear that no harmful behavior was intended.

Some thrashers, and stage divers too, engage in a stylized motion that is known as "shanking." This distinctive movement is characterized by a rhythmic flailing of the arms in front of the body while moving forward. Shanking is an audience behavior that typically accompanies reggae and ska music, an inherited dance style that originated with black listeners in Jamaica and London. The punk adaptation is a kind of extreme swimming motion.

There is a lot of feigned hostility in this ritual. Thrashers may push and shove each other, but the whole scene is a parody of violence. An important rule in this situation is that physical contact is *not* to be taken personally. Thrashing is an extreme violation of our culturally conditioned sense of personal space. When thrashing, you may be hit by another thrasher/ slammer at any time from almost any direction. It is not acceptable to become angry by this contact, and veteran thrashers appear to barely notice the source of the contact. They simply bounce in whatever direction they are pushed, perhaps ram into someone there and bounce off them, and keep bouncing and churning around in a circle until they are exhausted. The pit belongs to everyone. No one invokes any sense of territoriality, an attitude that runs counter to most of our social behavior, including other forms of dance, though it is not clear that "thrashing" is a dance. One does not "do the thrash."

Even under the most controlled and nonviolent conditions, thrashing, stage diving, and activity in the pit in general has a thoroughly masculine feeling to it. When girls or young women take to the floor they abide by rules that are informally instituted and reinforced by males. Often it is difficult to tell who the girls in the pit are, since they dress in a way that is not much different from the males. They are just as vulnerable to physical contact as anyone, and since no one is looking to see who is in front of them, they are rammed just as often as males when thrashing, fall to the floor, and receive no more attention because of their sex. Girls who stage dive, on the other hand, typically do so far more tentatively than boys. They usually ease themselves rather than throw themselves wildly off the stage into the audience. Unlike other forms of social "dance," thrashing and stage diving is done with no apparent sense of sexual coyness or attempts to gain attention from the opposite sex. The crowd in the pit is comprised of more than 90% males at a typical show. Sexuality and individual expression are downplayed. Thrashers obviously enjoy what they are doing, as they often smile broadly during the activity. One punk said that thrashing is a kind of sport: "It's a little like football without the footballs."

Media habits. Punk is not a homogenous subculture, so it is difficult to generalize about activity so broad as the exposure, consumption, and use of the mass media. There are some observations that can be made, however, particularly with respect to specialty media or programming from mainstream media that is useful to punks.

Television is least useful to the subculture. There is almost no programming on television that is of interest to punks, and some of them see the medium as an agent of cultural domination. Television viewing is considered to be passive activity, a medium "for sheep," according to one person. Mainstream radio stations do not play punk music, and members of the subculture are unlikely to appreciate other genres of music for any sustained period of time. There is a new wave rock radio station in San Francisco, KQAK ("The Quake"), but the music played is not hardcore enough for the punks. Rock music that makes a lot of money is suspect, and songs that are rotated regularly on commercial radio stations do not gain approval. During the Dead Kennedys' show, an audience member jumped onto the stage and took over one of the microphones between songs. He began to sing several verses to some unidentifiable song. After permitting him this access to the microphone, Jello Biafra took the mike back and mockingly said, "Wow, you should try out for the Psychedelic Furs!" a very popular English new wave pop band. The new music channels on television are also unacceptable to many punks. The Dead Kennedys have a song called "MTV, Get Off the Air!"

There are some opportunities for meaningful communication within the punk community on radio in San Francisco. The Jesuit school, the University of San Francisco, has a low-power, "alternative" radio station, KUSF, that plays mainly punk and other avant-garde music. A famous public radio station in Berkeley, KPFK, devotes 2 hours of programming on Tuesday night to punk music and information. Sunday night specialty programming on KQAK features some punk and reggae music.

Low cost print media are the more common instruments for the dissemination of information within the punk community. Print media connect punks of various cities and countries together, and also are used locally for spreading information about political issues, rallies and demonstrations, and music shows. Street media such as flyers and low cost "fanzines" (black and white magazines that concern punk music and other aspects of the subculture) are commonly distributed among the community. Punks carry these items around with them and share with their friends. They are trusted sources of information.

Money should not be made off the publication of these alternative media either. The editor of a 30-page political booklet concerning issues relevant to the punk community was chastized for making a little money off his last publication. Someone defended him, saying, "There's such a thing as breaking even," a comment that quieted the criticism. An attempt was made to fully democratize the publication of this editor's next booklet. Someone suggested that anybody in the punk community should be able to write an article for it, but another person said, "Forget it. Everybody don't read, much less fucking write." There is, nonetheless, a sense that no single person or entity should control the local media that are designed for punks.

SPECIAL CASE OF THE SKINHEADS

As one of San Francisco's most astute punks said, "There is a schism in the movement." She refers to the ideological and behavioral differences between punks and skinheads. In this report I have chosen to treat skinheads as part of the punk community, but this is a vision that is not shared by everyone involved. Some punks do not want to be associated with skinheads; some skinheads do not consider themselves to be punks. Nonetheless, they share many common orientations. Both are contemporary groups who define their cultural space as being outside of mainstream society. Both groups are young, male-dominated, and share an interest in the same basic music. They listen to many of the same records and tapes and they attend punk shows where they freely interact. In many ways they have the same attitude—a "punk" attitude that rejects traditional social expectations. They dress and cut their hair in a way that separates them from the mainstream. They coexist on the streets with punks and are generally categorized the same way by people outside the subculture. To most people, skinheads are simply radical punks.

Skinheads are males who shave their heads or have very closely-cropped hair. They wear the most simple clothing—t-shirts, denim or black cotton pants, and black leather boots that are fully exposed under rolled-up cuffs. They are often covered with tattoos but generally wear no jewelry, not even the tough-looking dog collars and chains that some punks like. They travel in groups ("packs") and almost always have an aggressive style in every aspect of their demeanor. They often display Nazi insignia and give the "heil Hitler" salute to each other and to passerbys who gawk at them.

Skinheads are violent, the fundamental characteristic that separates them from punks, who are active but generally reject the notion of inflicting physical harm on any other person. Three skinheads attacked a black man who was carrying an electric organ under his arm during a peaceful demonstration in the city during the observation period. An old man with a dog intervened and attempted to separate the fighters. The old man was beaten severely by the skinheads and his dog was also beaten with a lead pipe. There is always a cowardly dimension to skinhead violence, as they rely on the numbers in their group to overcome their adversaries, an orientation that closely resembles the way "bikers" conduct themselves. (San Francisco is home for the Hell's Angels motorcycle gang, who similarly have a reputation for engaging in group violence.)

Many skinheads say they identify with ultra-conservative, sometimes Fascist beliefs. One of the city's more well-known skinheads, "Animal," is representative of the skinhead attitude. Animal is a 21-year-old skinhead who spends much of his time in the Haight district of San Francisco, an interesting neighborhood that gained international attention as the "Haight-Ashbury" district during the 1960s. The legacy of that era still exits on Haight street. Punks, hippies, street blacks, and bums are interspersed with more affluent young adults who are attracted to the fashion boutiques and fancy little restaurants along the street. Haight Street is one of the more culturally diverse areas in this culturally rich city.

Animal has the word "lobotomy" tattooed on his shaved head. He walks fast and aggressively, yelling to his friends as they pass by in cars or walk on the other side of the street. He says he's "fucked up" (drunk or speeding) most of the time. He has welts on his neck and face, wears dirty and torn clothes with black boots. One day when I talked to him, his gums were bleeding profusely. He says the punk scene is dead, and refers to skinheads separately from punks. He said "I hate fags" as a way to describe the difference between skinheads and punks, who are considerably more tolerant of various lifestyles. He also hates "the fucking humanists," a quasi-political organization in San Francisco that occupied the streets during the observation period in the throes of a petition campaign. His hatred for them likely stemmed solely from street contact.

Animal said, "I am dumb. I like beer, sex, Reagan, and I like to beat people up." Many skinheads are pro-Reagan, claiming that his politics are consistent with their basic beliefs. There is a blue-collar backlash quality to the skinheads—workers who embrace right-wing politics and find themselves in competition with other specific groups, particularly Mexicans and blacks in San Francisco, for available work. Animal is employed full-time as a roofer. He says "every punk should have a job." He lives in an apartment, and does not approve of squatting. Animal often appears at punk music shows. He is likely to start the evening's thrashing, flying out of the audience and crashing into some onlookers, stimulating them to begin to thrash. During a set of music by Detox, he grabbed the microphone away from the singer and said, "All you fucking dinosaurs out there, get into premarital sex immediately! Argghhh!"

"Bagman" is another San Francisco skinhead who is well known in the punk community. He is a strikingly handsome man, tall with sculpted features and a broad smile. He is 19 years old. Bagman has a six-inch tattoo of a tarantula on the side of his neck, extending onto his face. He has an elaborate tattoo on his entire left arm that portrays a skull inside a Nazi war helmet with the words "Extreme Hate" inscribed above it. He is fearful of the police, since his brother was recently busted for drugs by undercover agents. Bagman drinks liquor out of a bag on the street.

Despite the fearsome aspects of Bagman's appearance, he is a warm and sensitive person in many ways. He is clever and charming in his verbal style, and women are very attracted to him. He reached out to gently touch and kiss a girl in front of the Mabuhay Gardens one night in a way that seemingly contradicted the vulgar, insensitive feelings that skinheads typically communicate.

Skinheads have a certain pathetic quality that they play upon. As Christy noted, "They have a victim mentality. They're into comparing scars." Skinheads often look beaten, having suffered in fights with other street occupants, particularly the Mexican gangs. Their rough and beaten appearance, together with frequent, intense states of intoxication, make the skinheads look tough but pathetic at the same time. Nonetheless, people, especially girls, stay out of their way generally. One punk said that skinheads are "okay, but they beat people up when they get into gangs and when they are drunk." This is a common perception of skinheads—they are fine as individuals but lose their heads in the group context, and that context defines the skinhead lifestyle.

FUNDAMENTAL THEMES CHARACTERIZING THE PUNK SUBCULTURE

In San Francisco at least, a strong argument can be made that punk subculture is a reasonable response to the pressures felt by youth in post-nuclear Western society, and an intense reaction to the realization that protest groups who have gone before, particularly the hippies, failed in their efforts to deter the dominant culture from its course toward world destruction.

A substantial number of punks are politically aware and motivated to change things. One punk said: "Our government wreaks havoc on people in my name. My commitment is to turn that around." Coming to grips with the abstract and mundane aspects of international, national, and local politics is a task that much of the punk movement is about. In that way, there is a robust optimism within the punk community. But change within the system seems impossible. "Keep your laws off my body," is the inscription on the black leather jacket of a punk who moved from New York to San Francisco because New York has "the most intense energy of competition." Another phrase that appears on the clothing of punks is, "If Voting Changed Anything, It Would Be Illegal!"

Voting was an important issue during the Fall of 1984, the observation period, since a presidential election was held. Jello Biafra yelled from the stage between songs, "We all voted, right? Because we have such freedom of choice! Reagan, Mondale, Mickey Mouse, Bugs Bunny." The singer from the Dicks announced from the stage the week after the election: "I hope all motherfuckers that voted for Reagan will burn up. And all the motherfuckers that voted for Mondale will burn up. It's too bad that we have to burn up with 'em." The band then played one of their anthems: "We don't want no fucking war. We don't want to fight no war." Similarly, Jello Biafra yelled from the stage, "Nicaragua, 1984. About time for a third world war!" He then screamed "No War" over and over as the band began to play while he dove into the crowd.

Biafra also commented during the Dead Kennedys show about other political issues: "Thirty to forty thousand dead in Central America so the bananas keep coming real cheap to Safeway." Regarding the police: "The

SFPD needs to masturbate in the streets, beating people up!" Regarding the multi-national corporations: "They say, we just want you to go home . . . turn on the TV . . . shut up . . . go to sleep." The band then played one of their well-known songs that begins with the lyric: "In the name of world peace. In the name of world profits!"

The punk community is concerned with racial issues too. There is a somewhat formalized movement called "Rock Against Racism" in the United States and England. This loosely knit organization of punks and others stage concerts to benefit the poor and needy, particularly the black community. There are very few black punks or skinheads. A few blacks play in punk bands, and one band, Bad Brains, is all black, fusing reggae and punk music but leaning on the latter. Some young black males show up at punk shows and engage in thrashing and stage diving.

The anti-materialism discussed in the early paragraphs of this paper is central to the punk community. In a demonstration against the enemy ("people with last names that are hyphenated two or three times"), the Scum of the Earth Guerilla Theatre Group in San Francisco stages a "Debutante's Debacle" outside an expensive hotel where a high society cotillion was being held. Urging people to join the demonstration, a 23-year-old woman with a Mohawk said it's "a good way to get out some of your anger at rich people."

The Punk–Hippie Relationship. There is an intricate association between these two groups. In San Francisco, the hippie subculture that bloomed in the sixties has not died completely. The atmosphere that the hippies created in parts of the city still exists, and many people still look like the stereotype—long hair on men and women, shawls and other loose-fitting clothes, headbands, sandals, etc. There are many people who fit this general description who are in their late 30s, 40s, even 50s. Many of these people were attracted to the Bay Area in the old days and remain here, relatively unchanged. There is also a substantial group of far younger people who have adopted the lifestyle and appearance of the original San Francisco "flower children"—these people are sometimes called the "new hippies." Old and young hippies are seen everywhere in San Francisco, and they make a stark contrast with the appearance of the punks.

There is an uneasy alliance between hippies and punks. The punks regard the old hippies as their ideological and lifestyle predecessors, but they believe that hippies were unsuccessful in their calling to change things. An 18-year-old punk girl who was raised by her hippie mother on a commune said: "The hippies said, 'All we are saying is give peace a chance.' We are saying, 'I want peace and I won't settle for anything else.' We will not get into the fetal position." A 17-year-old punk said that punks differ from hippies in degree of aggressiveness: "We say jump first and look later." A 19-year-old punk said: "What did the hippies do? We'll fucking bring a club or a bottle!"

Hippies are admired by punks because they lived outside mainstream society and were critical of it. They are faulted by punks because they withdrew inside themselves too much, not offering a sufficiently fierce resistance to the forces of oppression. Getting stoned every day and moving to the hillside to set up a commune is regarded by punks as escapist, self-indulgent, and nonproductive. Hippies lived inside themselves; punks live outside themselves. The hippie movement was rural; punk is urban.

Still, punks have inherited a fundamental ideology and various aspects of personal appearance from the hippies. Terms such as "pig" (police) and "freak" are commonly used by punks. Punks are battling San Francisco police much the same way, and in many of the same locations, that hippies did 10 to 20 years ago. Some punk art, including psychedelic designs on cars, clothing, and flyers, are derivatives of the hippie era. Both groups reflect admiration for the Native Americans in the way they dress and wear their hair—headbands, long hair, and pony tails among hippie men; now Mohawk cuts in the punk context. Hippies and punks have drawn much of their identities from the same sources, but their reactions to these conditions are very different. To be sure, punks want to display distance from the hippies in order not to diffuse their own strength, but a latent admiration for them is apparent.

Paradoxical symbolism. In order to understand the punk subculture, it is absolutely necessary to become aware of the codes, means of expression, and hidden meanings that exist in the unique worlds they create. Basic to this understanding is the concept of paradox—in the case of punk, the difference between appearance and reality.

Nearly every aspect of the subculture has a rough look to it. Punks are often abrasive and insulting, even to their friends and others who claim membership in the subculture. But these verbal and physical aggressions typically are not meant to hurt anyone. They are instances of cultural self-monitoring. The harshness of the forms of expressions they imply are confronting or confusing to the outsider. When one sees their actions as paradoxical, then the meaning is more clear (i.e., it can be perceived from the point of view of the punks, not from the biases of a nonmember). The most extreme cases of hostility can be viewed as harmless, even positive, evidences of cultural behavior.

The point about paradox can be made with a few illustrations taken from empirical observations. There are two primary forms to the paradoxes that were observed. In the first case, one behavior is followed by another behavior that seemingly contradicts the first act. In the second case, assertions are made that are the opposite of what is meant.

Of the first case, consider this observation: The equipment van for the punk band "Flipper" arrives at the Mabuhay Gardens. The driver gets out to look first-hand at what kind of maneuver will be required to back the van into the alley alongside the club. When the driver gets out, a punk standing on the busy sidewalk next to the street yells at the driver, "You fucking chump." The driver notices him, makes no comment, and gets back into the van to drive it into the alley. The same punk walks a considerable distance past the crowd to get into a position where he can guide the driver of the van safely into the alley for the unloading of equipment.

The band "Detox" plays excellent music featuring moody, dark textures. They are very good musicians and singers. When the band played a slow song, someone in the audience at the Mabuhay yelled, "Faster! This is punk music!" The singer responded by saying, "Now we're going to get real slow.' The band then played a very fast song. After another slow song later, someone else yelled, "Faster!" The singer said, "They just keep getting slower, and slower, and slower . . ." He slowed his voice down to a drawl, and the band resumed playing more slowly than before.

During the observation period, there was tension in the United States over what was originally reported as an effort by the government in Nicaragua to import MIG fighter jets from Russia. Lead singer Lee Ving from Fear announced from the stage: "The Rooskies, man. If they send MIGs in there, are we going to bomb 'em or what? Fucking A!" They then played one of their well-known songs that features the lyric, "Fuck you, I don't care about you." Similarly, the Dicks lead singer said at the Mabuhay: "They told you all the lies you need to know about the MIGs in Nicaragua. Well, I don't give a damn. I hope you all get drafted." Again, Lee Ving from Fear: "This song is called 'Foreign Policy.' We don't know what it means, we just saw it in the paper." These comments from the stage and the songs themselves often are designed to express the opposite sentiment held by the songwriter. They are stated in the most compelling, insulting way to get the attention of the audience. "Dumb" or "ignorant" are qualities that the bands try to foster as part of the parody. These comments are not taken literally by audience members who are truly members of the subculture. Their decoding skills immediately recognize the pervasive paradoxical content.

Sometimes, the harsh comments are communicated directly to a single person. A punk sang a Christmas carol to his friend on the street: "We wish you a merry Christmas; we wish you a merry Christmas; we wish you a merry Christmas; and *fuck* your New Year!" Gary Floyd of the Dicks told a punk who had jumped on the stage and started to sing into the microphone: "Get off the fucking stage. You don't even know the fucking song. You look fucking stupid." To the outsider, this surely appeared to be a confrontative interaction. It was not.

Contradictions exist everywhere in the punk subculture. The violent affectations of appearance, thrashing, and stage diving, for example, seemingly stand in contrast with the orientation toward peace and other humane issues that the vast majority of punks stand for. A major goal is to shock and outrage, a motivation that surely meets personal as well as subcultural objectives. Whereas the hippie movement was a slap in the face of their parents who were so supportive of discipline and toil, punk imagery successfully outrages not only parents, but also the hippies, serving to gain attention and advance a new noncomformist lifestyle. And punks slap their own faces too. Some punks, including members of various bands, have started to grow their hair long in order to disturb their own peers, suggesting a symbolic unwillingness to conform even with the subculture.

Normalcy within the subculture. There may be a wrongful tendency to believe that punks exist in a world that is completely external to the mainstream of society. Many parts of the lives of punks are no different than the "normal" reality of more conventional people. There is, for instance, a warmth and friendliness within the subculture that is just as intense and pervasive as other elements of society. There are gentle embraces, warm handshakes, helpful gestures, tender kisses, and other sensitive forms of physical interaction that may not be expected.

Punk girls are worried about what their mothers think just like other adolescents. When punk boys fight each other, it is likely to be over some issue having to do with personal feelings (over a girl, for example) rather than something stimulated by the lifestyle. On the day that the San Francisco Forty-Niners football team won its fifteenth game of the season, one of the roughest-looking punks in a San Francisco neighborhood ran down the street shouting, "Niners! Niners! Niners!" A punk tenderly stroked the back of another punk while the latter vomited into the gutter in front of the Mabuhay Gardens. A skinhead interrupted his aggressive march down a sidewalk to stop and pet a dog held on a leash by its straight owner. Two male punks discussed their hairstyles. One, whose hair stood straight up nearly a foot off the top of his head, said, "Some days I can make my hair look like this and other days I can't get it to do anything." His friend asked how he got it to stay like that: "I use gel, lots of it." And how do you get the gel out of the hair? "I have to wash it at least three times!"

CONCLUDING COMMENTS

Diverse in theory and practice, punk is nonetheless a place to go culturally for many young people and a consciousness that is little understood outside the subculture. There is a lot of anger directed toward punks from outside their community, some of it caused by genuinely conflicting ideological orientations, but much of it stems from a lack of understanding, or misunderstanding, of what the subculture is about. The rest of American society is generally repulsed by the appearance of punks, in much the same way that the hippies were suspected and feared in the preceeding two decades. This reaction is cultivated by the punks in order to demonstrate their separateness from dominant modes of thought and activity, a distance that creates attention but simultaneously may undermine efforts at meaningful outreach to agents of change. Much like the hippies had to cut their hair and embrace a liaison with blue-collar workers and minorities in the 1960s in order to further their goals (e.g., stopping the Viet Nam War, or democraticizing the workplace), punks are similarly challenged to step outside the comforts of their culture to create this kind of potential rapport.

Although punks are not well understood, even disliked or hated by some, they nonetheless have carved out a unique and fascinating cultural space in a vivid way. Most punks relish in their appearance, music, and identification generally, providing for them a certain social/psychological well being that others may actually envy. They are human envoys of a message of resistance carried to all of society by the way they prepare and use their bodies, hair, and clothing, by the ways they interact, and by the attitude they display on the street. Punks are public media in and of themselves. The subculture, while it exists only in the seams and cracks of mainstream consciousness, has a definite impact of some sort on nearly everyone in this city.

While a subtle optimism persists among San Francisco's punks as many of them dream of a better society, a 16-year-old punk reflects on the other side of the reality in which they live: "I'm depressed. Nothing I'm doing is doing any good. There will be no revolution." Indeed, there may not be. But there are always revolutionaries. In the United States, authentic punks may represent that romantic, if impotent ideal.

REFERENCES

1. Cashmore, E.E. *No Future.* London: Heinemann Educational Books, 1984.
2. Frith, S. *Sound Effects: Youth, Leisure, and the Politics of Rock and Roll.* New York: Pantheon Books, 1981.
3. Hebdige, D. *Subculture: The Meaning of Style.* London: Metheun and Company, Ltd., 1979.
4. Lull, J. "The Naturalistic Study of Media and Youth Culture." In K.E. Rosengren, L. Wenner, and P. Palmgreen (Eds.), *Media Gratifications Research: Current Perspectives.* Beverly Hills, CA: Sage Publications, 1985.

Chapter 12

Commentary on Qualitative Research and Mediated Communications in Subcultures and Institutions

Muriel G. Cantor

Department of Sociology
American University, Washington, D.C.

At first glance, my task—to comment on the articles in this section—seemed impossible because these articles apparently have little in common. One, Lindlof's "Ideology and Pragmatics of Media Access in Prison," reflects the title of the book, but the other two, although fascinating, are not about audiences who consume media. Rather they are about subgroups (or subcultures) who at least some of the time participate actively in the creative process. Because neither the Schwartz and Griffin article nor the one by Lull are about mass media audiences, formed naturally or otherwise, they should be discussed in a context different from the Lindlof article. However, the three do have one important element in common: each is based chiefly on the interpretative process and qualitative methodologies, rather than on a positivistic approach. In this commentary, I will not try to contrast the substantive elements in the articles, because of their obvious differences, but rather will discuss the methods and related theoretical orientations they share to show how each contributes to media (social science) research.

Two basic premises underlie this essay: that there is no difference between media research and other social science research, and that qualitative research can be as systematic and rigorous as quantitative research (5, 6, 13). The first premise is not defended, because it certainly has consensual validity. The same rules and norms apply whether one is studying religion, government, education, or media institutions and behaviors. However, in commenting on the three articles included in this section of the book, I will defend the second, showing how each research report did utilize qualitative research methodologies to provide information that could not otherwise be generated from the hypothesis-testing methodologies, such as experiments and surveys, more commonly advocated in the social sciences.

The appropriate methodologies and research techniques for the social sciences have been debated for several generations, and in introductory sociology textbooks, more often than not the hypothesis-testing model has been considered the primary model for social scientific inquiry. More sophisticated texts (5, 6, 13) consider still other methods, focusing on social action and interpretation to help students understand that research is more than merely collecting data. Hypothesis testing is, of course, much easier to justify, because the variables involved can be measured quantitatively and replicated more readily. Qualitative research, in contrast, can provide understandings about the social world unavailable to those who apply alternative methods of study. As the articles in this book reflect, recent years have shown a resurgence of interest in studies using the field methods pioneered by urban anthropologists and sociologists. Research approaches popular in one time period often can come in disrepute in another. Until a few years ago, just quantitative research would do for those studying the media. People did research either by developing hypotheses or by designing studies to generate descriptive, demographic data. Many of the problems studied taking these empirical, usually linear, approaches would have benefited from less formal and more interpretive methods of study. Quite often, the findings and conclusions presented, although highly sophisticated and very technical, were based on data that were obviously inadequate and conceptually unclear. The 1972 Surgeon General's papers on television and violence provide excellent examples (10) of how an unclear concept – aggressive behavior – was operationalized and then translated into sophisticated statistical analyses to suggest that direct causal relationships exist between media use and human behavior.

Qualitative studies in the United States, especially those relating to art, culture, and the media which were developed by sociologists applying interactionist theory, have been concerned usually with the creation and change of symbolic orders via social interaction (1, 9, 11, 12). While positivists tend to view methods as mere techniques for data-gathering, interactionists usually view the research process itself as still another symbolic order based on interaction. Norman Denzin (6), in his fine book on methods, states: "Methodology represents the principal ways the sociologist acts on his environment." He goes on to say that methods cannot be neutral instruments because they define how the topic will be symbolically constituted and how researchers will adopt a particular definition of self through collecting and analyzing data. Interactionists are therefore likely to define themselves as still another subject in the subject-to-subject relationships. All three articles reviewed here fall partially into that interactionist tradition. In reviewing these articles, my commentary will focus on the methodologies the researcher employed as well as the relationships of the methodology used to the substantive findings obtained and theoretical concerns involved. Because Lull does not elaborate on the actual techniques he used for data collection, I am limited in my ability to carry out the task for his article, although, as will be shown, his work as well is in an established social science tradition.

COMMENTARY ON ARTICLES

Thomas Lindlof is interested in how prison inmates will use media opportunities when allowed by prison authorities. He is also interested in why prison authorities in one prison have adopted a policy regarding media use. To investigate those concerns, he conducted in-depth interviews with prison administrators and staff and with 16 inmates. Three different, but related research questions concerned media use were asked: how media contribute to the prison's mission to control and rehabilitate prisoners; how inmates choose media (and programs), in a setting with relative freedom of choice; and finally, the most important question—what meanings do the media have for individual prisoners? Because Lindlof's work is in the interactionist tradition, one might ask why he chose interviews over participant observation, which would be the more appropriate method to examine naturally occurring events. The reason is obvious: it is extremely difficult to do participant observation in total institutions. The bulk of the data he reports on were gathered through interviews with a 16 prisoner sample selected through traditional survey techniques. Those selected were chosen because of their reported use of media as well as their ability to perform well in extended face-to-face interviews. Lindlof notes that this procedure did result in a sample somewhat more intelligent than the inmate population as a whole. In addition, some administrators and staff members were also interviewed.

Lindlof discusses some of the problems that can arise in using interviews to collect information for research. He notes that, although participant observation may have been the better methodology, it was clearly impossible in a prison setting. However, interviews such as the ones he conducted are a form of participant observation and provide rich data, although, as Lindlof himself warns, there is less confidence in the conclusions generated from such interviews. He cites the gap in status between the researcher and inmates and the consequent lack of trust as problems for face-to-face interviewing. The same lack of trust, of course, can be present when subjects know there is a stranger in their midst observing their actions. Status differentials always pose problems in doing face-to-face as well as other kinds of interviewing, whether the interviewer is higher in status or lower, as in the case of interviewing elites (2, 4). Almost all social scientists have used interviews as either a primary or secondary means of collecting data. Yet, as a technique, it continues to be widely criticized. The most important criticism is that the validity of the responses obtained themselves must always be considered suspect. Respondents are prone to tell interviewers what they think they want to hear. Interviewers must also take care not to transpose any information given to fit their own preconceptions of their subjects' theoretical orientations, prejudices, and world views. Aaron V. Cicourel (5) is very clear in his criticsm on this issue, showing no matter how "objective" the interviewer might try to be, he or she still functions in a social context where the interaction directs the course of the interview as well as the style of questioning. David Silverman (13), in his book *Qualitative Methodology and Sociology*, advocates interviewing as a realistic method to problem solving because it can often provide data often not available with other means. He and many others, including Denzin (6), recognize the advantage of interviews over surveys and experiments as richer sources of data, because interviews provide fuller explanations. For example, through interviews, people can account for their troubles and good fortune. In other words, interviews can provide knowledge about how people perceive their own conditions, which should never be confused with reality itself.

If interviews are not the best method to answer the questions Lindlof has raised, they were certainly the only possible method available under the circumstances. When reading studies such as this one, I ask myself how I would go about doing this type of research with all resources possible at my disposal. Clearly, a team of participant observers, either role-playing as prisoners or actual prisoners with training in the social sciences, would have been able to gather the 'most" or "best" information from the prisoners. Any status differential that rightly concerns Lindlof would not then exist, and the opportunity to observe first hand takes care of the other problems that arise from interviews (and surveys as well), such as false reports, intentional or not, about program choices. Also, with status equated, inmates are less likely to answer questions in terms of what they believe is expected of them.

This evaluation of methods does not do justice to the article and substantive issues raised. By using in-depth interviews, Lindlof shows the contradictions between the purposes and outcomes desired by the administration and the purposes of viewing and the meanings held by the prisoners. Would television have meant something different if access had not been made as available? Do prison officials believe that by providing information and entertainment, more prisoners will be passive and that passivity will become the prison norm rather than discontent? Lindlof raises many interesting questions that need addressing. Clearly, comparative studies would shed more light on the basic questions and show how prison ideology would affect viewing in more than one institution. Comparative studies would be especially valuable to show whether and how much media would vary under different control environments, and would provide more information on the meaning of television and other media to those confined in total institutions.

The article by Schwartz and Griffin on amateur photographers makes a valuable contribution on how art is organized and created. Throughout the last 15 years, I and others have advocated that to understand the "effects" of the media on audiences, it is necessary first to find out how media are created, by whom, and under what circumstances (2, 3, 11). My interest has been to either repudiate or support those critics of television who follow the lead of Horkheimer and Adorno (7) by assuming that entertainment as the products of culture industries are used as tools to impose an ideology on a malleable and somewhat willing populace, the "masses." Although this statement does not do justice to the complexities of critical analysis, the outcome of such criticism is more simplistic among the followers than the originators of this critical theory. For example, many critics, by failing to see the complexities and contradictions within popular culture, underestimate the involvement and intelligence of the audiences. There is no question that the "amateur" and the "creators of popular culture" are denigrated, and that those who produce the popular arts, not necessarily the stars but the committed amateur and the preprofessional, are not taken seriously by critics or scholars. This study and others like it, ranging from the production of television to amateur photography (see "References" for Schwartz and Griffin article), share both common methodologies and a theoretical orientation to the social organizations of artistic production which to be understood properly must be put in their social-historical contexts. The "production system," as Schwartz and Griffin define it, consists of the interrelated activities of the creators, the audience, and all others necessary to the realization of the symbolic events (in this case, visual). Rather than seeing the production of all art and culture as interrelated, they follow the model designed by others, particularly Rosenblum (12) and Becker (1), which show the production process as distinctive spheres of activity in which artistic work routines, styles, and evaluative standards differ sharply. The basic research question for this study, although not explicated, is similar to the analytic frameworks which many have used to describe the relationship between social processes and (what I call) "content." Content has two elements—the message and the form, or the 'aesthetic." They used several different methods to find the relationship between social process of production and pictorial aesthetic. Their overall interest was in the structural constraints on amateur photographers imposed by the values and the nature of the economy in the larger society. Most of the analyses they present come from their experiences as participant observers in an amateur photography club. As members, they helped organize the historical materials and attended meetings and special events, even taking photographs to submit to photo-competitions.

I am especially sympathetic to this type of research and the methods they adopted to carry it out. From personal experience, I have learned that we are limited in understanding if we just look at the powerful and at the system in which the powerful operate (11). By participating in the creative process, Schwartz and Griffin had an excellent opportunity to increase our understanding of what photography means to the club members and on the relationship of the creators to their art. This study shows the limitless variations and possibilities for personal creative activities in the world of "mass" entertainment and "mass" information and, along with related work (1, 9, 11, 12), shows that the American public cannot be conceptualized as a mass. Rather, the population consists of various subgroups which exist in a social matrix and vary in their interests, talents, and motivations to participate creatively in the production of culture in their everyday lives.

The methodology and the subject matter in this paper are praiseworthy, and I believe that, because of its perspective, the study provides a valuable model for research for students. Across the country, there are numerous groups of amateur and preprofessional artists, some with long histories such as this one and others of more recent origin such as the Romance Writers of America, which deserve study. Using this article as a model, students and others with limited resources can also do well-conceptualized and rigorous work to relate social-historical processes to artistic (creative) production. As more studies of this type are done, we will be less likely to conceptualize the audience as Americans pursuing leisure by just sitting in front of television sets 6 hours (on the average) a day.

The third article, "Thrashing in the Pit," is a descriptive ethnography, bringing to life the punk community in San Francisco. Jacqueline Wiseman (16), in her chapter on "Ethnography," asks: "Have you ever listened to a speaker describe a situation and suddenly in your mind's eye you were there? You could almost see the people." James Lull's article put me on Haight Street, and through his eyes I was able to imagine punk subculture more fully than I had before. Their clothes and dress were already familiar to me through visits to England over the last few years, and punks are now seen in the Washington, D.C. area as well. What Lull provides is the whole gestalt, a thick description of the totality of drugs, music, dress, and social relations. As part of the story, Lull calls attention to several aspects of the social fabric within which punks live, especially the relationships between punk bands and their audiences and punk men and women. There is no question that Lull has caught the flavor of punk life and the contradictions between their attitudes and behaviors. Punk shows, according to Lull, lessen the distance between the creator and the consumer. Band members are expected not to act "better" than their audiences, but rather merge with audience, sometimes symbolically and other times actually. "Thrashing in the pit" and "stage diving" are examples of the close relationship between the artist-creators and the audience members who also act as creators in their own ways.

The article is an important contribution because it provides insights into a small, but visible subculture in American and European societies. As a subculture, its members make a statement through unusual actions and appearance about their disappointments in the shortcomings of modern industrial life for them. More than a simple account of punks as thrashers and stage divers, the article presents a vivid picture of punk life, showing the contradictions that exist in the subculture. Lull presents a world that is not one dimensional, but rich in variations both within same persons and between members. As a study, it may eventually take its place with other select urban ethnographies, such as *Talley's Corners* (8), *All Our Kin* (14), and *Street Corner Society* (15).

Because no details are provided on the methods used, comments must be limited. However, the tools of the ethnographer, observation and interviews, are evident and, as with ethnographers, unobtrusive. This article is an excellent example of a research project where the researcher focuses his attention exclusively on the subjects, taking seriously their mores and folkways. In doing so, Lull carried out a research project in the best tradition of field work.

CONCLUSION

These articles are not about audiences, but are about subgroups (subcultures) which become interesting because they provide substantive information not available elsewhere, information that could not have been gathered through conventional empirical methodologies. Substantively, we learn that it is not correct to perceive Americans as a simple homogenized and passive audience, tapped at will by advertisers and professional communicators. Rather, these articles add to the growing body of data that show that the population is made up of numerous segments of people with varying interests, talents, positions, and motivations, people who both shape their environment and are shaped by it. A common element in all three articles is the desire of the authors to understand the social worlds in which the groups they studied live, and to try to understand both how those social worlds affect their members and, more important, how the members in turn affect their social environments.

To carry out the research agendas addressing interactive processes, such as the meaning of television programs for prison inmates, the aesthetic judgments of amateur photographers, and the contradictions between punk behavior and attitudes, researchers must be flexible and eclectic in the choice of methods used. Although not directly acknowledged, the researchers in this section have followed the advice that Denzin offers that multimethods be used, the approach he calls triangulation. Triangulation is not simply the use of exactly three methods, but can include two or more. Multiple triangulation is an attempt to combine various data sources, theoretical perspectives, and methodologies. Denzin (6) takes the position that one method alone is not sufficient to answer complex questions or to study social interactions, especially in natural settings. He advocates, and I agree, that interviews, participant observation, and unobtrusive analysis should all be combined when appropriate. In these articles, the researchers did just that to the best of their ability considering the difficulties inherent in doing research in field settings. It should also be noted that all three investigators know more than they were able to tell us in short reports. Lull, for example, was unable to describe his methodology in detail. Schwartz and Griffin, in the tradition established by Howard Becker, could probably write a book on "The World of the Amateur Photographer," and Lindlof, who investigated new territory in prison life, probably has views on how prisons with different philosophies and ideologies would affect the meanings media have for inmates. In conclusion, these studies provide excellent examples of how qualitative methods used in natural settings can enlarge our views on what art and the media mean in the lives of different subgroups in American society.

REFERENCES

1. Becker, H.S. *Art Worlds*. Berkeley, CA: University of California, Press, 1982.
2. Cantor, M.G. *The Hollywood TV Producer*. New York: Basic Books, 1971.
3. Cantor, M.G. *Prime-Time Television: Content and Control*. Beverly Hills, CA: Sage, 1980.
4. Cantor, M.G. "Using Interview Data for Media Research: The Social Construction of Fantasy." Paper presented at the Iowa Symposium and Conference on Television Criticism: Public and Academic Responsibility, Iowa City, 1985.
5. Cicourel, A.V. *Method and Measurement in Sociology*. New York: Free Press, 1964.
6. Denzin, N.K. *The Research Act: A Theoretical Introduction to Sociological Methods* (2nd. Edition). New York: McGraw Hill, 1978.
7. Horkheimer, M., and T.W. Adorno. *The Dialectic of Enlightenment*. New York: Herder and Herder, 1972.
8. Liebow, E. *Tally's Corner*. Boston: Little Brown, 1967.

9. McCall, M. "Who and Where Are the Artists?" In W.B. Shaffir, R.A. Stebbins, and A. Turowetz (Eds.), *Fieldwork Experience: Qualitative Approaches to Social Research*. New York: St. Martin's Press, 1980.

10. Murray, J.P., E.A. Rubinstein, and G.A. Comstock (Eds.), *Television and Social Behavior. Vol. II: Television and Social Learning*. Washington, DC: U.S. Government Printing Office, 1972.

11. Peters, A.K., and M.G. Cantor. "Screen Acting as Work." In J.S. Ettema and D.C. Whitney (Eds.), *Individuals in Mass Media Organizations: Creativity and Constraint*. Beverly Hills, CA: Sage, 1982.

12. Rosenblum, B. *Photographers at Work*. New York: Holmes and Meiers, Publishers, 1978.

13. Silverman, D. *Qualitative Methodology and Sociology: Describing the Social World*. Hants, England: Gower Publishing Company, 1985.

14. Stack, C.R. *All Our Kin*. New York: Harper and Row, 1974.

15. Whyte, W.F. *Street Corner Society* (2nd. Edition). Chicago: University of Chicago Press, 1955.

16. Wiseman, J.P., and M.S. Aron. *Field Projects for Sociology Students*. Cambridge, MA: Schenkman Publishing Company, 1970.

Author Index

Subject Index

A
Amateur, 203–205, 215, 220–222
  photography, 257–258
Art photography, 203–205, 208, 215n, 220
Attention to television, 33–34, 38–46, 54–55,
  121–122, 126–129
Audience concept, 1–2, 253, 259
  active, 121, 135–137
  mass, 2, 257, 258
  mediated communication, 1–2
Audio-visual tools in qualitative research, 8,
  15, 18–20

C
Camera club aesthetics, 213–221
Camera clubs, 199–205, 208–209
Children
  and movies, 109, 111–113
  and radio, 113
  developmental studies, 113–115, 117
  perception of audio effects on television,
    90–91, 93
  understanding of lighting techniques,
    88–89
  understanding of reality and fantasy, 66,
    79–80, 83, 85–87, 92, 93
Cognitive abilities and skills
  children's, 58, 64–65, 69–70, 74, 77, 81, 91,
    92
  formal tests of children's, 68, 81, 92
  traditional measures of, 92, 93
Cognitive development, 34–35, 50
Communication research
  history of, 109–111
  Payne Fund research on movies and
    youth, 111–113
  University of Chicago school, 109, 111,
    112–113
  violence studies, 254
Competence
  cultural, 10
  expressive, 14

C (cont.)
Comprehension, children's, 33–34, 45–46,
  54–55, 113–117
  recognition of special visual effects,
    87–89, 93
  story understanding, 65–67, 69, 75–77, 92
  television schemas, 83–85, 92–93
Computers in qualitative research, 6, 20
Contextuality, 7–8
Creative process, 253, 257

D
Data analysis, 67–70, 123–124, 126–127
Dramaturgical
  interaction, 162–163
  metaphor, 162–163

E
Ecological psychology, 5
Ethnomethodology, 5, 24–25, 139

F
Family
  as mediator of television, 122, 132–133,
    136–137
  defined, 161–162
  functions, 162
  nuclear, 161
  organization of time by, 122–124, 125–127,
    128–133, 167–168
  perspectives on, 162
  situated, 163
  structures, 163
  systems, 164, 167–170
  television viewing patterns in, 125–129,
    134–136, 164
  values relating to television, 134–135
Formal features, 34, 44–46, 55

H
Home mode, 200